W9-DIB-516

SPI
EGE
L&G
RAU

American Buffalo

— IN SEARCH OF A LOST ICON —

Steven Rinella

SPIEGEL & GRAU

New York

2008

Published in the United States by Spiegel & Grau,
an imprint of The Doubleday Publishing Group,
a division of Random House, Inc., New York.
www.spiegelandgrau.com

SPIEGEL & GRAU is a trademark of Random House, Inc.

For permission to reprint photographs, grateful acknowledgment is made to
the following: pages 6, 60, 132, 253, 255, and 256, courtesy of Danny Rinella;
page 9, courtesy of the Wildlife Conservation Society; page 42, photo by John
Hoganson, North Dakota Geological Survey (specimen exhibited at the North
Dakota Heritage Center); page 52, courtesy of Dr. Beth Shapiro; pages 74, 75, 79,
95, 124, 126, and 127, courtesy of Matt Rafferty; page 92, courtesy of Dr. Eric Kern;
pages 105 and 106, courtesy of Anna Baker; page 116, courtesy of Tony Baker;
page 142, copyright, Colorado Historical Society (Stephen H. Hart Library);
page 154, Julie Larsen Maher © WCS; page 179, Glenbow Archives NA-250-14;
page 182, courtesy of the Detroit Public Library; page 239, courtesy of Katie Finch.
All other photographs are courtesy of the author.

Book design by Ralph Fowler / rlf design
Map designed by Jeffrey L. Ward

Library of Congress Cataloging-in-Publication Data

Rinella, Steven.
    American buffalo : in search of a lost icon / Steven Rinella. — 1st ed.
       p. cm.
    1. American bison—Anecdotes. 2. Rinella, Steven. I. Title.
    QL737.U53R55 2008
    599.64'3—dc22

                                                              2008013624

ISBN 978-0-385-52168-0

PRINTED IN THE UNITED STATES OF AMERICA

10 9 8 7 6 5 4 3 2 1

First Edition

FOR KATIE

. . . they have the huge rump-like hump,
the giant head, the eyeball the size of a billiard ball.
What is not to like?

— PADGETT POWELL

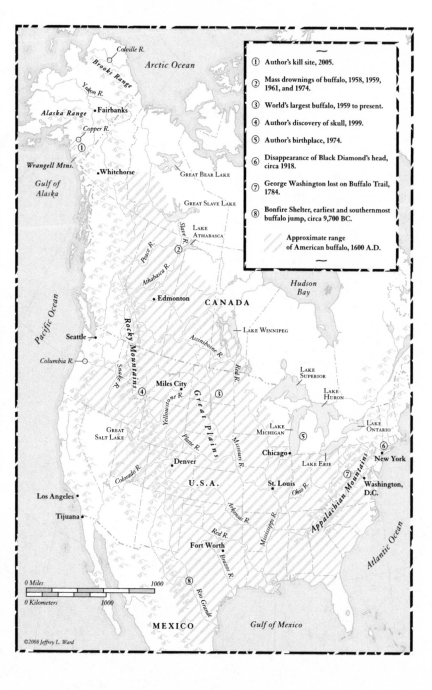

① Author's kill site, 2005.

② Mass drownings of buffalo, 1958, 1959, 1961, and 1974.

③ World's largest buffalo, 1959 to present.

④ Author's discovery of skull, 1999.

⑤ Author's birthplace, 1974.

⑥ Disappearance of Black Diamond's head, circa 1918.

⑦ George Washington lost on Buffalo Trail, 1784.

⑧ Bonfire Shelter, earliest and southernmost buffalo jump, circa 9,700 BC.

Approximate range of American buffalo, 1600 A.D.

Colville R.

Brooks Range

Arctic Ocean

Yukon R.

Alaska Range • Fairbanks

Copper R.

①

Wrangell Mtns.

• Whitehorse

Gulf of Alaska

Great Bear Lake

Great Slave Lake

Slave R.

Lake Athabasca

Peace R.

②

Athabasca R.

Pacific Ocean

• Edmonton

CANADA

Hudson Bay

Lake Winnipeg

Seattle →

Rocky Mountains

Assiniboine R.

Red R.

Lake Superior

Columbia R. ○

Snake R.

Miles City

Great Plains

③

Lake Huron

Lake Michigan

Lake Ontario

④

Yellowstone R.

⑤

Great Salt Lake

Platte R.

Missouri R.

Chicago •

Lake Erie

⑥

New York

• Denver

U.S.A.

St. Louis •

Ohio R.

⑦

Washington, D.C.

Appalachian Mountains

Los Angeles •

Colorado R.

Arkansas R.

Tijuana •

Mississippi R.

Red R.

Atlantic Ocean

Fort Worth •

Brazos R.

0 Miles   1000

0 Kilometers   1000

⑧

Rio Grande

MEXICO

Gulf of Mexico

©2008 Jeffrey L. Ward

— 1 —

I N THE PAST WEEK I've become something of a buffalo chip connoisseur. The perfect specimen has the circumference of a baseball cap, with folded layers like a sheik's turban. It's as dense as a gingersnap cookie, with the color and texture of old cardboard that's been wet and dried out again. Of course, when I say "buffalo chip," I'm talking about buffalo dung, or what's left of vegetation after it passes through the digestive circuitry of North America's largest native land animal, also known as the American bison (*Bison bison*). These chips will burn with an orange-colored halo of flame surrounding a coal black center; they let off a good heat, not many sparks, and a blue-hued smoke that smells nothing like you'd expect it to. At times I've dipped my face into the smoke and picked up the odors of cinnamon and cloves, dried straw and pumpkins, and sometimes the smell of walking into a bathroom after someone smoked a joint.

If I were to leave my buffalo chip fire right now, it would take me about a half hour to stomp my way through the thickets of spruce and alder that separate me from the Chetaslina River, a fast-flowing torrent of glacial runoff that drains a collection of fourteen-thousand-foot peaks in the Wrangell Mountains of south-central Alaska. If I tossed a stick into the Chetaslina River, it would drift through three miles of narrow canyon before dumping into the cold gray swirl of the much larger Copper River. From there the stick would flow more or less southward, past a couple of small villages and dozens of fish traps that were recently dragged onto the banks by their owners to save them from the crushing floes of winter ice. After dodging past mountains and winding through canyons, the stick would enter the Gulf of Alaska outside of Prince William Sound. As the crow flies (or, as is more likely in these parts, the raven), that's about eighty miles from here. Along the way, the crow would cross one two-lane highway and any number of wolves, coyotes, lynx, black bears, grizzly bears, wolverines, mountain goats, Dall sheep, and moose.

And perhaps a herd or two of wandering buffalo. Earlier in the morning there were about twenty of them in this valley; one of them, a cow, or female, is now lying just uphill from me within arm's reach. Probably about six hundred pounds of hide, bone, horn, and innards. Another four hundred or five hundred pounds of meat. When it fell dead, after I shot it, it slid down the steep slope across the wet slush and crashed into a snag of aspen trees. I've been working on it all day. I made skinning cuts up the legs and then opened the carcass from the underside of the tail to the chin before removing the entrails. With short, fast slices from my skinning knife, I pulled the hide away from the upper half of the carcass as if I were slowly turning down the covers of a bed. I skinned over the brisket, ribs, and paunch, then up and over the shoulder all the way to the animal's spine. If you touch the base of your own neck and feel the pebble-like shapes running up the center of your backbone, you're feeling the neural processes of your thoracic vertebrae. On a buffalo, those things can be over twenty inches long; they act as a sort of mooring post for tendons that support the animal's shag-haired, curve-horned head. The hump gives the buffalo its distinctive look, its front-heavy, bull-dozer, mass-shouldered appearance.

I've been rationing my food for the last few days, and now I can eat all I want. I cut some slices of fat from behind the hump and then pull the hide back in place to keep the carcass from freezing too solid to work on. The fat has an orangish color, not like the white fat you see on grain-fattened beef. The orange is from a diet of wild plants that are rich in fat-soluble carotene, the same substance that colors a carrot. The heat of the fire liquefies the fat and leaves the cracklings floating in the oil of my pan like if you melted hard candy and all the wrappers came to the surface. Whenever a crackling becomes rendered out, I pinch it out with the pliers on my Leatherman and blow on it until it's cooled off and crispy. I was keeping my salt in a film canister sealed with duct tape, but sometime over the last week, when I was crossing a river or standing in the rain or snow, the salt got wet. I scrape a chunk out with my knife and then grind it back into grains between my fingers. With a bit of salt, the cracklings taste like pork rinds but much better. They taste wilder.

You can say all you want about Coca-Cola and hot dogs and apple pie, but this is the real original American meal right here, buffalo meat; when the first Americans arrived in the Western Hemisphere, having crossed from eastern Siberia to Alaska, buffalo meat was one of the things that they were after. The animals were bigger then, with longer horns and probably shaggier hair, but it takes a trained eye to tell those skeletal remains apart from the ones I'm cleaning up with my knife.

The red-stained snow and the odor of blood in the air mean that I will not be alone here for long. Already gray jays are squawking around above my head and zipping in and out of the

Steven Rinella

spruce trees. I hear the croak of a raven passing by. Yesterday morning I saw a wolf; last night I saw two grizzly bears, not a half mile from here. The bears were eating rose hips on a hillside in the falling snow. They were young but good-sized, a couple of four-hundred-pounders. I'll bet they hear these excited birdcalls. When the sun ducks down toward the horizon, the thermal currents are going to switch direction and carry the smell right to them.

After I eat the fat and fry some little squares of meat, I load about a hundred pounds of the buffalo into my backpack and start through the trees toward the Chetaslina. From there it's about a three-mile walk down to my main camp along the Copper River.

When I get to the Chetaslina, I see just what I didn't want to see: two sets of grizzly tracks in the fresh snow, circling around near the riverbank. I check the air; sure enough, the tracks are downwind of the carcass. They already smell it. Shit. I unload the meat on the riverbank and drape it with some well-worn clothes and a sleeping bag to give it human odor. I light a little fire next to the meat and then march back up to the carcass and strip down out of my long underwear. My skin breaks out in gooseflesh before I can get dressed again. I drape the pants over the buffalo's horns and make a little scarecrow with the top. Then I piss on a few trees to mark my territory. That's as much as I can do, unless I want to sleep here and take my chances in the dark.

And nope, I don't want to sleep here. I gather up my pack and head back to the Chetaslina. There's a set of grizzly tracks on my boot prints from just an hour ago, backtracking up my trail and then veering off into the spruce trees. I'm going to have to come back up here first thing in the morning, and I'm not looking forward to it. I get a rush of adrenaline at the thought of sorting out who's going to get this buffalo meat, them or me. I'm planning on it being me.

— 2 —

FIRST BECAME INTERESTED in buffalo because of a kick from my brother Matt's boot on a mid-September afternoon in the late 1990s, at an elevation of about nine thousand feet above sea level in the Madison Mountains of southwest Montana. Matt and I, along with our brother Danny, had been up there for a few days bow hunting for elk. Snow had been on the ground a few days before, but it had turned sunny and you could smell the heat coming off the pine needles. The lodgepole pines on the mountainside were so thick that we sometimes had to turn sideways to pass between them—people call them dog hair pines when they're like that. The slope was steep, but here and there the ground leveled off into room-sized benches. As we were crossing one of those benches, Matt kicked at something on the ground. It was just a half-assed kick, and he didn't even slow down.

As I passed that spot, I looked to see what he had kicked at. It was a small circle of bone poking out of the forest floor. I gave it a kick, too, but it didn't budge. I gave it a couple more kicks. Still nothing. The circle of bone looked like it might be the eye socket of an old elk skull. I was wondering if there were any antler stubs attached, so I pushed a stick into the circle and pried. The stick broke. I dug away enough dirt to see that the hole was actually a foramen magnum, the opening in the back of a skull where the spinal column passes through to the brain. But this foramen magnum looked different from an elk's. I dug a couple gallons worth of dirt from around the object's perimeter. After I wiggled it a few times, it popped free from the little roots with the sound of dry spaghetti snapping in half. I stood up with the skull and held it at arm's length. It was the color of hot chocolate mix. The whole thing was woven over with green moss and roots. Everything below the eye sockets was missing: no jaws, no nose. But the moment that I saw it, I knew I'd just found a buffalo skull.

Ever since that day, I'm always a little surprised by the ways in which buffalo can come out of nowhere and suddenly pop up into one's life. It's actually become a game that I like to play with other people. The game has to do with random associations. I'll be talking to friends or acquaintances at a party and I'll try to seduce their interest with compelling buffalo-related facts and trivia. For

instance, I might explain that there's a town or city named Buffalo in eighteen states, though the most famous of these, Buffalo, New York, is the only one that never had a population of wild buffalo living in its vicinity.

Such discussions often make my partners in conversation uncomfortable or bored, and it's amazing how often they bring up the word *tatanka* as an avenue of partic-

Finding the skull in the Madison Mountains, September 1999.

ipation into the conversation. *Tatanka* is a Lakota word for buffalo. It was popularized by its frequent and animated use in *Dances with Wolves*, the 1990 film starring Kevin Costner. When a friend mentions this word, I build on the conversation's momentum by adding a related tidbit of my own: during the filming of *Dances with Wolves,* I'll say, which was shot in Canada, the filmmakers used buffalo that were owned by the Canadian-born musician Neil Young. Young once recorded a popular song called "Cortez the Killer" (1975), which was banned for a while by the Franco regime in Cortés's native country of Spain. Hernando Cortés is of course the famed Spanish conquistador, and in A.D. 1519 he happened to be the first European to ever see an American buffalo. The animal was housed in the menagerie of the Aztecs' godlike chief, Montezuma, in the Aztec capital of Tenochtitlán, which now lies in ruins beneath Mexico City. Cortés had no way of knowing it, but the captive buffalo was hundreds of miles south of its native range. Cortés hung around Tenochtitlán for a few years before he completely destroyed the place, from the Aztecs' written records to Montezuma's collection of hundreds of thousands of human skulls.

Before he recorded "Cortez the Killer," Neil Young was an influential member of the band called Buffalo Springfield, known for their instrumental interplay and vocal harmony, put to use in antiwar songs such as "For What It's Worth" (1967). The band's name was inspired by the Buffalo-Springfield Roller Company, an American manufacturer of road-building equipment founded in 1916 with the merger of the Buffalo-Pitts and Kelly-Springfield companies. To put the words "Buffalo" and "Springfield" together was an interesting choice, however coincidental. The Springfield Armory of Massachusetts manufactured many of the weapons used by the Union in the Civil War. After the Civil War, many of those federal soldiers took their Springfield weapons westward and provided the military backbone for the suppression of the remaining free-ranging indigenous buffalo-hunting cultures on the Great Plains.

By now I'll be on a roll: The most famous Plains Indian of all time was Crazy Horse, I'll continue, the renegade Oglala Sioux warrior who was instrumental in the annihilation of General George Armstrong Custer's command at the Battle of the Little Bighorn. As it happens, Crazy Horse was also the name of the band that Neil Young usually performed "Cortez the Killer" with. Crazy Horse, the man, would have certainly used the word *tatanka,* though most other assertions about his life are, as the novelist Larry McMurtry put it, "an exercise in assumption, conjecture, and surmise." However, it is fairly certain that Crazy Horse had an affair with a married woman named Black Buffalo Woman. It's less certain but still possible that his maternal grandfather was named Black Buffalo, and his maternal grandmother was named White Cow (as in white-colored female buffalo). It's also rumored that one of Crazy Horse's maternal uncles, One Horn, or Lone Horn, was gored to death by a buffalo. Crazy Horse himself died from bayonet wounds. There's a legend that his deathbed statement mentioned the Tongue River. I used to live less than a mile from where the Tongue River flows into the Yellowstone River, in Miles City, Montana. When I lived there I liked to visit a place where Indians chased buffalo over a cliff's edge hundreds of years ago. The buffalo jump, as such cliffs are known, is on the property of my brother Matt's employer, the U.S. Department of Agriculture's Fort Keogh Livestock and Range Research Laboratory. The laboratory takes its name from Captain Keogh, an Irishman who was rumored to be the last of Custer's men to die while battling Crazy Horse at the Battle of the Little Bighorn.

Often, my game associations will take me to a discussion of the most famous buffalo in all of American history—that is, the one who touched the most human lives. Black Diamond was the buffalo from the buffalo-head nickel. His path to fame began in 1911, when the U.S. Mint was seeking a replacement for the Liberty-head nickel, which had been in circulation for twenty-eight years. The mint commissioned the sculptor James Earle Fraser to come up with a concept. Because the Liberty-head nickel had a Romanesque theme, Fraser thought that something more "American" was in order. He began researching his nickel in 1911. "And, in my search for symbols," he later explained, "I found no motif within the boundaries of the United States so distinctive as the American buffalo or bison."

Looking back on it, Fraser's choice was peculiar. He was crafting a coin based on what was then a national embarrassment, as if

Black Diamond.

today the U.S. Mint were to strike a coin featuring the American prison at Guantánamo Bay. At the time when the concept of the United States was first taking shape, in the mid-eighteenth century, the distribution of wild, free-ranging buffalo on the North American continent looked very roughly like this:

<u>Northwest Territories.</u>

British Columbia. **Alberta.** **Saskatchewan.** <u>Manitoba.</u>

Washington. **Montana.** **North Dakota.** **Minnesota.** <u>Wisconsin.</u>

Oregon. <u>Idaho</u>. **Wyoming.** **South Dakota.** **Iowa.** <u>Illinois.</u> <u>Indiana.</u> <u>Ohio.</u> *Pennsylvania.* *Maryland.*

Utah. **Colorado.** **Nebraska.** **Kansas.** **Missouri.** <u>Kentucky</u>. <u>West Virginia.</u> *Virginia.*

Arizona. <u>New Mexico.</u> **Oklahoma.** **Arkansas.** <u>Tennessee.</u> <u>North Carolina.</u> *South Carolina.*

Texas. <u>Louisiana.</u> <u>Mississippi.</u> *Alabama.* *Georgia.* *Florida.*

Northern Mexico.

KEY: *Italics:* very limited, intermittent distribution.
<u>Underlined</u>: regionally abundant.
Bold: prolific, widespread abundance.

Buffalo ranged across the continent in herds numbering from fewer than ten to more than ten thousand. The buffalo was one of the most—perhaps *the* most—numerous large mammals to ever exist on the face of the earth. Around thirty-two million lived on the Great Plains alone, the thumb-shaped band of arid grasslands paralleling the eastern flank of the Rocky Mountains from the Texas Panhandle to southern Canada. Four to eight million more buffalo were thought to be scattered to the north, south, east, and west of the plains.

Let's think of all those buffalo in terms of meat. For discussion's sake, say the total population of buffalo living in North America averaged out at one thousand pounds apiece. That's forty billion pounds of buffalo. If a butcher is thorough and careful, a buffalo will yield about 60 percent usable meat. So let's say twenty-four billion pounds of buffalo meat ranged across North America in the early seventeenth century. If every man, woman, and child now living in the United States, all 300 million of us, got together for a buffalo meat party of those proportions, that party would well outlast the Woodstock Festival of 1969. We'd each have eighty pounds of buffalo meat to go through. However, people who relied on buffalo meat as their sole source of food did not usually divide it evenly. At one nineteenth-century trading post, men lived on a ration of twelve pounds of fresh buffalo meat a day.

Fraser's cast of buffalo nickel. Photograph courtesy of the National Cowboy & Western Heritage Museum, Oklahoma City.

Women got half of that. Children, half of that again. With the twenty-four billion pounds of buffalo meat divided thus by age and gender, the 300-million-person buffalo party would last ten days. At the time of European contact, when maybe around 10 million people lived in what is now the United States, the party would have lasted closer to one year.

Fast-forward to 1911—the year that James Earle Fraser started working on his coin. There were only about twenty-two hundred buffalo left on the North American continent, or about two million pounds of buffalo meat. Then the buffalo meat party would have lasted only about forty-five seconds. The distribution of wild, free-ranging buffalo living on their native range looked like this:

Canada

Montana

In all probability, Fraser, who was born toward the end of the wild buffalo's reign on the Great Plains, in 1876, would never have seen a free-roaming buffalo. Fraser claimed that the model for his coin was a buffalo named Black Diamond, which lived in a pasture at the Bronx Zoo. This is somewhat conjectural, as the Bronx Zoo never had a Black Diamond. However, the Central Park Menagerie did. The bull had been born to a pair of buffalo that once belonged to the Barnum Circus, and it lived in a very small cage. People have argued various theories concerning this confusion, either that Fraser was correct about the buffalo's name and confused about its location or that he was correct about the location but got the name wrong. Most evidence suggests right buffalo, wrong location. The coin itself is the most compelling piece of evidence for that, because the buffalo on it looks as if he's accustomed to tight confines. One critic of the nickel summed it up: "Its head droops as if it had lost all hope in the world, and even the sculptor was not able to raise it."

On January 27, 1913, twenty-five presses at the Philadelphia Mint began stamping out three thousand buffalo nickels a minute. Production continued until 1938, and Black Diamond's profile became the most widely distributed image of a buffalo in the world. In the midst of that production, in 1915, Black Diamond himself was put up on an auction block in New York City. There were no bidders. His keeper, Bill Snyder, then offered Black Diamond for private sale. Snyder was hoping to get $500, but the best he could do was $300, this from a dealer in meat specialties named August Silz. The purchaser hauled the still-alive buffalo to 416 West Fourteenth Street, in New York's meatpacking district. The carcass yielded 1,020 pounds of meat, and his head went up on the wall of Silz's office.

Black Diamond's head hung in Silz's office at least until 1918, but no one knows where it is now. On my first-ever trip to New York City I hailed a taxicab in front of Madison Square Garden, where Buffalo Bill Cody's entire herd of twenty buffalo was killed by pneumonia while he performed there in the winter of 1886–87. The driver took me to 416 West Fourteenth Street, but I found that Mr. Silz's enterprise had been replaced by a store called Esthete that specializes in expensive clothes. The store, decorated in the industrial-chic style, with exposed beams and brickwork, was selling a shirt for over eight times the selling price of Black Diamond's entire carcass. I walked up to the clerk, a woman with her legs crossed and her back arched, and I said, "You know what happened in here? They slaughtered Black Diamond in this building and hung his head on the wall. That's the buffalo from the buffalo-head nickel. Isn't that crazy?" She glanced down nervously at her telephone and placed her hand on it. I thanked her and walked out.

Next I took the subway to the Bronx Zoo, where Fraser claimed to have sculpted Black Diamond. It was raining a cold spring rain. The zoo's buffalo were in their pasture, soaking wet but content next to a haystack and a large stump that they like to scratch themselves against. A woman was standing under an umbrella at the fence with a small child, and she laughed when the kid looked at her and said, "I wouldn't want to go in there. Those are big."

In the early twentieth century, a group of well-to-do Easterners, including the artist Frederic Remington and the industrialist Andrew Carnegie, established the American Bison Society at the zoo.* President Theodore Roosevelt, a onetime buffalo hunter and the honorary president of the ABS, believed that the total annihilation of the buffalo would do irreparable damage to the manly mystique of the American West and that it would have overall negative impacts on the American psyche. Society members financed a search for a suitable range in the West where buffalo could be restocked and protected, and they settled on land in Cache, Oklahoma. One of America's great ironies is that not only did New York's aristocrats help save the West's buffalo from extinction, but they used New York's buffalo to do it. On Friday, October 11, 1907, fifteen buffalo left the Bronx Zoo's buffalo pasture and began a two-thousand-mile journey out west. A photog-

---

*The Wildlife Conservation Society at the Bronx Zoo revitalized the American Bison Society in 2005. The original ABS had been founded a hundred years earlier and was disbanded after the buffalo had been saved from extinction. The new incarnation of the ABS will take on what it describes as a "long-term, large-scale, international, multi-purpose, and inclusive" initiative "to restore the ecological role of bison across their original range."

rapher and editor from the zoo rode in the car with the buffalo and complained of how the animals reached out of their cages with their tongues to nab the straw that he was using as a bed. In Oklahoma, the train was approached by a group of curious Comanche Indians. The adults remembered buffalo, though the children had never seen one.

I went inside the Bronx Zoo Library to talk with the librarian, Steven Johnson, about the potential whereabouts of Black Diamond's head. Johnson has sleepy eyes and a slow, precise way about him. He told me that I'm not the first person to come looking for the head. He's sometimes visited by numismatists, those who study and collect coins. Johnson shared with me his freshest clue about Black Diamond's head. In the 1980s, shortly after he started working at the Bronx Zoo, a man called and said he had the head. At the time, Johnson didn't know what the man was talking about. Later, when it occurred to him, he scoured his desk for a note or a phone number, but there was no trace of the caller.

"You think that person threw it out or something?" I asked.

"I don't think it's the type of thing you throw away," said Johnson. "I think it's still around. If there was a story in the New York papers—'Who Has Black Diamond's Head?'—I think the answer might emerge. Until then, we'll just have to wait and see."

THE BUFFALO'S RELATIONSHIP with man has been so complex and dramatic that it's sometimes difficult for us to explain. We lean on patriotism, mythology, spirituality, even religion. The Blackfoot Indians of the northern Great Plains believed that the buffalo once hunted and ate humans, but then the Maker of People gave humans bows and flint knives and instructed them to eat the buffalo instead of the other way around. Some plains tribes did not eat the thymus glands, or sweetbreads, of buffalo, believing that they were chunks of human flesh still stuck in the buffalo's throat. A Crow narrative explains that humans received the buffalo from giants who rode buffalo but did not eat them. The Cheyenne believed that buffalo originated from a magical sack that hung from the lodge pole of an old man who was afraid of geese. The Kiowa believed that buffalo were related to the sun.

I have to say that the buffalo was given to me by Lady Luck. There's really no other way to explain it. I was lucky to find the buffalo skull on that warm mid-September day in Montana's Madison Mountains. And I got lucky again in the summer of 2005 when I was walking through downtown Oxford, Mississippi, with my friend Anna Baker. She and I had spent the previous evening in Clarksdale, Mississippi, the "Official Home of the Blues." There I ate fried catfish, fried okra, and fried hush puppies before drinking so many drinks that I decided to sell my soul to the Devil at the same crossroads where the blues legend Robert Johnson allegedly sold his. Anna wouldn't stop the car to let me out at the proper place, and so she and I got into a big fight. My soul was still my own in the morning, but my head felt like someone was trying to take it away with a set of rusty pliers. In short, I wasn't feeling lucky.

Just then my phone rang. It was my brother Danny up in Alaska.

"Lucky fucker!" he yelled into the phone. "You drew a buffalo tag for the Copper River!"

Earlier that year, in the spring of 2005, the state of Alaska announced that it was issuing twenty-four hunting permits for the Copper River buffalo herd. The herd wanders freely throughout hundreds of square miles of roadless wilderness in Wrangell–St. Elias National Park and Preserve, a twenty-three-million-acre chunk of federally owned land in the south-central portion of the state. Along with 1,303 other people from around the country, I filled out my form and mailed in my ten bucks. My odds were one in fifty. Danny was right—lucky indeed.

A GAME OF ASSOCIATION, a skull, a coin, the luck of the draw. It seems to me that each represents an important aspect of our relationship to the buffalo. The game, which allows me to see the interconnectedness of the world through the buffalo, represents the often hidden though pervasive presence of the animal in our culture. The skull, which sent me on its own journey, represents the buffalo itself, an animal of flesh and bone. The coin and its unsolved mystery represent man, particularly in the way that he has struggled to put the buffalo to use as an icon, a resource, and a trophy. The lottery drawing, which led to my own physical encounter with the buffalo, represents the forces that continue to draw us toward the buffalo, to join it in nature in the ancient dance of predator and prey. In my efforts to understand the buffalo, I had to follow the animals. I've tracked them through mountains and prairies, zoos and ranches, libraries and laboratories, museums and tourist traps. Sometimes even my own dreams. This book is my attempt to follow their trail.*

---

*Cortés was the first European to see a buffalo, but the prize for the first European to see a *wild* buffalo goes to the Spanish explorer Álvar Núñez Cabeza de Vaca. Cabeza de Vaca sailed for North America in 1527 as second-in-command of the Narváez expedition, an armada of five boats under the king's orders to "conquer and govern" the land of Florida, a vast expanse of ground with an indefinite western boundary. Three hundred men and forty horses departed the ships and headed cross-country into the Florida Peninsula in April 1528. They had loose plans of traveling to the north and west, where they'd meet up again with the men who remained on the ships. After five months of trudging through swamps, they hadn't found their ships and they hadn't discovered any cities of gold, but they did manage to kill or harass every native Floridian they ran into. Word of the Spaniards' open hostilities spread from one native village to the next, and soon the Indians were stealthily slaughtering the Spaniards with arrows.

By the time the Narváez expedition hit northern Florida, they were down to 250 men. They hatched a plan to build makeshift rafts and sail along the coast toward the Spanish colonies in Mexico. While they labored, they were forced to eat the last of their horses. They used horsehair to weave cord for lashing material, and they tanned the legs of the horses to make canteens. During construction, Indian arrows picked off ten more men. The survivors boarded the rafts and paddled up the Gulf Coast. One of the rafts vanished without a trace near the Mississippi Delta. The other rafts got split up. Five men died from drinking salt water. A couple more drowned. On November 6, 1528, two of the rafts were shipwrecked on Galveston Island, Texas, which Cabeza de Vaca dubbed the Isle of Misfortune. It was one of the homelands of the Karankawa Indians, who dressed in woven grass. The Karankawa took great pity on the suffering Spaniards; they fed the survivors and mourned the Spanish dead for an entire night, crying and wailing and sobbing. Things changed, though, when the Karankawa learned that some of the Spaniards had practiced cannibalism. The Indians were so distraught by this moral transgression that the Spaniards feared they would be put to death. What saved them from capital punishment is that they started to die on their own. Dysentery and malaria felled them. Soon the eighty or so men who landed on the Isle of Misfortune were down to fifteen. Then the Spaniards' luck went to shit.

The survivors were dispersed among bands of Indians. They fell into slavery and got further whittled down. They died of exposure and starvation. One Spaniard killed another Spaniard. Indians killed them for reasons that must have struck the Spaniards as very odd. Several were killed after insulting an Indian host by moving from his lodge into that of another man. More were killed when an Indian dreamed that he should kill them and then followed through with the dream. Some were sold off as slaves to distant tribes, where they were abused and killed.

Cabeza de Vaca survived only through luck and fortitude and the kindness of his hosts and keepers. Because he prayed to a God that he claimed was very powerful, the Indians asked him to heal their sick. Cabeza de Vaca explained that he did not have that kind of sway with God, but the Indians withheld his food until he relented. He genuflected, prayed, and made crosses with his hands over the bodies of the sick, and he laid his hands on them. The Indians were very pleased with the results. Once, he was credited with bringing a man back to life. In another village, he cut a man open with his knife to remove an arrowhead that had long ago punctured him in the back and lodged above his heart, where it caused him "great pain and suffering." Cabeza de Vaca closed the incision with two stitches and became the first European to practice surgery in the New World.

By 1532, after four years of wandering, the Narváez expedition was down to four men: Cabeza de Vaca, two other Spaniards, and an African Muslim. The four of them were freed from captivity and reunited through a series of spectacular adventures, and they again continued westward on their quest to find the Spanish colonies in Mexico. They didn't make it far. Just around the time they got into central Texas, they fell into the hands of two new tribes, the Mariames and the Yguazes. Again they were divided up and enslaved. Things got even weirder. Cabeza de Vaca encountered humans who burned their religious leaders' bodies and drank the ashes mixed with water; he encountered men who lived with eunuch lovers, the eunuchs being "more muscular and taller than other men"; he encountered humans who ate the flesh of poisonous snakes, and when the meat was gone, they roasted the bones and ate those, too; he encountered humans who fed their infant daughters to dogs because it was considered taboo for tribal members to marry women born within their own clan and they feared that female babies would grow up to bear the children of their enemies.

Somewhere amid this mayhem in south-central Texas, Cabeza de Vaca finally encountered the buffalo. "Cows come here," he later wrote in his *Relación*.

I have seen them three or four times and eaten them. It seems to me they are about the size of the ones in Spain. They have two small horns, like Moorish cattle, and very long hair, like a fine blanket made from the wool of merino sheep. Some are brownish and others black. It seems to me they have more and better meat than cattle here in Spain. From the small ones the Indians make blankets to cover themselves, and from the large ones they make shoes and shields. These animals come from the North all the way to the coast of Florida, where they scatter, crossing the land more than four hundred leagues. All along their range, through the valleys where they roam, people who live near there descend to live off them.

— 3 —

I HAVE THREE RECURRING NIGHTMARES. In order of increasing frequency, they are (1) that I'm reaching into dark, murky water to retrieve a muskrat from a trap, but instead of feeling the fur of the muskrat, I clasp the hair of a drowned human; (2) that I did not, in fact, graduate from college; and (3) that I'm in a small airplane that's about to crash into an entanglement of overhead power lines.

I'm thinking of the third nightmare right now, as I happen to be sitting in an airplane on a landing strip along the western bank of the Copper River. My pilot, a man my brothers and I know as Bushpilot Dave, is sitting directly in front of me in the cockpit of his Super Cub—a small, single-engine airplane made of cloth stretched over a wooden frame that serves as the work horse, or I should say the work pony, of Alaska's bush pilots. If I were to try to slide a chopstick between the roof of the aircraft and Dave's head, it would be a tight fit. A deck of cards placed between his shoulders and the side windows would probably be held in place. My only view forward is when I press my cheek on the window and try to look around him. Doing so, I see up the runway. The strip ends at a low line of stunted spruce trees and then, beyond, power lines. Dave starts the airplane, then fiddles with some controls and messes with the cockpit GPS unit. Over his radio, he converses with someone about the weather. Then he gives the plane some throttle and adjusts it on the airstrip. I lose sight of the power lines for a moment. Then Dave turns the plane into the wind and there they are again, dead ahead.

It's October. Over three months have passed since I drew my buffalo permit, and I've hired Dave to fly me over Wrangell–St. Elias National Park and Preserve so I can get an idea of where I'll be going when I head into the woods tomorrow. Dave was born in the valley of the Copper River, and he's been flying it for almost his entire life. When I arrived in the town of Glennallen this afternoon, I found Dave in his office. He was wearing the unofficial Alaskan bush pilot uniform: jeans, flannel shirt, sneakers, and a mustache. Besides airplanes, his hangar contains rubber rafts, tents, boxes of freeze-dried food, plane parts, shotgun and rifle ammunition, building materials, steel drums, and landing gear. Dave has kayak-shaped floats for landing planes on water, skis for landing on ice, and large balloon tires for landing on gravel bars or tundra. On a series of shelves covering one of the walls, I noticed rows of parcels labeled with dates. "What's with those?" I asked.

"That's stuff that needs to go places at whatever time is written on them," said Dave. The parcels were prepackaged shipments of food and gear put together by gold prospectors working in the mountains. When the date on a given package comes up, Dave knows to fly the gear into whatever remote airstrip is nearest to the gold miner's claim. Flying gold miners and their gear into the mountains is just a fraction of Dave's business. He also flies scientists to remote field camps on top of glaciers, hunters into the mountains, hikers to alpine trails, fishermen to lakes, whitewater rafters to the headwaters of rivers, and, in my case, people who just want to get a look at the ground.

The plane lifts. The wings rock gently as we come level with the power lines. Despite my nightmares, we continue to climb, and the wires pass easily beneath us. It is the only clear sky that I will see for several days, and I take in the view. I can see Glennallen out the right window. From this perspective the town seems to be positioned in a donut hole. It is encircled by four mountain ranges—the Alaska Range to the north, the Wrangell Mountains to the east, the Talkeetna Range to the west, and the Chugach Mountains to the south. The U.S. Census Bureau classifies Glennallen as a census-designated place (CDP) of 115 square miles. The population of the CDP is 550 people, at a density of 5 persons per square mile (Manhattan's population density is 66,490 persons per square mile). It's the largest CDP along the entire length of the river.

The bulk of Glennallen's citizenry lives at the intersection of the Glenn and Richardson highways. The Richardson Highway connects Valdez and Fairbanks, and the Glenn Highway connects the Richardson Highway to the town of Palmer, which is north of Anchorage and about 150 miles away.

The forest that surrounds these highways is dominated by coniferous trees, or evergreens, with scatterings of small-leaf deciduous trees such as birch, alder, and willow mixed in. In most places, the ground is frozen into a layer of permafrost that lies just a couple of feet below the soil's surface. Precipitation from rain and melted snow does not easily penetrate permafrost, and organic matter breaks down very slowly in the cold climate, so the ground is very spongy with water, moss, and accumulated debris. Trees do not get very big in this biome; the roots have a hard time penetrating the layer of ice, and since the ice traps and holds surface water from rain and melting snow, the ground is often wet enough to drown deep-rooted plants. To survive, the trees sink only shallow roots. And because a tree's roots act as its anchor and support, the trees tend to stay low to the ground lest a big load of snow and ice renders them so top-heavy that they tip over. In what seems like a form of compensation for their diminutive size, the trees grow so densely that foresters refer to this type of landscape as closed forest.

When people build homes in closed forest, they'll sometimes use earthmoving equipment to clear the trees and scrape away the spongy layer of ground. This is often done in very unimaginative ways, and building lots tend to occur in perfect rectangles and squares. People with small businesses will abut their lots directly on the highway, so the asphalt forms one side of the box. People who want some privacy will plow a small driveway through the trees and then create their square of open land back in the woods a ways. These are the places that I get most curious about. When Dave and I level off, at about eight hundred feet, I sneak a couple looks at these citizens' lives. I see magnificent arrays of utilitarian items: log living structures, stacks of firewood, work sheds, dismantled cars and trucks, dog kennels, miscellaneous sections of stovepipe and plumbing, propane tanks, boat motors, bleached moose antlers.

Glennallen passes in seconds and we veer directly over the course of the Copper River, a wide gray swirl of water flanked by broad gravel bars. The river forms to the northeast of here, at Copper Glacier, a mass of melting ice on the north end of the Wrangell Mountains. We're headed downriver, toward the south. Out across the river, toward the east, there is no visible evidence of man. That's Wrangell–St. Elias National Park and Preserve, where the buffalo live. The forest stretches for twenty miles or so and then gives way to mountains that rise out of the land at severe angles.

The next road to the east is 160 miles away, in Canada. It's exhilarating to think that there's a herd of buffalo running around out there. Of the 500,000 buffalo living on the continent today, only 4 percent are allowed to roam free; the remaining 480,000 are held captive behind fences because most people think the animals are too big and bad and dangerous to roam free. The story of how these animals came to be here is part legend and part fact, though it's likely that the legend portions actually contain a few nuggets of truth. It begins in the early 1870s, when North America's last remaining buffalo herds were on the verge of their final collapse. The southern Great Plains were just about cleaned out; the northern plains still had fairly abundant herds, but the animals would be gone in a decade or so.

Enter a man named Sam Walking Coyote, a.k.a. Sam Short Coyote, Running Coyote, or just plain Walking Coyote. He was from the Pend d'Oreille tribe of the Idaho panhandle, but he was married to a Salish woman who lived on the Flathead Indian Reservation on the Flathead River of northwestern Montana. The people of the Flathead valley had always been buffalo hunters, though their own land had never had many. Every year, hunting parties would voyage across the Continental Divide to hunt on Blackfoot land to the east of the Rockies, where the animals were thick. These hunting trips dismayed the Jesuit missionaries who lived among the Flatheads, because they caused significant interruptions to their job of "civilizing" the Indians. Father Jerome D'Aste complained bitterly about this in the 1870s. "The passion for buffalo is a regular fever among them and could not be stopped."

This "fever" was certainly part of Sam Walking Coyote's

makeup, and when he fell out of favor with his wife, he crossed the Continental Divide to go hunting and decided to stay for a couple years in the valley of the Milk River. He took a new wife, a Blackfoot woman. This was a serious violation of the Catholic ban on polygamy, and Sam Walking Coyote worried about it so much that the Blackfeet told him that maybe he should go back home and patch things up with the Jesuits. As a goodwill token to his first wife's people, he tamed six buffalo and herded them back across the mountains. He and the buffalo arrived in the Flathead valley in the spring of 1873. He was promptly beaten by the Indian police, either of their own volition or else under the orders of the Jesuits. This pissed off Sam Walking Coyote, and he decided to keep the buffalo for himself. By 1884 his herd had increased to thirteen head. He sold the buffalo to two ranchers on the reservation for $3,000 in gold and then went down to Missoula to get drunk. Days later, he turned up dead and penniless beneath the Higgins Street Bridge.

The two ranchers, Michel Pablo and Charles Allard, bragged that their buffalo were "as good an investment as real estate." They ran the herd like a business, and the business grew and grew. In the latter years of the 1890s there were fewer than one thousand buffalo in the United States, but the two ranchers owned more than half of them. Just ten years earlier, complete buffalo hides were selling for $2 or $3 apiece, but now a person could sell just a severed head for $100 and then sell the same animal's hide for another two to five hundred bucks. Pablo and Allard refused to sell breeding-aged pairs of the animals because they didn't want to create competition for themselves. Instead, they sold single bulls to zoos and parks, and also to private individuals who wanted pet buffalo, which was a developing fad.

Charles Allard died just before the new century, and his family sold off his share of the buffalo in small bunches—some to taxidermists, some to private collectors, a small herd to the Conrad family of Kalispell, Montana. Pablo kept his until 1907, when he was up to six hundred head. Then trouble struck. Because he was married to a Salish woman, he had been allowed to graze his buffalo free of charge on reservation lands. But that year the federal government essentially deregulated the reservation and opened tribal lands to purchase by white settlers. Whites bought prime reservation land from Indians who wanted cash instead of land, and other whites received free land that they acquired through squatter's rights. Soon Pablo had no place to graze his buffalo.

He sought land in the United States for his herd to roam free, but the U.S. government didn't want them, because it already owned close to a hundred buffalo and didn't see the need to have more. Pablo made arrangements to sell the herd to Canada at $250 apiece. He spent the next five years trying to round them up. It was a fiasco. Some years he caught a couple hundred, one year he caught only seven. What he did catch was shipped to Canada's Wainwright Preserve, east of Edmonton, Alberta. Some died in transit, literally rampaging themselves to death inside the train cars. Others had to be shot to protect the cowboys who were trying to corral them. Pablo ordered twenty-five killed because they were too wild to deal with. In the meantime, the buffalo that remained on the reservation continued to breed. By the time he finally quit trying to round them up, in 1912, Pablo had shipped 695 buffalo to Alberta and had grossed $170,000 on the sale. About seventy-five buffalo remained on the reservation, too wild to catch. A valley that held the United States' largest buffalo herd just six years before now contained just a remnant.

The American Bison Society countered the U.S. government's belief that it already had enough buffalo by arguing that a single prairie fire or an outbreak of disease could easily kill off half of the publicly owned buffalo in the country. This worried President Theodore Roosevelt, who signed legislation enabling the United States to purchase thirteen thousand acres of Flathead Reservation from the Indians for $30,000. The American Bison Society spent over ten grand to purchase the nucleus herd for the Flathead Reservation land. It bought thirty-four animals from the Conrad family of Kalispell, who had purchased them from Charles Allard, who had purchased them from Sam Walking Coyote. Three other buffalo were donated, and two of those were also direct descendants of Sam Walking Coyote's original six animals.* In October 1909, these thirty-seven buffalo were released into the fences of the National Bison Range and then watched as the remainder of Michel Pablo's now-wild buffalo were killed off by poachers outside the fence.

---

*The intermingling and swapping of small buffalo herds during the establishment of the National Bison Range was emblematic of buffalo management in general during the early twentieth century. Basically, conservationists were desperately trying to gather up whatever scattered herds had survived the slaughters of previous decades, and they gave little thought to the particular histories of each herd—as long as the animals looked like buffalo, they were regarded as buffalo. However, this wasn't always a good test, because many of the private individuals who helped "save" the buffalo from extinction were not acting out of altruistic impulses. Rather, they wanted to breed the buffalo with cattle in order to make a sort of mythical super-beast known as a cattalo. The goal was a docile animal with "less hump and more rump" than buffalo, but with the buffalo's tolerance for extreme weather conditions and its apparent immunity to such devastating livestock diseases as Texas fever. Most of these early crossbreeding experiments were failures, though they succeeded in creating a lot of buffalo with significant amounts of genetic introgression from cattle. Today, only three herds of government-owned buffalo—those at Yellowstone and Wind Cave national parks and a state-owned herd in Utah—are known to be genetically pure. Of privately owned buffalo, which constitute about 96 percent of all buffalo in existence, only one herd, at Ted Turner's Vermejo Park Ranch, in New Mexico, is known to be genetically pure.

At the end of World War I, the American Bison Society conducted a census and counted 12,521 head in North America. The buffalo had been saved from extinction. Now conservationists who were once worried about too few buffalo were worried about too many. Yellowstone National Park couldn't feed all of its, despite efforts to farm portions of the park and put up hay. It began slaughtering. The herd in Wainwright grew so rapidly the animals ran out of range. The Canadians slaughtered a thousand in the first batch and then continued butchering all through the 1920s. They turned the meat into pemmican—dried meat mixed with buffalo fat—and sold it at thirty cents a pound in ten-, twenty-, thirty-, or fifty-pound sacks.

The National Bison Range had similar problems. The founders of the range had thought that the land could support over a thousand head, but in truth it couldn't hold half of that. By 1924, the range had been degraded by overgrazing. Surrounding cattle ranchers didn't want wild buffalo running around and trashing their fences, so the range manager slaughtered a few hundred. In general, the public was uneasy with this large-scale buffalo killing. The practice brought back fresh memories from just thirty or forty years earlier, when the last of the millions were killed off for their hides during a ten-year bloodbath. Under pressure, the U.S. and Canadian governments began making room for them elsewhere. Most often, that meant toward the north. In 1925, Canada shipped buffalo to the newly founded Wood Buffalo National Park in northern Alberta, where the government had discovered a remnant wild herd of five hundred buffalo that had somehow survived the nineteenth century. Almost seven thousand buffalo left Wainwright, but no one knows how many survived the trip to the park; it's been estimated that three thousand died in transit.

The U.S. territory of Alaska also acquired excess buffalo from the National Bison Range. The acquisition was spearheaded by a group of hunters from Fairbanks, Alaska. They had wanted to introduce Rocky Mountain elk to the region, but at the time no one was selling elk. They settled for buffalo and got a good deal. The range charged only for crating and shipping and sent up twenty-three head. The animals traveled by rail to Seattle, where they were loaded on a barge and shipped by sea up to Whittier, Alaska, near the base of the Kenai Peninsula. From there they rode the train up to Fairbanks and arrived on June 27, 1928. After a short stopover, the buffalo were loaded on trucks and driven a hundred miles to the southeast and let loose near their final destination, which is now the town of Delta Junction. Because Alaska was still thirty-one years away from statehood, the animals fell under the jurisdiction of the U.S. Fish and Wildlife Service. The government wanted to protect the buffalo herd until it was large enough to withstand a limited amount of hunting by humans. The plan worked: by 1940 Alaska had become home to upwards of five hundred descendants of Sam Walking Coyote's buffalo.

It's hard to say what might have happened to the buffalo herd if it had been allowed to expand without any constraints on its habitat, but in many ways World War II sealed the herd's fate. The U.S. Army was looking to supply its Russian allies with a northern route that was safe from German and Japanese aerial assault. It established the Big Delta Army Air Field and started building highways to connect it to the Lower 48. People started moving in. After World War II, the airbase used to supply Russia became a key strategic point in our emerging national defense plan against Russia.

The buffalo herd's habitat was being invaded by people. The animals destroyed the army's landscaping. Large bulls, gone crazy with the hormones of breeding season, charged trucks. By 1950 the government was looking to get rid of some of the buffalo, and this time to a place where they wouldn't cause any future hassles. That summer, employees of the U.S. Fish and Wildlife Service rounded up seventeen buffalo from Delta Junction and herded them into a sturdy corral. They loaded the buffalo into trucks and drove them about 170 miles to the southeast, near the town of Slana, and then hauled them up the Nabesna Road.

On contemporary maps, the Nabesna Road is a dotted line next to the words "Closed in winter." It leads into Wrangell–St. Elias, and the National Park Service describes it as "short on services but big on wilderness." Somewhere along the road—no one knows exactly where—the U.S. Fish and Wildlife Service employees released the buffalo. For the next ten years, the fate of the Nabesna Road herd was unknown. Reports of lone, wandering buffalo trickled in from various points across hundreds of square miles. There were rumors that the buffalo had been killed off by wolves and grizzlies. Some people thought that disease had killed them all. Eventually, though, the reported whereabouts of the buffalo herd started to focus in on a particular tract of wilderness about 130 miles downriver from the release site at Slana, or about fifteen hundred miles from where Sam Walking Coyote had originally picked up their ancestors.

This tract of land is now beneath Bushpilot Dave and me as we fly along in his Super Cub. I have a map of the area spread across my lap, along with a legal description of the hunt area. The area has a name, DI454, which comprises nine hundred square miles, or over a half-million acres. It's described in terms of physical landmarks. I read the description to Bushpilot Dave: "East of the Copper River, south of the Nadina River, Nadina Glacier and Sanford Glacier, and west of the line from Mount Sanford to

Mount Wrangell to Long Glacier, and west of the Kotsina River, and that portion of Unit 13D east of the Edgerton Highway."

When I get done reading, Bushpilot Dave taps the left window and points to a canyon that slices through the forested expanse beneath us. "That's the Nadina River," he says. "You've got the Nadina Glacier up there at the head of it. In a second here we'll be at the Dadina River. I hardly ever see them above the Nadina, but they're fairly common below the Dadina."

"How often do you see these buffalo?" I ask. "I mean, anywhere around here?"

"Depends. If they're crossing a gravel bar or feeding in the willow patches, I'll see them. But if they're over in there"—Dave sweeps his hand across the vast forest to the east—"you don't see them from up here. They're big, but, boy, they can vanish on you. You'd have to get down in there and look. But I got to tell you, everything down here along the river is Ahtna, Incorporated land. Whatever you do about that is none of my business . . . I'm just telling you."

Bushpilot Dave is referring to something that's been plaguing me for the last few months. Right after receiving the news that I'd won the permit, I began studying up on the applicable rules as established by the Alaska Department of Fish and Game. While some of the rules of the hunt were presented in terms of what you *may* do (you may kill a buffalo of either sex, and you have seven months, from September 1 to March 31, to do it), the bulk of the rules were in terms of what you couldn't do. You *may not*: shoot from roads; use motorized vehicles (airplanes, boats, ATVs, snowmobiles, trucks, and so forth) to chase animals; use a helicopter in any way that has anything to do with hunting or transporting hunters or hunting gear; use a machine gun; use bait; pursue animals with the use of fire, artificial light, laser sight, electronically enhanced night vision scope, radio communication, cellular or satellite telephone, artificial salt lick, explosive, expanding gas arrow, bomb, smoke, or chemical; shoot buffalo while they are swimming; or hunt on the same day that you fly in a bush plane.

Those rules are all great, and they're essential to a fair-chase hunt. However, I was floored when I received the following letter from the Department of Fish and Game:

July 19, 2005

Dear Hunter:

Congratulations on winning a Copper River Herd Bison Permit. You must provide Fish and Game with a written notification of intent to hunt by September 1, 2005 . . . After we receive your notification we will mail to you a hunt information packet and map. You are still required to pick up your permit at the Glennallen Fish and Game office. At that time we will discuss with you the important land access issues that affect this hunt.

Much of the land where the bison are found is private land. Opportunities to hunt bison on private land are extremely limited. You may want to spend some time researching land ownership in the area before you commit to the hunt.

My first thought was, Important land-access issues!? Private land!? Extremely limited? Before you *commit* to the hunt? What the hell? This is Alaska, for God's sake. The Last Frontier, the Great White North, God's Country, a state that is about 70 percent public lands. My dismay turned to disbelief, and I fired off my intent-to-hunt letter in hopes that I'd get some clarification. Then, in early August, I received a packet of information. On the enclosed map, the thousands upon thousands of acres of land within the DI454 area were colored green for public land (Wrangell–St.

Elias) and orange for private property. The map was mostly green, except for strips of orange that bordered the Copper River on both sides. So that was the important land-access issue: if you were hunting by raft, which was the only way to do it, you couldn't get from the river into the wilderness without crossing private land. It was as if you were allowed to travel on a highway and on the land alongside the highway, but you weren't allowed to cross the shoulder.

The entity that owned all of this private property was Ahtna, Incorporated, one of thirteen regional corporations established under the Alaska Native Claims Settlement Act in 1971. The act distributed 44 million acres of land and $1 billion in cash to citizens who could claim at least one-quarter of native Alaskan descent. Rather than being paid out on an individual basis, the money and land were piled into large corporations that operate on a for-profit basis and issue shares to stakeholders. Ahtna, which holds over 1.5 million acres, is one such corporation. Because their profit-making ventures lean toward somewhat destructive extraction industries—mining, logging, highway construction, pipeline construction, rock crushing—I assumed that they probably wouldn't care about something as comparatively benign as a guy cutting across their land. I wrote a letter to Ahtna explaining my predicament and asking permission. The letter went unanswered. I made several phone calls and left messages. No reply.

Then, one day in late August, I was thumbing through the *Anchorage Daily News*, and a large advertisement caught my eye. It was headed: "Notice to the Public." The notice was from Ahtna, and it explained that they were going to throw the books at anyone who dared to "hunt, camp, fish, pick berries or park any type of vehicle on Ahtna property." They promised that they'd be stepping up patrols for trespassers throughout the fall and that their lands would be "heavily patrolled by air, land and water." Violators could expect fines and ninety days in the slammer, and then face additional civil claims for damages.

This left me wondering what in the hell Fish and Game expected a fellow in my situation to do. As it turns out, their solution involves a law that makes it legal to travel through private property as long as one stays below the average high-water mark of a navigable river. On the Copper, the high-water mark is usually above the actual level of the river and includes many small islands and riverside willow thickets. Thus, you could feasibly find and shoot a buffalo that's standing near the river. It seemed kind of cheap to try to float up on a buffalo; and even if I did, there was the risk that the wounded animal would run into the river and die out there. Then I'd be in trouble, because there's no way that I'd be able to drag a wet, thousand-plus-pound animal out of the river before it washed away.

But there was one loophole, sort of, and that was one of the reasons that I am up here with Dave. Several streams, such as the Nadina, Dadina, and Chetaslina rivers, flow from the mountains and through the private land before dumping into the Copper River. If I can locate buffalo up one of these rivers, I'll be able to follow the river below the high-water mark and perhaps access the public land. I've got a GPS unit on my lap, and I'm ready to punch in a waypoint at the sight of something . . . anything. But there's nothing. Several times Dave takes the Super Cub in spiraling dives to check out suspected sets of fresh tracks and suspicious shapes, but we don't see any convincing evidence of buffalo on public land. We're forty minutes out now, or about forty miles, and this plane isn't free. Even if we head back now, I'll be looking at a few hundred dollars.

"Here's the Chetaslina River," says Dave. "I don't know if I've ever seen buffalo below this river." He points out the left window, toward the head of the Chetaslina. "They do hang out between here and there, even up by those glaciers."

"How far is that?" I ask.

"Twenty miles or so. They could be up there somewhere. They'll stay in those hills until the weather gets too bad." Dave circles around and starts following the Copper back up toward Glennallen. Along the way, I keep my nose scrunched against the glass in hopes of seeing buffalo along the Copper, but there's nothing. This isn't going to be so easy, I think. How am I going to find a buffalo? What am I going to do with the thing if I kill it? How will I get it back to the raft? How will I keep from getting busted on private land? How long will I be out here? I get the nagging though familiar sense that winning this permit was something of a curse. It's as if someone who is obsessed with outer space were invited to go to the moon. Of course he'd have to say yes; he'd be a fool not to. But at some point the initial euphoria wears off, and then there's nothing left but the fear of doing it.

— 4 —

WHEN I FOUND the buffalo skull on that September day in Montana's Madison Mountains, I padded it carefully with a fleece jacket and strapped it to the outside of my backpack with a few bungee cords. There was something very enticing about the skull; it seemed so perfectly symbolic, as though it stood for much more than the one animal that died and left it behind. At night, sitting around the campfire, I stared at the skull so much that I started to feel like Shakespeare's Hamlet, when he finds the skull of his old friend Yorick and launches into a speech about how even the great and mighty can be reduced to dust.

My fascination with the skull was accompanied by a nagging curiosity about its rarity and value. I wondered whether it was cool in only a personal way, like a painting your niece makes for you, or in a more general and universal way, like that other people would be jealous. After a few days of lugging it around in the mountains, I finally got a chance to find out. I left my brothers and walked down Sentinel Creek to the trailhead where I'd parked my van. When I got there, I was happy to see a few guys loading some horses into a trailer. I figured they'd be a good audience for the skull; anyone who owns a horse is sure to understand the value of Western iconography. I handled the skull in such a way that they couldn't miss it. Facing them, I unlashed it from my pack, loosened some dirt in the brain cavity with a stick, and poured the dirt out. Some small beetles and rodent-chewed pine nut husks spilled out as well. I held it up over my head to give the underside a careful study. I stayed in that position for some time, waiting for a collective *Good Lord! He found a buffalo skull!* But they said nothing.

This worried me. I started to think that maybe I hadn't found a buffalo skull, and that I was getting all excited about some wayward domestic cow that had wandered into the mountains and died. Maybe it was a weird breed of cow with a weird-shaped head that I was unfamiliar with. I anxiously got in my van and drove down a long forest service road to its inter-section with highway 287. I turned to the west. The road curved through the mountains for a while and then dropped down to the northern bank of Earthquake Lake. The lake began to form at 11:37 p.m. on August 17, 1959, when an earthquake along the face of the Madison Range dumped a mountainside into the Madison River. The debris completely blocked the river's flow and buried nineteen people, mostly campers. The chimney on Old Faithful Inn, miles away in Yellowstone National Park, fell through the roof.

I drove through the earthquake's debris field and entered the broad, grassy valley of the lower Madison River. When I got to the town of Ennis, the Madison River split away from the road to flow through Bear Trap Canyon. I continued along northward until I hit I-90, and then I headed west, crossing the Continental Divide and dropping down into the town of Butte, where I bought a bean burrito. From there I paralleled the headwaters of the Clark Fork River, which flows all the way to the Columbia River and into the Pacific Ocean. I drove through long expanses of ranchland punctuated by short spurts of town, looked at passing cattle, particularly the horned varieties, and was visited again and again by my pestering suspicion that I was driving around with a cattle skull on my front seat. Where the Clark Fork River receives the Blackfoot and Bitterroot rivers in the town of Missoula, I exited I-90, crossed over Rattlesnake Creek, and pulled in to my local public library. I grabbed *Skulls and Bones,* by Glenn Searfoss, from the stacks, checked the index, and turned to page 32. There it was, the same thing that I'd dug out of the ground. I'd found a buffalo skull.

I hung the skull from my living room ceiling by a length of nylon cord. At night, with the floor lamp next to it, the skull would cast a huge shadow against the opposite wall, as big as a buffalo. When one of my housemates slammed the door, the shadow would sway in eerie patterns. In the evenings, before I'd go out and hit the town, I liked to sit beneath the skull and read. As it happens, I was around this time reading Francis Parkman's *Oregon Trail,* which chronicles the author's journey to the Great Plains in the summer of 1846. My friend Sandy had given me the book because Parkman does a lot of hunting in it; but because I happened to be thinking about buffalo skulls, I noticed something else entirely: when Parkman, a historian, isn't complaining about his travel mates, or discoursing on tobacco, or eating a puppy, or complaining about his physical ailments, he is usually describing a Great Plains covered so thick with the skulls of buffalo that it must have been hard to get from place to place. In a meadow full of wildflowers, he sits down on one of the many available buffalo skulls and lazily contemplates the skulls surrounding it. Near the

Arkansas River, he sees a white wolf skulking through camp at night and fires a shot at it. When he runs over to what he believes is the wolf's carcass, it turns out to be nothing more than a large sun-bleached buffalo skull. At another point in his trip, up near the Black Hills of South Dakota, Parkman gets lost. There's a big thunderstorm headed his way, and he's terribly afraid of being caught and killed by Pawnee Indians. He writes, "I felt the most dreary forebodings of ill-success . . . the passage was encumbered by the ghastly skulls of buffalo."

Reading Parkman inspired me to read more about buffalo skulls. I became especially interested in stories about the things that people can learn by digging them up. For instance, a guy named William Fisher in 1932 unearthed a large buffalo skull while digging water lines in downtown Toronto. The skull had settled into sediments predating the Great Lakes, and it was estimated to be somewhere around ten thousand years old. The find was interesting, because the skull did not look like a modern buffalo and it was found in a locality that was not known to have ever had any of the animals.

About twenty years later, on the other end of Canada, a warden named Ulysses La Casse found a buffalo skull along the upper Bow River in Banff National Park. La Casse noticed a steel arrowhead stuck into the skull, with "I. & H. Sorby" stamped into the metal. As it happens, John Sorby (back then, people used *I*s in place of *J*s when registering trademarks) was a toolmaker from Sheffield, England. He and two of his sons, Edwin and John, had long produced "edge tools," shears, spades, saws, blades, and so forth, under the trademark I.S. In 1827, his third son, Henry, joined the business and they changed the trademark to I. & H. Sorby. Through unknown but no doubt interesting circumstances, one of their tools ended up buried in a buffalo's head about four thousand miles away.* Before La Casse came along, it was not known that buffalo had lived so far up the Bow River valley. And not only was this proof of their existence there, but it showed that they were present until at least 1827.

Another interesting story came out of Alaska. In 1979, a husband and wife named Walter and Ruth Roman were mining for gold near Fairbanks when they happened to unearth the skull of a type of Ice Age buffalo known as *Bison priscus.* The flesh and skin were still attached to the skull, and so was the animal's body; it had been frozen in the permafrost and almost perfectly preserved. The animal had been killed in the fall or early winter by an American lion, an extinct cat that was quite similar in appearance to, though larger than, the African lion of today. The lion opened up the buffalo's hide along the spine and ribs and upper limbs. On the buffalo's body, pockets of coagulated blood were still visible beneath its wounds. It had died thirty-six thousand years ago. Dale Guthrie, a professor emeritus at the University of Alaska, cooked and ate part of the animal's neck. He reported it to be "well aged but still a little tough."

While reading about old buffalo skulls, I encountered a lot of arguments and speculations about the various species and subspecies of buffalo that lived in North America at one time or another. This was initially very confusing to me, and since then I've found that it's confusing to other people as well. First off, it's important to be clear that there is no difference between the

---

*I was warned about the veracity of La Casse's claim by Dr. Michael Wilson, a vertebrate paleontologist with Douglas College, in British Columbia. Though he did not specifically refer to La Casse's skull (he'd never even heard of him), he explained that it was once common practice to artificially wed human artifacts with buffalo skulls. The pairing increased the value of the artifacts, both as museum exhibits and as curios for the tourist trade.

American buffalo and the American bison. The word "buffalo" likely originated in a roundabout way involving the English. In Shakespeare's time, military men often wore a type of protective jacket known as a buff coat; these coats were thick and soft and made of undyed leather. When Englishmen arrived in the New World, they would often describe any animal that yielded such leather as a "buff," be it a moose or a manatee. Eventually all of the other North American animals acquired their own particular names, and the largest of them, the American buffalo, walked away with exclusive rights to the title. The name bounced around a bit—buffs, bufle, buffle, buffelo, buffaloe—but it had begun to settle into its modern form by the time of the American Revolution.

The problem with the word "buffalo" is that it had already been given away a couple of times earlier, once to the water buffalo of Asia and once to the Cape buffalo of Africa. Taxonomists, the people in the business of naming and classifying organisms, saw this as a problem, particularly because the American buffalo is not closely related to either of those creatures. As a solution, they began promoting the word "bison," which had already been used in the Latin name of a closely related European animal, the wisent (*Bison bonasus*). It seems as though these efforts to clarify the situation were in vain: we've now got an animal with two perfectly serviceable names, and many discussions about the animal inevitably begin with the question, "What's the difference between buffalo and bison?"

The scientific system for classifying organisms, whereby an animal gets two names, such as *Bison bison,* is known as binomial nomenclature. Under this system, the first word is the generic name, or genus. The second word is the specific name, or species. Carl Linnaeus, who invented binomial nomenclature, was born in

Bison latifrons *skull recovered in North Dakota.*

1707 and believed that all of the world's species were distinct creatures independently created by the hand of God; more simply put, he didn't know about evolution. This excusable bit of oversight, considering his time period, makes his system less than ideal for naming fossils.

Here's why: Over the years, archaeologists and paleontologists (and guys like me) have unearthed many buffalo skulls that look a lot different from the skulls of modern buffalo. For instance, a full-grown modern buffalo has a horn span, from tip to tip, of about three feet. Some ancient buffalo skulls, however, have a horn span of seven feet. And while the modern buffalo's horns sweep upward and backward, these seven-footers were mostly straight with slight forward-facing curves toward the tips. Other skulls fall in between the two extremes, and each has its own idiosyncratic shape and horn configuration. Logically, taxonomists gave these skulls different names. The really big ones became *Bison latifrons*; other, smaller types of skulls picked up their own names, including *Bison priscus, Bison athabascae, Bison alleni, Bison antiquus*, and *Bison occidentalis*. For much of the twentieth century, the relationships between these different buffalo were not very well understood. Scientists believed that at least some of them coexisted in the present-day United States, where they interbred to produce the modern buffalo. We now know that this is not the case; in fact, the different "species" of "extinct" buffalo were just discrete points along the continuous path of a single species' trajectory of change.

The bulk of buffalo history is set in the geologic epoch known as the Pleistocene, which spanned from about two million years ago to ten thousand years ago. Of the geologic epochs, the Pleistocene is by far my favorite. Its relationship to the modern world reminds me of my own relationship to my grandparents: their lives were distant and obscure enough that it's difficult for me to really know and understand them, but what I do know about them helps explain a lot about how I turned into the kind of person I am.

However, whether or not bison history actually began in the Pleistocene depends on how you define "began." If we think in terms of life beginning at conception rather than at birth, we might say that the bison "began" during the epoch that preceded the Pleistocene, called the Pliocene. During the Pliocene, it must have felt as if the gods had turned on an air conditioner and a dehumidifier—imagine a hot and swampy earth cooled off and dried out. Savannas and grasslands had spread across most continents, giving rise to a great diversification of long-legged grazing mammals. One of these mammals was a now-extinct critter known as the Proleptobos, which appears in the fossil record of Asia at about four million years ago. By the end of the Pliocene, the Proleptobos had split into two different groups, cattle and bison. The bison at that time were small and slightly built, and they were soon to enjoy a great expansion of their range; during the early Pleistocene, they spread across most of Eurasia.

The earth more or less continued to cool off during the Pleistocene, which is known somewhat generally as the Ice Age. Really, it's more accurate to say that the Pleistocene epoch contained many ice ages. There were at least seventeen glacial episodes during the epoch's two-million-year span. The episodes varied in terms of severity, but each one followed a cycle that lasted about a hundred thousand years. Each cycle was marked by a glacial period, when ice sheets expanded and climaxed, and an interglacial period, when ice sheets receded. Sometimes the changes were extremely rapid, occurring in just a matter of decades. During the interglacial periods, global temperature averages were as warm as or warmer than today.

Some geologists refer to the most recent glacial episode as the Wisconsinan. It peaked about twenty thousand years ago, and it was a doozy. Glacial ice covered much of the Northern Hemisphere; the Great Lakes region of the United States was under one and a half miles of ice.* With so much of the earth's water tied up in glaciers, ocean levels were much lower. This caused a phenomenon of tremendous ecological significance: dryland cor-

---

*The great weight of that ice caused the earth's crust to sink down into the mantle (a three-mile-thick covering of ice would "sink" the crust one mile). At the end of the Ice Age, the great burden of ice melted away. Because the crust is buoyant, the earth's surface is rising back up in a process known as isostatic rebound. It often rises in lurches, so that seismologists record (and feel) earthquakes in southern Canada, New England, and northern Europe. In all, it's an excruciatingly slow process. Siberia, Canada, and the Great Lakes are all currently rising at average rates of centimeters or less annually, and it will take another ten thousand years before the job is done. I own a cabin that's on pilings over the ocean on an island in Alaska, and friends keep telling me that I'm going to lose the place thanks to the rising ocean levels brought on by global warming. Not quite, I say, as the island is currently undergoing isostatic rebound.

ridors formed between landmasses usually separated by immense bodies of water.

There were many such corridors that opened between various landmasses during the Pleistocene, but for our topic here—the advent of the American buffalo—one of them is particularly important: the Bering Land Bridge. When I was a kid, the Bering Land Bridge always baffled me. I pictured it as a long, narrow hallway running between two continents, with walls of ice and water mounded up on the sides. When I heard about animals and man crossing it, I imagined them making a mad dash, like Moses crossing the parted Red Sea. Actually, though, that is not a good way of looking at it. Instead of picturing a "bridge" connecting Siberia and Alaska during times of lower ocean levels, one should imagine them as being connected by a landmass. That landmass has a name—Beringia—and it was huge. Basically, the entire western border of present-day Alaska stretched out to join the entire eastern border of present-day Siberia. That's one thousand miles from north to south, or about the distance between Miami and New York City. Beringia was dominated by rolling hills, grasslands, and broad valleys. It did not get much snow and was free from glaciers. The dire wolf fed on horses where king crabs now feed on clams.

Several times during the Pleistocene, the dryland corridor of Beringia was open long enough to allow a nearly complete homogenization of wildlife between Siberia and Alaska. That is, animals were able to move freely back and forth between the continents. Of course, these migrating animals would probably have had no idea that they were "going" anywhere. They were just moving along, heading where there was food and a more suitable climate. Individual animals would have been born and would have died on land that is now underwater, and it may have taken several generations for a population of animals to actually "cross" the land bridge.

While there was some interchange going from North America to Siberia, such as the horse, the predominance of faunal exchanges went in the other direction, from Siberia to North America. It seems that the first of several bison migrations happened during the second-to-last glacial episode, about 140,000 years ago. Scientists often refer to these early arrivals as Eurasian steppe bison (*Bison priscus*). In the cave art of Paleolithic European hunters, the steppe bison is often portrayed with curvaceous horns, a large shoulder hump, and a mane so thick that it almost appears to be a second hump. The steppe bison shared the North American landscape with a host of bizarre and fascinating animals that I wish were still around: flat-headed peccaries and beavers that were the size of modern pigs; an armadillo the size of a black bear; the ox-sized Jefferson's ground sloth, which had lips capable of gripping things; the twenty-foot-long, elephant-sized Rusconi's ground sloth, which dragged itself along on its knuckles and used its tail as a support when it stood up to feed on leaves; the one-ton giant short-faced bear, which had catlike teeth and a skull that was almost as wide as it was long; as many as six different camels, including one that was seven feet tall at the shoulder; two horses, including one that may have been striped like a zebra; several elephants, including the five-ton Columbian mammoth, the ten-ton woolly mammoth, and the forest-dwelling American mastodon; and also an impressive array of large cats, including the 275-pound dirk-toothed cat, the 400-pound Ice Age jaguar, the 600-pound scimitar cat, the 700-pound saber-toothed cat, the 850-pound American lion, and two American cheetahs of indeterminate size.

The steppe bison thrived alongside many of these mammals on

the semi-arid grasslands of eastern Beringia, where it was confined by the same factors that had allowed for its arrival. That is, the glaciers that caused the ocean levels to drop also served to block the animal's southward migration into what is now the Lower 48 of the United States, or the mid-continent.

Eventually, during the interglacial period that separated the last two glacial periods, a north-south corridor opened through western Canada. Bison passed through the corridor maybe a hundred thousand years ago, emerging on the Great Plains near the location of Edmonton, Alberta. During the next and final glacial period, the Wisconsinan, that corridor was closed again by advancing glaciers. The bison in the south would never again interbreed with those in the north, and they would each follow their own evolutionary paths: the northern path led to extinction, the southern to the American buffalo.

Populations of animals that are colonizing new territory sometimes undergo sudden and dramatic evolutionary changes. There are a couple of reasons for this. First, the colonizing population is likely to be numerically small and may contain only a fraction of the original population's genetic diversity. Thus, the new founder population can turn out to be slightly different from the parent population, and there's less genetic anchoring, or genetic stability, to "pull" the founder population back into line. When it comes to colonizing postglacial territory, the new population is also likely to have abundant access to food and a low population density. The Russian-born zoologist Valerius Geist has linked these conditions to the phenomenon of "giantism" in ungulates such as buffalo. The animals develop what Geist describes as "altered body proportions" and "huge and often bizarre horns."

That's what happened to *Bison priscus*; the animal experienced an evolutionary growth spurt and turned into the monster-horned

Bison latifrons. It was one and a half times as big as the modern form of the animal, with horns as long as an NBA player. That relatively quick move toward giantism, however, was followed by a much longer movement in the opposite direction. For whatever reason, the large horns and body size of *B. latifrons* became disadvantageous to the animal. Perhaps *B. latifrons*'s predators learned to exploit the animal's ungainly size, and quicker, more agile animals were more likely to survive. Or perhaps a reduction in the available food supply, or greater competition for that food, gave an advantage to animals with smaller body sizes. The evolutionary trend toward smallness, or diminution, continued for thousands of years. By around twenty thousand years ago, the long, straight horns of *B. latifrons* had given way to the shorter, curved horns of *B. antiquus.* The animal continued to get smaller, and by about five thousand years ago it had assumed the basic shape and size and behavioral characteristics of the buffalo that we know today, *Bison bison.*

Of course, the buffalo is still changing—maybe more rapidly now than at any other time. We may not know until much later, maybe thousands of years from now, when we have a distant point of perspective from which to look at it.

I often wondered how my own buffalo skull fit into the grand scheme of the animal's history. Was it actually what I'd been calling it, an American buffalo, or was it from one of those remnant forms of the past? I worried that perhaps it belonged in a museum, or maybe had some value to science. I studied a system of bison skull diagnostics known as "cranial characteristics and horn-core morphology"; you take a bunch of measurements of a buffalo skull, with particular focus on the horns, and those measurements help you extrapolate what sort of skull you're looking at. I got my hands on a list of twenty-six of those measurements and felt like I was holding a secret code that would unravel a great mystery. However, the measurement descriptions were somewhat puzzling; I was supposed to measure the "rostral width at maxillary-premaxillary suture," the "transverse diameter of core at right angles to longitudinal axis," and the "width of skull at masateric process above M1." Not only did I not know what any of those parts were, but I felt that the measurements were callously indifferent to the reality of my skull's condition: it wasn't all there, and much of what was there was crumbled and chipped.

My next attempt at identifying the skull brought me all the way to Oxford University, in England. I had read an academic article titled "Rise and Fall of the Beringian Steppe Bison," which appeared in a 2004 issue of the journal *Science*. The article provides a timetable supporting a claim that the bison began sliding toward extinction across the northern extent of its range about thirty-five thousand years ago. The article's primary author is Beth Shapiro, a leading expert on ancient DNA who works at Oxford University. In researching the article, Beth and her colleagues had extracted genetic material from the skeletal remains of around five hundred bison that lived in Alaska and northern Canada thousands of years ago. Ancient DNA tends to be highly degraded and eroded—it would be virtually impossible to use it for cloning—though it can be used to reveal the effective population size of a breeding group, as well as how the particular animal fits into the overall evolutionary history of its species. I called Beth Shapiro one day, introduced myself, and asked if she could work some of her magic on my buffalo skull. She told me she'd be happy to try.

It was wintertime when I arrived in Oxford. The snowfall was so light that the flakes looked like drifting campfire ash. Underdressed students hustled from building to building with their chins tucked into their collars and their hands pulled up into their sleeves. I walked to the Henry Wellcome Ancient Biomolecules Centre and waited outside for Beth Shapiro.

Beth arrived on a bicycle. She mentioned that she was suffering from a mild hangover as she fiddled with her belly button ring, which seemed to have snagged itself on an article of her clothing. Beth grew up in Rome, Georgia, where she landed a job in tenth grade as the news anchor on her local television station. She'd go to work at 6:00 a.m., do the news, and then get to school during the second hour. After school, she'd go back to the television station and work until 6:00 p.m. After graduating from high school with honors, she got a university degree in ecology in 1999 and then landed a Rhodes scholarship to study evolutionary biology at Oxford. She's been there long enough to pick up a touch of an accent, and she's fond of words such as "bloody" and "rubbish."

Beth led me around to the back of the biomolecules center. No one is allowed to use the front door because they've found that genetic contaminants have a way of coming in off the street. Beth told me several stories of people who'd made "great" discoveries with ancient DNA only to find that they hadn't: a genetic researcher looking for DNA from an extinct saber-toothed cat found some feline DNA all right, but it turned out to come from someone's house cat.

Another time, a team of researchers working in England claimed to extract from salt crystals a form of bacterial DNA that was tens of millions of years old. Until then, the oldest successfully extracted samples of DNA came from organisms that were only forty to eighty thousand years old. "We got their data and looked at it and said, 'Piss off,' " Beth told me. "We later got the same DNA from dirt that I collected on the roof of Oxford University's Museum of Natural History. So either that roof has bacterial

DNA that's associated with salt crystals that are a hundred million years old, or they were dealing with a contaminant."

To avoid such contaminants, we stripped out of our outer clothes and stepped into one-piece white lab outfits with rubber bootees, latex gloves, skintight hoods, and full face masks. We looked like we were going to clean up a chemical spill. Then we stepped through a series of doors, closing each set behind us before opening the next. We arrived in a room that was piled here and there with sealed plastic bags containing some alarming labels. There were several bags of "unused plague samples." There were samples of thirty-five-thousand-year-old giant ground sloth shit, taken from a cave in South America. ("Poop's great," said Beth. "You can get the animal's own DNA, and also the DNA from its intestinal parasites.") There were mammoth bones, bones from extinct horses, saber-toothed cat bones, and short-faced bear bones. Beth opened a freezer to show me two complete human skeletons. "Dead Victorians," she said. "Some archaeologists turned them up. No markings on the graves. I'm trying to give them away because they're taking up space. I've offered to throw in this bloody freezer to whoever will come and get them."

We went into a small room containing workbenches and several devices that looked like elaborate refrigerators with labels reading "Thermo Cryotechnics." I unsheathed the skull and laid it on the counter. Beth fitted a cutting wheel that was the size of a quarter to a Dremel tool and plugged the tool in. It made a faint whirring sound. "With bison, I like to cut right here," she said, pointing to a thick section of bone between the horn's base and the eye socket.

To reduce surface contaminants, Beth used the tool to scrape away the outside of the bone. She only needed about a gram, so the area she cleaned was less than an inch square. The bone on the surface turned to fine powder, and the smell of burning hair filled the room and penetrated my face mask. "Ancient DNA is already in shitty condition," she said, "so I want to get as good a sample of bone as I can. Usually, I can tell by the way they smell whether they still have good DNA in them."

"Does it have the right smell?" I asked.

"Pretty good," she said.

"So you think it's going to work, then?" I asked.

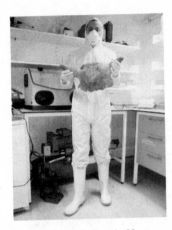

Author and skull at the Henry Wellcome Ancient Biomolecules Centre at Oxford University.

Beth continued cutting. "I give it fifty-fifty," she said.

When she turned off the saw, Beth picked up a small tool that looked like a dentist's implement and used it to pry out the rectangular block of bone that she'd cut. It was about as big as two Chiclets set side by side, and twice as thick. She cut the block into two squares and gave me one in case I decided to submit it to a laboratory for radiocarbon dating. She placed the second sample of bone in a heavy-duty stainless steel canister containing a steel ball bearing. The canister was fitted into a machine labeled "Mikro-Dismembrator." The machine shook the canister so fast that it was a blur. The ball bearing inside the canister pulverized the bone into a fine powder. Beth then poured the powder into a test tube and capped the tube. She labeled it No. 43, and it went into a rack of a hundred such tubes containing powdered bone from extinct species of Siberian yaks and bison. Mixed in at random were empty tubes. She makes sure that the results from those empty tubes are negative, to ensure that they are not contaminated with ambient bits of modern DNA.

That was as much of the process as Beth could show me, and it was as much as I could readily understand. The actual act of extracting the DNA is mind-boggling in its complexity, and mostly takes place inside elaborate, sensitive machinery. As Beth walked me to a bus stop, she told me that it would take about a month before she had results. I flew home, as anxious as if I were waiting for the outcome of a girlfriend's pregnancy test. I counted down the days until I hit the number thirty, and then I placed a call to Beth's office. She sounded dejected. "I was hoping to get some really old bison DNA from Montana," she said.

"So it's not old?" I asked. "It's not some weird, ancient form of bygone buffalo?"

"I can't tell you how old it is," she said. "But I can tell you that, genetically, it matches a modern bison."

"A regular ol' American buffalo?" I asked.

"If that's how you want to put it, then yes," she said. "An American buffalo."

At this point, the gram-sized piece that Beth had given me began to burn a hole in my pocket. It costs about $700 to get a radiocarbon date from a piece of bone, and I'd been waiting for Beth's results before I dropped the money. If she determined that my skull was from an ancient form of the animal, I'd save my cash. But if it was from a modern form of the animal, I thought it would be cool if I could link it to some specific date that pertained to human history. Plus, by now I'd become addicted to the highs and lows of scientific inquiry. I padded a one-gram piece of the skull with cotton balls and stuffed it into an empty Tic Tac container along with a check for $675. I placed that into a padded envelope and addressed it to Beta Analytic of Miami, Florida. Again, the pleasure of anticipation coursed through my veins.

Radiocarbon dating works something like this: Through photosynthesis, plants take up carbon-14, a naturally occurring radioactive isotope that is produced by cosmic rays entering the earth's atmosphere. Through the consumption of plant materials, or through the consumption of organisms that eat plant materials, the carbon-14 passes into every other living organism on earth—it's inside of you, your dog, your goldfish, your house plants, and your goldfish's food. Organisms accumulate the isotope at the same ratio as it occurs in the atmosphere, and the accumulation process stops when the organism dies. From then on, the carbon-14 begins to decay with a half-life of 5,730 years. Through some laboratory wizardry, it's possible to examine the rate of decay of the remaining carbon-14 in an organism's tissues and then infer how long the thing's been dead.

I waited over a month for my results. In the meantime, I followed a somewhat related series of articles that appeared in the *Billings Gazette* about the U.S. Mint's ten-year, fifty-state commemorative-quarter program. Montana's quarter was scheduled for a 2007 release, and the state had begun its selection process in the summer of 2005, when Governor Brian Schweitzer's office put out a call for designs.

Hundreds of proposals were submitted. Suggestions included a flaming skeleton riding a motorcycle; a can of beer and a pork chop sandwich; a grizzly bear; "dudes riding three-wheeled ATVs on a hill"; a picture of Lewis and Clark; and the Unabomber's cabin in Lincoln, Montana. Some ideas were thrown out for being obscene, some were thrown out for being illegal (you can't use the state symbol on a coin), and others were rejected for being non-coinable, which is the U.S. Mint's term for a design that is too complicated. The governor proposed the novel idea that Montana's quarter be minted in palladium, a white metal mined in Montana, but federal law mandates the use of silver.

The six-person selection committee appointed by Schweitzer eventually nominated four ideas: a bull elk; a landscape featuring the sun; a landscape featuring a river; and a buffalo skull. The four ideas were submitted to the U.S. Mint for preliminary design, and the U.S. Mint returned the four ideas in coin form. The images were placed on an Internet-based ballot. The *Billings Gazette* announced the final decision on June 30, 2006, just as I was struggling with my radiocarbon purchase. The story appeared amid a collection of state headlines dominated by stories about car crashes, crystal meth, murder, and a plan to give birth control to wild horses: the elk pulled 30 percent, the sun and the river each nabbed around 18 percent, and the buffalo skull landed 34 percent of the vote. The choice seemed to tear the state apart. Someone pointed out that more people had voted against the skull than had voted for it. Comments flooded in to the *Gazette*:

"That quarter is UG-LY."

"Man, that coin is dumb! A floating cow skull, what the heck does that have to do with anything?"

"The skull is easily the worst of the four. Carrion has always been such a great beacon for prosperity."

"I think it was a wonderful choice. We were competing in the ugly quarter contest, weren't we?"

"Why in the world would Montana choose a symbol of death for its new quarter?"

"Can't Montana do anything right? A quarter to honor Montana and we choose a dead animal's skull?"

"UGH!"

The entire process made me feel as though my personal feelings (and cash expenditures) were being put to a public forum. By now, a couple of years had passed since I'd found the skull, and I'd been carrying it from home to home and state to state, trying to find some way to describe what it meant. Not just what it meant to me, but also what it *meant* meant, in a larger way. All I could come up with was that I liked being near it and that I enjoyed staring at it. I described it as somehow symbolic of the American experience, but I could never really put this sentiment into the proper words. Now I felt as though my whole enterprise with the buffalo skull was being mocked. I pictured myself as an oddball variant of those folks who spend their time and money trying to prove that they are descended from European royalty.

But the story with the skull had a satisfactory ending after all. When my radiocarbon results arrived in the mail, I discovered that my buffalo skull's official age was, in the jargon of radiocarbon dating, 150 +/– 40 BP. Calibrated to calendar years, that meant the buffalo was no older than A.D. 1660. Because the bone did not contain radioactive bomb carbon from atmospheric testing of nuclear warheads, it was no younger than A.D. 1960.

The first thing I said was, "A three-hundred-year span of time was the best that these people could do for $675?" I was tempted to call the Better Business Bureau, but first I dialed up Darden Hood, of Beta Analytic, to see what he had to say for himself. He politely explained a few things to me, such as the "heliomagnetic modulation of the galactic cosmos," "geomagnetic variations," and the "intercepts between the average radiocarbon age and the calibrated curve timescale." That information helped him to explain, in a roundabout way, why organic materials from the past few hundred years are less reliably datable than materials from the past few thousand years.

I sank into a mild carbon-dating depression. Then one day I was reading something by an archaeologist with the National Park Service named Kenneth P. Cannon. He was discussing a buffalo skull with the exact same radiocarbon date as mine, 150 +/– BP, which was analyzed by Beta Analytic of Miami, Florida. Cannon writes, "Statistically, this bison likely died in the early to mid-18th century."

I called Kenneth Cannon at his office in Lincoln, Nebraska, and told him about my little problem.* He knows Darden, has worked with him for years. He explained that Darden's job is to accurately calculate radiocarbon dates, "not interpret results." "There's always going to be a level of variability in calculation and interpretation," explained Ken. But he did help shed some light on my results. He explained that there's a 95 percent chance that my buffalo died between A.D. 1720 and A.D. 1880, and a 66 percent chance that it died within a few decades of A.D. 1750. For the sake of patriotic nostalgia, it's fun to think that my American buffalo might have died in 1776. And because the animal was found at such a high elevation, nine thousand feet, it's apparent that he died in the snow-free season of summertime. While I'm not going so far as to suggest that he died on July 4, 1776, you can't say for sure that he didn't. Now, when people come over to my house, I'll usually point at the skull and say, "See that? That

---

*Because I had found the skull on national forest land, Kenneth Cannon encouraged me to report the find to the proper authorities. I resisted this at first, fearing that I'd broken a law by removing the skull from federal property and now it would be taken away from me. Eventually the guilt was too much for me to handle, and I confessed my crime to Mark Sant, a federal archaeologist whose jurisdiction includes the Beaverhead National Forest. We discussed the skull, and he informed me that I fit into a sort of gray area between rules governing anthropological specimens. Because the skull does not show direct evidence of obvious human tampering, such as carvings or brain extraction, it is not necessarily a cultural artifact. And since the bone is not yet fossilized, it isn't considered a fossil. He granted me immunity in exchange for information. I submitted photos, a copy of the radiocarbon report, and a marked U.S. Geological Survey quadrangle map. With these materials, Sant promised to compile an archaeological site form on the skull.

buffalo might have been alive when they signed the Declaration of Independence." I can never decide if there is irony in that statement, or nostalgia, or what, so I usually just let the statement stand on its own. People fill the silence by walking over and picking it up.

— 5 —

THINK OF THE SHAPE of the letter D. The curved arc of the letter's right side is the fifty-mile stretch of the Copper River that I'm going to float in search of buffalo. The vertical line at the letter's left side is the forty-mile stretch of highway south of Copper Center, a small village that lies just south of Glennallen. Where the two lines meet, at the top and bottom of the D, are two places where my partners and I can get a truck close enough to the river to load and unload gear into a raft. The lower part is near the town of Tonsina, where there's a little road off the highway that salmon fishermen use to access their fish traps. I've got a buddy's truck parked down there with the keys hidden under the front-left tire. We'll use that truck at the end of the trip, rather than hitchhiking back to where we are now, at the top of the D.

Specifically, the top of the D is where the Klutina River passes below the Richardson Highway just before flowing into the Copper River, which is less than a mile downstream from me. My brother Danny and I are staring at a bunch of gear strewn up and down the riverbank while two of our buddies, Matt Rafferty and

Jeff Jessen near the Copper/Klutina confluence.

Jeff Jessen, inflate the raft with a pair of hand-powered pumps. The four of us are going to travel downriver and hunt together for a few days. If we don't find a buffalo in that amount of time, I'll stay behind in Wrangell–St. Elias and they'll come back with the raft to pick me up at some later date.

Right now, we're sorting through gear, trying to determine how much we can bring. Usually you can pack everything you want in a raft, right down to cases of beer. But this situation is different, because Danny and I are trying to imagine what the raft's going to look like with eight hundred pounds of buffalo parts in it. It's highly speculative work. For starters, we don't really know if we're going to find a buffalo, let alone how big it will be. Second, we don't know how much water we'll have to float the raft in. The air temperature dropped into the teens last night, and the edges of the Klutina are frozen in a skein of ice. Boulders in the middle of the river are capped with frozen splash water, so they look as slick and shiny as greased bowling balls. A few more cold nights like this will set off a chain of events: the glaciers that feed the Copper's tributaries will slow down in their melting; water levels in the Copper River will drop; more and more rocks and gravel bars will rise above the water's surface; the raft will drag on the bottom more often; we'll have to unload the boat to get it unstuck; we'll start wishing like hell that we hadn't packed so much gear.

My brother Danny is particularly in tune to the workings of rivers because he's a freshwater ecologist with the University of Alaska. He's coming along because we have an unspoken brotherly tie that says he has to. Our companions, Rafferty and Jessen, are in tune to the doings of rivers because they're both whitewater enthusiasts. They're coming along partly because it's their raft and partly because they're hoping to get their hands on a bit of free-range organic buffalo meat. I first became aware of Jessen, a hospital administrator, and Rafferty, an environmental activist, while hanging around at backyard barbecues in Anchorage. The town has a thriving community of people in their twenties and thirties who moved to the state looking for wilderness thrills, and these folks get drawn into summertime salmon cookouts like raccoons to garbage. You'll find out about common acquaintances while talking about getting lost on a mountain, or digging clams, or flipping a boat in a river while hunting caribou. During such conversations, I heard that Jessen once spent ten days holed up in a snow cave during a blizzard on a mountain. I heard about how Rafferty was watching a grizzly bear one day when another grizzly bear came along and killed it and ate its guts. Another time, I heard a story about how the two of them were rafting with some friends when a landslide peeled off a mountain and came ripping down the slope, trees and all. A descending tree limb grabbed a girl's life jacket and, as my friend described it, "deposited her in the river like an anchor. She just vanished. Then the limb broke, and she came popping back up." The landslide caused a minor tsunami that beached the raft so far up on the riverbank that they had to drag the boat back down to the water.

The number of weird things that happen to a person in the wild is directly proportional to how much time that person spends in the wild, and I figured that these would be some useful guys to have around. Danny had met Rafferty a couple times but he'd never hung out with him for that long; he knew Jessen a little bit better, and described him to me as having an infectious enthusiasm that would be suitable to a used-car salesman. He arranged for the three of us to meet for a beer at Humpy's, a popular downtown Anchorage bar on West Sixth Avenue. Jessen is short and stocky, with a square build and slightly crooked teeth. He was wearing a wool jacket with a yoked back and oversized buttons, and his fingers were nicked up with many little cuts. I'd been prepared to talk Jessen into making the trip, but no such persuasion was necessary. He ordered a beer and a blackened-halibut sandwich, rolled out a few maps, and jumped right into the nitty-gritty details of what it would take to float the Copper River. When we left, Jessen said, "I can't totally commit until I talk this over with Rafferty. It's his raft, too."

I awaited Jessen's call for a week, but he never got back to me. I called him, and he didn't call me back. I couldn't imagine what the problem was. I'd been blown off, and for no good reason! After eight days had passed, I started to work out a whole new set of plans that didn't rely on anyone else's input. Then one night Danny was hanging out at a party and talking about buffalo hunting with some guy, and the guy says, "I heard that Matt Rafferty's going on a buffalo hunt, too."

"What?" Danny said. "Are you serious? With who?"

"I don't know. I guess Jeff Jessen knows someone who has a brother who drew a buffalo tag for the Copper River."

"That's *my* brother," said Danny. "That's us!"

NEAR ITS CONFLUENCE with the Copper River, the Klutina flows through a narrow channel bracketed by heavy stands of spruce trees and steep banks formed by fist- and head-sized rocks. We can only see what is immediately in front of us on the sharp bends, so our course down the river relies on snap decisions. Danny and I are sitting toward the bow of the raft, me on the starboard side and Danny on port. We're each wearing a dry suit, these one-piece jobbies with watertight zippers, built-in bootees, and neoprene gaskets that cinch around your neck and wrists to prevent the intrusion of liquid. Basically, it's like wearing a body-sized latex condom, except it's your neck that emerges through the opening rather than the base of your pecker. Pulled over layers of heavy clothes, the suits restrict our movements and make our paddling sluggish. Rafferty and Jessen are at the stern, shouting out commands. "Hard on left . . . No, hard on right . . . Hard on right, go, go *go*." We maneuver the raft like a tank on tracks; the sharpest turns are executed by moving one side forward and the other side backward. When I turn around, I see that Rafferty has a big grin on his face. He's got a runner's build, tall and thin, with blond hair capped by a tasseled hat. He seems like the kind of guy who'd be happy even if he had to shovel horse shit—so long as it was next to whitewater.

The confluence of the two rivers reminds me of the junction where an alleyway meets an expressway. During the peak spring runoff, the Klutina dumps an average of 7,080 cubic feet of water per second into the Copper River, which itself carries an annual average of 57,400 cubic feet per second. That's like having 57,400 soccer balls roll past you in the time that it takes you to say "one-Mississippi." But the soccer balls do not roll by in one heavy mass; instead, they are broken into many different channels, or braids. In places, the Copper River is split into six or more braids, stretched across a mile-wide floodplain. The braids twist together and split apart like frayed rope, tangling themselves around scores of long, narrow islands. The river is constantly moving these islands, at once destroying some and creating others. If an island can hold for a few years, it becomes armored with a carpeting of sedges and willows that help to hold it in place.

I'm struck by the lunar appearance of the river, its stark grayness. Essentially, the river's floodplain is composed of a vast, deep expanse of glacial debris. Eighteen percent of the Copper Basin is covered in glaciers, which pulverize the surrounding mountains into something known to geologists as glacial till. The finest glacial till is called rock flour, particles so small and fine that they turn the water the color of potter's clay. Every year, the Copper River carries about sixty-nine million tons of debris to the ocean, or about thirty-five times the total amount of debris that was hauled away during cleanup after the destruction of the World Trade Center.

In places, the meandering channels of the Copper River are eating away at the steep hillsides, which border the floodplain. The river takes away slices of the hillsides in vertical chunks—think of cutting a meat loaf into slices that fall away intact or else crumble into the pan. Some of the eroded slopes are one hundred or more feet high. Within the first few miles of our float, I watch erosion happen several times. As we float along, little pebbles and puffs of dirt fall away from the banks and trail into the river. Sometimes the falling debris knocks off more rocks and dirt, creating miniature landslides. Above these eroded banks, the vegetative mats of the forest hang over the precipices like heads of foam tilting over the lips of overfilled glasses of beer. Trees that reach too far over the cliffs tend to lose their footing and plunge down into the river en masse. We pass several places where dozens of trees have come down at once in great tangles of wood. The limbs, still springy with life, wave in the current and emit swishing sounds. Trees that have spent a season or two in the river are stripped of their limbs and bark. They look like perfect telephone poles, except they are still attached to their root wads. If you sank one of these trees in the ground upside down, it would look like a long-stemmed flower with a wooden blossom.

In part, the buffalo chose to live in this specific area because of the erosion. There are steep bluffs a half mile away from the water, evidence that the river has changed its course and volume many times over the millennia; with the river no longer sloughing away at their bases, the cliffs taper off and vegetation takes hold. Sedges, grasses, and wildflowers carpet the soft soil of the hillsides, but trees don't hold as easily. The lack of trees exposes the bluffs to the sun and wind. In the winter, the wind carries the snow away, and the sun helps to melt it. While the buffalo might prefer to winter among the thick stands of willows along the river, at times these bluffs provide the only food for many miles that is not encased in snow and ice.

When it comes to the cold, buffalo have a lot of anatomical tricks up their sleeves. Proportionate to body size, the buffalo's trachea is larger than that of any other large land mammal; when it takes a breath of cold air, the air is pre-warmed inside the trachea before it moves down to the animal's lungs. This way, ambient air temperatures have a diminished effect on the animal's core body temperature, which is 101.6 degrees Fahrenheit. A buffalo's coat of hair is another handy adaptation. The hair above its eyes is so short that it looks like someone buzzed it with an electric clipper. This shortness prevents freezing water from accumulating against sensitive eye tissues. Domestic cattle have longer hair around their eyeballs and are commonly blinded by gobs of ice. With dark hair growing out of black skin, buffalo can absorb much more warmth from the sun than light-skinned and light-haired critters. And their hair is thick. On their mid-rib, female buffalo calves have about 2,992 hair fibers per square centimeter, while males have a bit fewer, at 2,182. (The total number of hair follicles on an animal is constant throughout its life. So as it gets bigger, the hairs are less dense because they're spread over a greater amount of space.) The hair densities of cattle are highly variable between individual animals, but Holstein cattle have hair densities ranging from 550 to 1,095 follicles per square centimeter.

In the late 1970s, Professor Robert Hudson, the director of the Alberta Veterinary Research Institute, and a team of colleagues attempted to put numbers and figures to the buffalo's cold tolerance. They selected the six-month-old calves of four creatures: the Tibetan yak, Scottish highland cattle, Hereford cattle, and American buffalo. The researchers put the animals into airtight, insulated boxes resembling horse trailers and subjected each calf to increasingly cold temperatures. They were looking for the moment when the animals' metabolic rate increased as a response to the cold. They monitored the animals' breathing with a device that measures the oxygen and carbon dioxide levels going into and coming out of the box. With the input constant, changes in the output represent changes in the animals' breathing patterns. Hereford cattle hit their critical temperature at 14 degrees

Fahrenheit. The yak and the highland cattle hit theirs at −13 degrees Fahrenheit. At −22 degrees Fahrenheit, the buffalo's metabolic rate was still *decreasing* as an energy-saving strategy. The buffalo's critical temperature remains unknown, because no one's gotten a box cold enough to find it.

While buffalo can tolerate the extreme cold, Mother Nature does have her ways of toppling them in great numbers. Lightning sometimes killed dozens of buffalo in a single zap, leaving their smoldering carcasses on the open ground. Near the great bend in the Arkansas River, a Sioux war party watched a tornado overtake a buffalo herd. It deposited the animals' carcasses in a quarter-mile-long row that was stacked several buffalo deep. The Indians said that the air pressure from the tornado popped the buffalo's eyeballs out of their sockets. Disease killed them. In the 1820s, the Sioux described a great disease that killed almost all of the buffalo in southeast Nebraska. Seven warriors were returning from a war with the Missouri River tribes, and they nearly starved while crossing this corner of the state. They found a dying bull with a swollen and rotting tongue. Six of the seven Sioux ate it, and they all died. From then on, they referred to 1825 as "When the Six Died from Eating the Whistling Buffalo." Wildfires killed them. In 1864, a nineteen-year-old captive of the Oglala Sioux named Fanny Kelly passed through the aftermath of a prairie fire and reported so many buffalo "that had fallen victims to the embrace of the flames" that her captors' horses had a hard time passing through the pile. Another man watched a herd of buffalo fleeing from a prairie fire near his camp and witnessed "a large number" plunge over a steep riverbank and fall hundreds of feet to get dashed on a rocky shoreline. A Canadian man traveling in North Dakota found herds of burned buffalo that were "dead and dying, blind, lame, singed and roasted." He said the wounded were "staggering about, sometimes running afoul of a large stone, at other times tumbling down hill and falling into creeks not yet frozen over." And they got stuck, mired in mud bogs, river bottoms, quicksand, and tar pits. In the summer of 1867, a herd of four thousand buffalo went into the mud at the confluence of the Platte River and Plum Creek, and only two thousand came out. The remaining two thousand—or around 2.5 million pounds of buffalo—joined the riverbed. South of the Platte River, along the Arkansas, an army officer named Dangerfield Parker attempted to stalk a herd of buffalo that were wading in the water. When he got close enough, he realized that the buffalo were perfectly dead. Stuck fast in the mud, the carcasses had become mummified in the dry prairie air.

It's been estimated that accidental deaths—from fire, falling, drowning, tornadoes—claim an annual 3–9 percent of the continent's population of wild buffalo today. If you accept that the rate of 3–9 percent was constant through time (and there's no reason to think it wasn't), you see that North America was once home to one to three million accidental buffalo deaths every year. At first glance that figure is hard to digest, but just look at a collection of statistics from Wood Buffalo National Park. In 1974, three thousand of the park's buffalo, or about one-third of the total population, drowned in the Peace-Athabasca Delta. Thirteen years earlier, in 1961, roughly the same number drowned in the same place. In 1959, a thousand drowned there. In 1958, five hundred drowned there.

As the data from Wood Buffalo National Park suggests, water is the No. 1 enemy of buffalo. The substance has likely killed more buffalo than all other factors combined, including human hunting. The Spanish conquistador Coronado was perhaps the first European to witness the aftermath wrought by the mixture of

American buffalo and large bodies of water. In 1540, he was traveling the American Great Plains and encountered a mound of buffalo bones piled along the leeward edge of a lake. His men estimated the mound of bones to be eighteen feet wide, as tall as two men, and about as long as a crossbow shot—maybe four hundred or five hundred yards.

While Coronado was treated to an image of cleaned and bleached bones, many other explorers witnessed sights and smells of drowned buffalo that were much less appetizing. In May 1795, the fur trader John McDonnell descended the Qu'Appelle River and spent a day counting dead buffalo that were either floating in the river or mired along the banks. By the time he made camp for the night, his count had reached 7,360. In several places, McDonnell got out and walked across the carcasses and remarked that the animals were stacked three to five deep. John Bradbury, a Scottish-born botanist who traveled the Missouri River in 1811, spotted his first drowned buffalo on April 2 when he was 240 miles upstream from St. Louis.* Two weeks later, writes Bradbury, "we began to notice more particularly the great number of drowned buffaloes

---

*Bradbury had an eventful, though ultimately fruitless, trip. He came to the United States to collect plants, but he got a whole lot more than he bargained for. Traveling the Missouri River, he hunted for grizzly bears and buffalo, got chased by a skunk, and was sexually propositioned by many Indian women, of whom he remarked that "chastity . . . is not a virtue." At the end of his trip, he shipped his botanical specimens to London and attempted to return home by taking a detour down the Mississippi River to New Orleans. He passed through New Madrid, Missouri, on December 14, 1811, and complained that the city was shabby and poorly stocked. Much of New Madrid was destroyed two days later, when the first of several powerful earthquakes struck the region. It was the most powerful series of earthquakes to ever hit the Lower 48. The aftershocks were felt across one million square miles (the great earthquake that destroyed San Francisco in 1906 was felt across only six thousand square miles), large areas of the earth disappeared into faults, rivers flowed backward, 150,000 acres of trees were destroyed, and the Mississippi River changed its course. Bradbury was

that were floating on the river; vast numbers of them were also thrown ashore, and upon the rafts, on the points of the islands." In 1829, a man named Sir George Simpson saw "as many as 10,000 of their putrid carcasses lying mired in a single ford of the Saskatchewan, and contaminating the air for many miles around." The German explorer and ethnologist Prince Maximilian traveled up the Missouri River in the early 1830s. He wrote of how "whole herds were often drowned in the Missouri" and described places where eighteen hundred or more dead buffalo were collected in some of the sloughs of the river. Along the Red River, another traveler noted that "drowned buffalo continue to drift by in whole herds throughout the month, and toward the end for two days and nights their dead bodies formed one continuous line in the current." He watched thousands come to rest against the banks. It smelled so bad that he refused to eat his dinner, and he wondered if he was witnessing a rare tragedy. When he put the question to his Indian guides, they told him that every spring was "about the same."

All of these drowned buffalo carcasses had dramatic effects on the ecology of large rivers. Along the Missouri River, the annual "runs" of dead buffalo were an important part of the environmental cycle. People passing near Great Falls, Montana, reported congregations of grizzly bears gathered there in the spring to feed on drowned buffalo that came over the falls and got bashed against

---

actually on the river, near Memphis, Tennessee, when the quake hit. His boat was upset by tsunamis, and hours later the current was transporting hundreds of human bodies. Bradbury continued his journey toward home, making it to New Orleans in time for the War of 1812, when the United States rehashed the Revolutionary War in a series of battles with Britain. The war delayed Bradbury's return home by several years. In his absence, a rival botanist pirated his treasure trove of specimens and published a book based on Bradbury's findings. Bradbury's bitterness over the fraud lasted him throughout his life, and he died in obscurity in 1823.

the rocks.* John Bradbury described how the carcasses on the Missouri "attracted an immense number of turkey buzzards." Prince Maximilian reported that many of the river's islands were formed by the collection of silt against rafts of drowned buffalo. Other explorers watched living buffalo cross the river on mushy bridges made from the bodies of drowned buffalo. Still others claimed to see the entire river dammed by accumulations of beached carcasses.

"HARD LEFT," Rafferty yells. "Left, left, left. Go, paddle." We've been floating down the river for seven hours, and we've just rounded a bend to see the mouth of the Dadina River go shooting past. It flows into the Copper through a broad, shallow channel of water that you could cross in three running jumps. Doing so would cause you to bust your ass, because the river rocks here are as slippery as vegetable oil. I jump from the raft with the bowline in my hand; the raft hits the bank like a bumper car and bounces away. I put the line in a double wrap around the trunk of a dead cottonwood and use the friction to slow the raft. The force of the current nearly uproots the small tree. Danny and Jessen jump to the bank and drag over a large drift log. We run two lines from the log to the boat, one fore and one aft, and then mound the log with four hundred or five hundred pounds of rock. The raft isn't going anywhere. We load enough gear in our packs to get us through a couple days, some extra clothes, food, skinning knives, a tarp. Then we start heading up the tributary.

Flying over the backcountry in a bush plane messes with your

---

*Today, when scientists with the U.S. Department of the Interior's National Biological Service discuss the disappearance of grizzly bears from 95 percent of their range in the Lower 48 over the last two centuries, they cite the termination of the supply of drowned buffalo carcasses on the Great Plains as one of the causes.

mind. You're going about eighty or ninety miles per hour at an elevation of a thousand feet, and the ground crawls along beneath you. The land looks relatively flat, the brush low and thin, landmarks close together. It feels as if you could walk faster than you're moving, as though you'd cross the ground like a greased hog. Reality hits when you hit the ground. You see that the waisthigh brush really reaches ten feet over your head. Land that looked as flat as a pool table is actually marked by steep hills and crevices so deep that you can't tell where you're going or where you've been. Bodies of water that appeared to have shorelines as solid as golf course water hazards turn out to be open pockets of water amid vast expanses of boot-sucking muck.

Those are the conditions we run into as we try to move up the banks of the river. The alder is of mind-boggling thickness. Alder is a shrub-like tree belonging to the birch family, though it plays the role of the birch tree's evil bastard cousin. The trunk of an alder, about as thick as a professional wrestler's forearm, rises out of the ground just a little higher than a person can raise his leg and then branches out in multiple, twisted, horizontal angles. Going through it makes every ten feet of progress feel like breaking out of a maximum-security jail. Some limbs shoot out over the water, so we can't walk in the shallow edges of the river; other limbs are shooting back into the woods, so we can't walk on the immediate banks. Despite Rafferty's advice that "you have to love the alders, be one with them," I hate the alders.

There are two ways for us to get out of the alders, the first being hazardous and the second being illegal. The hazardous option involves climbing into the middle of the Dadina River and wading upstream. The river is waist high and moving fast, and the rocks on the bottom are slick as snot. Even if we aren't bowled over by the current, our gear will get soaked. The illegal option involves striking off into the timber away from the immediate edge of the river, which would put us on land owned by Ahtna. Not that anyone would ever know we're here. Even if you buzzed directly overhead in a bush plane, you'd have a hell of a time seeing us down in this alder-choked hellhole. But our concerns are beyond the simple fact of getting upstream, because that isn't even half the problem.

In fact, that's not even one-tenth of the problem. The four of us are moving upstream with maybe a hundred pounds of gear between us, but if we killed a buffalo up here, we'd be walking out with hundreds of pounds of meat, hide, femurs, fat, and skull. That can't be done in one trip. Even if we really loaded our packs to backbreaking capacity on each trip, with maybe a hundred pounds apiece, we'd be going back and forth to the raft three times.

There's a fine line between being practical and being a candyass, which is a word that my father used to describe someone whom he considered to be the opposite of tough. When I'm in the woods and I run into a situation that seems like a bad idea, whether it's climbing up a steep icy mountainside or taking a canoe through a nasty stretch of rapids, I always ask myself which of these two words, "practical" or "candyass," best defines my decision making. Sometimes, it's a difficult determination to make. Because I'm very afraid of becoming a candyass, I'll sometimes do things that I know to be impractical just so I don't have to worry about being a candyass. I guess that's why we're still struggling up the Dadina an hour after getting started. We haven't gone a half mile, and dusk will be coming soon. I turn to Danny, who's fighting the alders like they're a pack of extraterrestrial dryland octopuses.

"This is ridiculous. I just don't think we could pack an animal

Grizzly tracks at the mouth of the Dadina River.

out of here. I mean, I suppose we *could* . . . but give me a break." Danny looks at me and then turns his head back and forth to survey the tangle of vegetation. He looks down into the current of the Dadina. Without saying anything, he gestures back toward the way we came and turns around.

When the four of us get back to the raft, we've only got an hour of daylight left. We pick a good spot to camp on a dry gravel bar just below our raft. Grizzly bear tracks are all over in the mud, especially along the shallow channel of water separating our gravel bar from the river's main stem. The channel is littered with the partially decomposed carcasses of sockeye salmon. I prod a carcass with the toe of my boot, and Danny gives me a look that says, "You jackass." He's right about that. Within minutes the entire area stinks like rotten fish.

Rafferty and Jessen volunteer to fetch the raft and unload it while Danny and I walk down the Copper to have a look around. Here and there we can steal views of the grassy bluffs to the north and east of us. We study the bluffs with binoculars, looking for

buffalo trails or, better yet, the animals themselves. I cut a fresh set of
wolf tracks just down from our
campsite. The prints look like those
of a supersized dog trotting along in
a straight line. They're fresh, maybe
from this morning. The tracks cross
a few shallow channels of water and
disappear in narrow patches of
brush, always emerging on the other
side in the same steady gait.

Wolf tracks along the Copper River.

I abandon the tracks to inspect a
shallow stream flowing out of the timber at the base of a hillside.
The water in the stream isn't gray like the water in the Copper; instead, it's clear, with just a slight brownish tint from tannins
leached out of tree roots. Where the clear water hits the Copper, it
forms a trailing, bedroom-sized pool of clear water that is infil-
trated on the edges by wisps and swirls of gray glacial water.
Salmon pass lazily through the clear water, moving sideways to
the current and disappearing into the gray. I follow the creek upstream from its mouth and into the alders. The mud is plastered
with bear tracks, mostly grizzly, though there's one set of black
bear.* Just inside the alders the creek is blocked by a beaver dam,
with a deep pool of water below the dam from where the beavers
have excavated mud by scooping it up in clumps and clasping the
clumps between their chests and forearms while rushing forward

---

*A black bear track has an arced, rainbow-shaped toe pattern, like your fingertips
when your hand is stretched out flat. The tips of the claw marks fall within one or one
and a half inches of the toe marks. On a grizzly's footprint, the toes are arranged in a
more or less straight line, so you can take a ruler's edge and hit all five. Their claw
marks can be two or three inches out from the toes.

with their back feet. The pool swarms with half-dead coho salmon, drawn to the promise of a spawning stream. But this promise was probably a lie, and the fish have been waiting at this impassable barrier for who knows how long. Some of the salmon cut frantic circles in the pool, while others loll in a half-dead stupor. For salmon, a trip upriver to spawn is invariably fatal; but for these fish, the trip upriver is looking to be fatal and futile. They have accumulated many wounds and skin abrasions from their journey, and their wounds are infected with saprolegnia, a parasitic fungus that attacks damaged tissues in freshwater and causes a mycosis that looks like cottony gauze. One salmon is missing a section of its back. It looks like a wedge of melon with a bite missing. There's no telling how it happened: a raptor, a seal, a sea lion, a bear, the moving parts of a fish trap. The fungus on the wound wisps about in the gentle current like a sea fan. The banks are strewn with the naked spines of his fellows, dragged ashore by bears and stripped clean of meat. Their eggs are scattered about, as if some kid spilled little orange marbles in the dirt.

Throughout the day the air has slowly warmed up, and now it's edging above freezing. It starts to rain. I pull my rain jacket out of my pack, and Danny and I climb up a big pile of drift logs to get a look around. We've got a good view of several grassy bluffs rising out of the forest a couple miles to the east and north. All of it is Ahtna land. I watch the slopes with my binoculars while Danny adjusts the tripod beneath a spotting scope. The slopes are distant and foggy, but I could see a big animal if it was there.

Danny pulls his hood out far enough to act as a rain shield for the optical lens of the scope as he fiddles with the focus knob. "When you get that thing set up," I say, "check out the bluff that's farthest to the left. Up at the crest. There's some dark shapes up there. Probably nothing, but check them out."

Seconds later, Danny says the word that I've been wanting to hear for a very long time. "Buffalo," he says. "Those gotta be buffalo."

"Are they moving?"

"No, it looks like they're bedded down. It looks like four, maybe. One's a lot smaller than the others. Maybe a calf. You see that tan-colored line cutting across the hill below the shapes? Like a game trail? It's for sure a game trail."

"You sure?" I say. "They look like rocks."

Just then, I watch one of the shapes shift a bit. Then the shape next to it shifts as well. The third shape rises up to a standing position. At that distance its legs are invisible, so it looks like it's floating above the ground. The others stand up. Two buffalo, three buffalo, four. For the first time in my life, I'm a buffalo hunter looking at a group of buffalo, and for a beautiful moment or two I'm paralyzed by the joy of it. In the final moments of daylight, I find myself running a simple word through my head again and again. Buffalo . . . buffalo . . . buffalo . . . It's as though something from the prison of the past has stepped into the sunlight of the present.

— 6 —

My second day on the Copper River breaks cold and gray, with clouds thick like barroom smoke laid low over the land. I pull on my boots and step outside of the tent to take a leak. I can't see the hills because of the clouds. The horizon is just beyond camp; I could throw a rock to it. It rained on and off through the night, and the tracks in the mud became dappled by the raindrops and then froze solid. Now I can walk across my old boot prints without leaving any new ones. In a couple hours the ground will probably be soft again. This kind of weather is the norm rather than the exception; climatologists describe this region as one of the most variable solar environments in the world. Sun, clouds, sun, clouds, sun, clouds. When you average out all the daily temperatures recorded here throughout the year, you get a figure that's below freezing.

I grab my rifle and explore the horizon, enjoying the way it moves out ahead of me in a slow revelation of the land. A hundred yards out from camp I see where a grizzly bear passed through before the surface of the ground froze. I follow its tracks long enough to see that it stopped to dig a salmon carcass out of the

Confluence of Dadina and Copper rivers.

mud. The bear rolled the fish around and flipped it into a pool of water, then left it lying there. The fish's eyeballs are missing, and its tail fin is gray with fungus. In the low light, the water in the river looks as viscous as half-and-half. If you pump the Copper's water through a handheld filtration system, the particulate matter will clog the filter and destroy it. If you don't filter it, you can feel the crunch of it between your teeth. We filled a collapsible bucket with river water last night to make drinking water, and the silt settled to the bottom as a light layer. The top is capped by ice.

We can't do much of anything until the clouds lift, so we look at a topographical map to double-check the location of last night's buffalo. The animals were quite clearly on Ahtna land, and I'd have to hire one of O. J. Simpson's lawyers if I wanted to make the case that they were within the high-water mark. Still, I'm curious enough to hang around in order to get a second look at their whereabouts. Large animals are remarkable both in their propensity to move and in their propensity to stay put. I've gone to sleep in the vicinity of two hundred head of elk, fixing to stalk one of them in the morning with my bow, only to have the sun rise and find that they've traveled so far that it takes me two days to find them again. At other times I've watched elk sleep and feed on the same little knife-edge ridge for a week without moving. While I wait for the clouds to lift, I roll up my extra clothes and stuff them into a rubberized bag with a roll-top watertight seal. The four of us shake the dew from our eight-man tent and brush the bottom free from river gravel and then pack it into its sack. The cookware gets cleaned and goes into its own bag. I stack all of the food into an improvised and probably ineffective bear-resistant container that we jury-rigged from a heavy-duty sealed plastic box wrapped in nylon compression straps. I check the inside of my waterproof rifle case, more like a giant sock, for condensation. It's dry. I check the lenses of the rifle's scope. Dry and clear. I wipe the rifle's metal parts with a lightly oiled rag and slip it into the case. The rag goes into a Ziploc; the Ziploc bag goes into my shirt pocket.

By the time everything's loaded into the raft and tied down, the clouds have lifted enough for us to see that the buffalo are in fact gone. I'm almost glad; my decision about whether or not to trespass has been made for me. We shove away from the bank, and the river carries us away as if we were a balloon taken by the wind. Drifting along, I can't stop thinking of the trespassing issue. I've thought about my reluctance to trespass, and I believe that it has to do with the fact that it's owned by a Native Alaskan corporation; as a white person of European descent, I feel as though I don't really have any business screwing around on their land.

I think of the Treaties of Medicine Lodge, struck in October 1867 between the U.S. government and five thousand Kiowa, Comanche, Cheyenne, and Arapaho from the southern Great Plains. The tribes wanted to protect their buffalo hunting grounds to the south of the Arkansas River from Euro-American encroachment; the United States wanted to protect settlers to the north of the river, and also railroad workers who were laying tracks in the Arkansas valley. In settling the agreement, the United States formulated a clause that only a lawyer could love, giving the Indians exclusive hunting rights south of the Arkansas River "so long as the buffalo may range thereon in such numbers as to justify the chase." Immediately following ratification, the military turned a blind eye while Euro-American hide hunters went in there and killed most of the buffalo. The subsequent lack of food forced Indians to seek provisions from the government, which—you guessed it—suggested that buffalo no longer ranged thereon in such numbers as to justify the chase. That effectively undid the treaty and opened the door for more hide hunters to go down there with military protection and kill whatever buffalo were left.

However, another part of me views the issue within the context of a much deeper history, which is the long saga of humankind's involvement with buffalo—a saga that predates racial collisions. If that history shows one thing, it's that humans have seldom regarded the wishes of other humans when it comes to following and killing buffalo, and this has caused many thousands of years of warfare and violence. One could blame human behavior for the trouble, but it's probably just as useful to blame buffalo. Left to their own devices, the animals just refuse to locate themselves in convenient places at convenient times. Many historians have argued that buffalo followed very "predictable" and "regular" migration patterns and that early human cultures in North America exploited those patterns to get what they needed from the animals while avoiding conflict with one another. This understanding is one of the many pleasant and naive fallacies that we entertain with regard to the balancing act performed between buffalo and humans. It holds that buffalo occurred across the landscape in a fairly constant distribution, with each buffalo more or less belonging to a specific "herd." These herds had names, usually based on where they spent the winter. There was the Republican herd of the Republican River, the Yellowstone herd of the Yellowstone River, and so on. To explain the constant movement of buffalo from place to place, people thought that each herd was perpetually migrating in response to the ebb and flow of the seasons.* Northward for the summer, southward for the winter. For example, buffalo that wintered in New Mexico would summer in Colorado. Buffalo that wintered in Colorado would summer in Montana. Buffalo that wintered in Montana would summer in southern Canada. Buffalo that wintered in southern Canada would summer in central Canada. When I think of this theory, I imagine the land between the Mississippi River and the Rocky Mountains as the lid of a shoe box. The shoe box is almost filled

---

*The historian Mari Sandoz argued vehemently that buffalo always, without exception, traveled into the wind. If this were true, every buffalo in the western United States would have eventually ended up congregated in great masses on the coasts of the Pacific and Arctic oceans. (Or else they'd swim, lemminglike, to their deaths.) However, she believed that seasonal wind changes routinely saved buffalo from such a disaster. Sandoz relates a story told to her by a Sioux man, which itself does a good job of illustrating the troubles that her own theory, if true, would cause for buffalo. The man described an unseasonably warm fall that allowed a massive herd of buffalo to push so far into northern Canada—perhaps into the predominant winds—that they weren't able to go back down south in time for the winter. When Sandoz asked how many died, the Sioux man used hand signals to show that it was a hundred times a hundred times a hundred, or a million.

by a single layer of marbles, each representing a buffalo herd. The edge of the box close to your body is the south, the distant edge the north. Tip the box slightly downward and away from you for spring movements; slightly upward and toward you for fall movements. When you do this, each marble maintains a constant position relative to its neighbor while still moving back and forth.

The north-south migration theory, which advocates strictly latitudinal movements, is like a small-scale version of the annual movements of migratory birds, such as ducks and geese, which are capable of traveling hundreds of miles in twenty-four-hour periods and which can move from the Arctic to South America in a matter of weeks or months. Being bound to the land, buffalo obviously move much more slowly; they aren't really capable of making the concerted, long-distance treks necessary to make such a system worthwhile. Rather, buffalo migrated in a much more localized sense: older, more experienced animals led younger animals across a vast though largely familiar landscape. They *tended* to respond to seasonal weather patterns by moving from higher elevations to lower elevations in the fall, and vice versa in the spring; they tended to seek out open country in good weather and sheltered country in bad; when food was scarce, they tended to split apart into small roving bands; when food was abundant, they tended to come together in large herds; if they felt safe and were well fed, they tended to stay put; if they were hungry or threatened, they tended to move. If such movements dictated that they were going north in the winter, or south in the summer, so be it.* Perhaps the buffalo's movement patterns are best described by the

---

*A couple of examples: In Yellowstone National Park, the largest seasonal migration is a midwinter movement toward the north, where there tends to be less snowfall. Along the Copper River, the herd's fall migration is eastward, moving away from glaciers and toward a major river valley.

Canadian historian Frank Gilbert Roe. The buffalo's movements, he writes, "were utterly erratic and unpredictable and might occur regardless of time, place, or season, with any number, in any direction, in any manner, under any conditions, and for any reason—which is to say, for no 'reason' at all."

Because the buffalo has no concept of boundaries or private land, Native American buffalo hunters have historically forsaken those concepts as well. Or, as was more often the case, the hunters have tried to have it both ways: when buffalo were on their land, they defended their land against human trespassers; when buffalo were not on their land, they trespassed onto the lands of others. These disputes over buffalo hunting grounds likely dated back to the arrival of humans in the New World, but for most of human history the wars were probably low-intensity affairs that claimed few lives and required only small amounts of energy and resources.

All of that changed when Cortés introduced the horse to the Americas. From then on, buffalo-related warfare became the defining aspect of intertribal politics. The transition was sudden and dramatic. The horse arrived in Mexico in 1519, and within thirty years there were thousands of horses in Mexico. By 1700 the Pueblo Indians had acquired the horse through warfare and theft, and they quickly became master horsemen and breeders. The Pueblos made no attempt to keep a lock on their newfound treasure. They established a thriving business in the horse trade and helped spread the animal throughout the United States as rapidly as the buffalo would later disappear. The Navajo got horses from the Pueblos and traded them up the western edge of the Rockies. The Comanche traded them up the eastern edge of the Rockies, along the Great Plains. The Nez Percé and Shoshones, way up around Idaho, had them by the 1730s. The Crows bought horses from the Nez Percé, and the Blackfeet stole them from the Crows.

When the Crows had excess horses, they herded them toward the Missouri and sold them to tribes there. The Sioux, in the vicinity of the upper Mississippi, on the extreme northeast fringe of the Great Plains, had the horse by 1750. Their animals had come from tribes to both the south and the west. By that time, there were perhaps more than a million wild horses in the western United States that had no owners whatsoever.

Pre-horse hunters usually only ventured out on large-scale buffalo hunts during the summer breeding seasons, when the herds congregated in terrific numbers along major rivers. In the fall, when the herds broke up and traveled in erratic directions, the Indians returned to their permanent villages to fish catfish and harvest crops of corn, beans, and squash. But the horse made it possible to give up farming and have no permanent home, because, in essence, the horse was your home: with a travois, the horse could pull all of one's possessions, including family-sized tents that could withstand winter.

The Indians' rush to get horses and hunt buffalo on the Great Plains was like a slow-motion version of the westward exodus that accompanied the California gold rush of 1849. Many of the tribes that we now think of as dominant Great Plains buffalo hunters—the Crow, Blackfoot, Sioux, Pawnee, Kiowa, Comanche—were either weak, small tribes before the horse or part-time horticulturalists. The horse made them extremely powerful. These tribes initiated new wars with neighboring tribes, and old wars amplified in intensity. The Comanche left their traditional homeland at the interface of the Rocky Mountains and the Great Basin, and then displaced the Apache from the buffalo-rich lands of the southern plains. The Sioux routed the Kiowa from the Black Hills and chased them into the southern plains. At various times, the Sioux and Cheyenne fought the Crows for control of buffalo herds along the Powder River. The Crows fought the Blackfeet over herds along the Yellowstone River. When Kansa war parties traveled through the hunting grounds of the Osages, they killed and left to rot whatever buffalo they could find so the animals wouldn't be available to feed their enemies. For tribes to the west of the Rocky Mountains, such as the Nez Percé and Flatheads, it was a rite of passage for young men to kill buffalo on lands claimed by the Blackfeet. Such activities could turn grotesque and deadly. A fur trader named Ross Cox once ventured into Blackfoot territory with a Flathead hunting party and witnessed a startling set of events when his companions caught an enemy. While the Blackfoot prisoner was still alive, the Flatheads shortened his fingers knuckle by knuckle, scooped out his eye, cut his nose in half, and then put an arrow through his heart. The Flatheads could have expected the same treatment or worse if the tides were turned. The Blackfeet would murder entire enemy villages down to the babies for the crime of killing buffalo on claimed land.

One has to wonder, why bother with it at all? Is the hunting lifestyle so great, is the thrill of chasing buffalo so tremendous, that it warrants the risk of life and limb? Apparently so. When Europeans first made contact with Native Americans, they were sometimes astounded by the unstoppable desire of the people to wander in search of buffalo even when it apparently contradicted their own economic self-interests. A Frenchman initiated contact with a band of Blackfeet on the Canadian prairie in 1754 and tried to convince them to begin hunting beaver for the fur trade. He promised them material wealth, but the chief rebuked him by saying that he didn't need the beaver or the fur trade. "We hunt the Buffalo and kill them with the Bows and Arrows," he blithely explained. Nathaniel Shaler, a writer and scientist, complained of how buffalo interfered with the Indians' adoption of agriculture. Buffalo hunting, he said, caused "the gradual decadence of the slight civilization which the people had acquired." A Canadian writer argued that it's impossible to civilize a hunter until you take away his means of making a living The buffalo-hunting lifestyle rankled missionaries as well. A Jesuit complained about the allure of nomadic buffalo hunting because "it is the same thing in a Savage to wish to become sedentary and to believe in God."

The allure of searching for buffalo was not always lost on Europeans. The administrators of Spanish colonies in Mexico were so troubled by buffalo hunting that they instituted legislation forbidding it. The governor of a Spanish province handed down the law and its reasoning in January 1806: "Buffalo hunting expeditions in the settlements of this province are the cause of the neglect of families. The expeditions cause settlers to lose interest in stock raising. Hereafter, settlers are not to go out in organized parties for the sole purpose of hunting buffaloes." The same troubles came out of Kentucky and Tennessee, where settlers couldn't be bothered with agriculture so long as they stood a reasonable chance of finding buffalo. In the vicinity of Big Bone Lick, Kentucky, a man complained, "buffaloes were so plenty in the country that little or no bread was used, but that even the children were fed on game; the facility of gaining which prevented the progress of agriculture, until the poor, innocent buffaloes were completely extirpated, and the other wild animals much thinned."

WHEN I THINK of the early buffalo hunters, I can't help but think of the word "nomadic." It's a favorite word of mine, especially when it's joined with the word "hunter." Sometimes, sitting around, I'll realize that I've been silently mouthing the words "nomadic hunter" over and over again to myself. Taking off to wherever the animals are strikes me as a perfectly noble reason to move around. In my life, maybe half of my moves around the country have been with that goal in mind. The other half were meant to get me close to particular women. (I've been frustrated to find that one move seldom accomplishes both of those things.) When I first left my parents' home, I moved from Twin Lake, in Michigan's more civilized Lower Peninsula, to Sault Sainte Marie, in the animal-rich Upper Peninsula. I ran traplines for beaver, mink, river otter, and muskrat, and caught steelhead, salmon, and whitefish out of Lake Superior. I got into a big fight with a professor because he refused to grant a deer-hunting exception to his mandatory attendance policy for a 9:00 a.m. class. I stormed out in a huff and went hunting anyway, feeling like an outdoorsy version of those kids in the Robin Williams movie *Dead Poets Society*. The next morning I got incredibly lucky right at daybreak and made no attempt to hide the deer blood on my hands when I tromped into the classroom just ahead of the bell. Take that!

I stupidly moved back downstate, to Grand Rapids, to get closer to a girlfriend. I was depressed as hell down there, and as soon as the girl and I broke up, I moved out to western Montana, to Missoula. Fantastic things happened there. I approached a pine marten so close that I touched it with my bare hand. I watched sandhill cranes feeding on steeply pitched ground that had been cleared of snow by an avalanche. I saw thousands of snow geese rise out of a steamy lake and swirl into a coiled cone that reminded me of a tornado. One time a bobcat stepped in front of me with a dead ground squirrel hanging from its teeth, the way it would carry its own kitten. I ran into four mountain lions and many grizzly bears. I hunted elk with my bow. I ate the flesh of black bears. And, perhaps best of all, I found my buffalo skull on a warm September day. After that day, I started to spend time watching the buffalo north of town, in the National Bison Range. I'd look at them as if I were watching something that happened a long time ago, the way you might look at Civil War reenactors. It bothered me that I felt that way. So I kept watching them, in hopes that someday my feelings about buffalo would drift away from the past and move toward the present.

I left Missoula a total of four times before I actually stayed away for good. One time I moved east of the Continental Divide, to Bozeman, Montana, because they have more animals over there than they do in Missoula. Then I moved back to Missoula to be closer to a girlfriend. That girl threatened me with a shotgun one day, and they locked her up in jail. I got the feeling that I should move again, so I went down to Thermopolis, Wyoming, where a small herd of buffalo lives right outside of town. I'd go jogging in –10-degree temperatures, with clouds of steam coming off the Bighorn River so thick that cars would turn on their headlights while crossing the bridge. The buffalo would watch me with mild interest as I ran through their pasture. One time I kicked up a cottontail rabbit that ran out ahead of me; the buffalo looked back and forth between me and the rabbit the way you'd glance back and forth between a water skier and the boat that was pulling her.

Next I moved to Miles City, Montana, which lies on the Great Plains at the confluence of the Tongue and the Yellowstone rivers.* Miles City has had roughly the same population for the last one hundred years. The town came into existence in 1876, in the aftermath that followed General Custer's defeat along the Little Bighorn River. Its first boom came in 1882, when it served as the hub of operations for the professional hunters who were busy killing off the last big herd of wild buffalo in North America. In 1888, William T. Hornaday reported to the Smithsonian

---

*There are several competing theories about the origin of the Tongue River's name: (1) the river is crooked like a white man's tongue; (2) there's a tongue-shaped formation of trees and rocks near the head of the river, in the Bighorn Mountains of Wyoming; (3) Indians called it the Talking River, and whites mistranslated it as the Tongue River; and (4) someone killed a bunch of buffalo along the river and only kept the tongues.

Institution that Miles City was one of only three places in America that had any buffalo left. He thought there were maybe a couple hundred in the breaks of the Musselshell River and a smaller bunch hiding in the badlands around Big Dry and Big Porcupine creeks. It's never been clear what happened to those buffalo—it's almost as if they vanished into the dirt. Hornaday also reported on the fate of the buffalo hunters who were still hanging around Miles City. The majority "cherished the fond delusion that the great herd had only 'gone north' into the British Possessions, and would eventually return in great force. Scores of rumors of the finding of herds floated about, all of which were eagerly believed at first. But after a year or two had gone by without the appearance of a single buffalo, and likewise without any reliable information of the existence of a herd of any size, even in British territory, the butchers of the buffalo either hung up their old Sharps rifles, or sold them for nothing to the gun-dealers, and sought other means of livelihood. Some . . . became cowboys."

When I was hanging around there, either drinking in the Bison Bar, or looking at the bullet holes in the window of the Montana Bar, or field-dressing an antelope so close to town that I could wave at motorists who were exiting the highway, or staring at the unmarked graves of poisoned and gun-shot buffalo hunters outside of town, I sometimes got the feeling that I had become one of those men, that like them I was there waiting for the return of the herds so that I could continue the hunt.

Even with almost a half-million buffalo living in North America, I still figured that I'd never have a chance to hunt one. Like I said, 96 percent of those animals are privately owned livestock. They live within the confines of fenced ranches, under the management of individuals who are looking to use the animals to generate income. The bulk of this revenue is made through the commercial sale of buffalo meat, but many buffalo ranchers specialize in selling buffalo to people who want to pretend to hunt them. This type of "hunting" is popularly known as canned hunting, because the results are prepackaged. You go to a farmer, buy one of the animals that are fenced on his land, and then walk or drive out and shoot it with a gun. It's estimated that about two thousand canned-hunting operations exist in the United States, ranging from places that specialize in native species of North American birds to African big game. To get a sense for the aesthetic of the canned-buffalo-hunting business in America, all one has to do is type "buffalo hunting" into an Internet search engine and then peruse the hundreds of hits for "guaranteed success" hunts.

When I did such a search on Google, I discovered that killing a "trophy" buffalo on CNN founder Ted Turner's Flying D ranch in Montana would set me back about $4,000. The High Adventure Ranch, in Missouri, was offering a "huge herd reduction sale." For $4,285 (a $500 savings from last year's prices) I could hunt a trophy-sized bull inside a fenced enclosure. If I didn't get a buffalo, I didn't have to pay a dime. If I was looking for something a little more "Western," I could consider the Rockin' 7 Ranch of Wyoming. They offer a fairly straightforward package: "We drive you out into a 2500 acre pasture and you shoot the buffalo you want." There were more full-service operations as well. At Thousand Hills Bison Ranch, in Colorado, $4,550 would get me full accommodations as well as a "fair-chase" hunt: they separate a breeding bull from a domestic herd and then haul the animal away and release it inside a pasture. The rancher would then take me out in a truck to find the bull while the bull tried to find his way back to where he came from.

Because there's little romance or genuine experience in shoot-

*One of Ted Turner's buffalo herds; Turner owns
more buffalo than exist in the wild.*

ing a penned-up animal, companies that offer such services try to
build up the experience with adventurous and dashing language.
The Web site of an outfit in Iowa asks whether you have "the passion . . . the drive . . . the determination" to shoot down a buffalo
inside its fenced pasture. Other places invoke the Wild West, as
though shooting a penned animal is like a trip to the past.
Thousand Hills Bison Ranch goes so far as to acknowledge that
it's mighty peculiar to use such newfangled technologies as the
Internet to discuss something as old-timey as a buffalo hunt. The
Two Heart Buffalo Ranch tells would-be customers that "the
mighty American Buffalo still roams the virgin prairie of their
ancestors and thrive on their prairie home." Pipe Creek Buffalo
Hunts invites customers to "slip back in time to when pioneers
were filtering into Kansas and big herds of bison roamed the lush

prairie." I suppose this sort of language is necessary, because when you're selling a captive buffalo, you're selling the illusion of something rather than the thing itself.

It was thanks to my brother Danny that I learned about Alaska's Copper River buffalo herd. Danny had moved to Alaska some years before, and in snooping around the state, he heard rumors that a wild buffalo herd lived in the foothills of the Wrangell Mountains. As soon as he told me this, I downloaded an application form from the Alaska Department of Fish and Game's Web site. Timing was my first bit of luck. While the state usually issues only a dozen or fewer permits every year, the number made a surprise jump to twenty-four in 2005. If any thanks are due for that, they should go to global climate change. A series of mild winters with unusually light snowfall had allowed greater survival rates for buffalo calves. What's more, the lack of ice on the Copper River had prohibited hunters from accessing the area on snowmobiles during the winter months, a time when the buffalo herd is more easily located.

Since its foundation, the Copper River herd has been open to hunting only intermittently. The hunt was instituted in 1964, fourteen years after the animals were dumped off the truck on the Nabesna Road and three years after they wandered into their present location. There were about a hundred animals. Back then, the hunt was not administered under the permit lottery system. Instead, it was run as a registration hunt: if you wanted to hunt buffalo, you simply signed up and went. The season stayed open as long as it took for the hunters to kill whatever quota was set by the state, which ranged from just a few animals to a dozen. When a hunter bagged a buffalo, he was to report the kill to the Department of Fish and Game within two days. When the quota was hit, the hunting season ended.

This system caused problems. First off, it created something of a free-for-all, with too many hunters converging on the area in the first days of the season out of fear that they'd miss their chance if they waited too long. Also, there was an effective delay between reaching the quota and ending the season; the quota could be surpassed before anyone even had a chance to report his kill.

State wildlife biologists had determined that for the long-term viability of the herd, their numbers should not drop below a population of sixty-five adult animals (as estimated through aerial surveys in the spring); a series of rough winters in the late 1980s had knocked the herd size down to a critical level. The state canceled the hunt in 1989 and didn't open it again for ten years.

When it was reopened, in 1999, the lottery system was put into place. It's a far better system, in my mind, as it erased the competitive aspect. It changed the dynamic of the hunt in other ways as well. Under the registration system, successful hunters were almost exclusively local residents. For one thing, they were more likely to hunt because they were already up there. Also, they had access to information that outsiders didn't; a local guy has his own regionally specific experiences, plus he can pick the brains of other locals and bush pilots who might not be so forthcoming to some jackass from the Lower 48.

But with the advent of the lottery system, locals were effectively shut out. Or, rather, they had the same chances of hunting a buffalo as anyone else—a paltry 2 percent. The hunt became a thing for anyone and everyone—Joe Blow from New Jersey had as much chance of hunting a buffalo as someone from Fairbanks. But a lot of these outsiders apply for permits without knowing what they're getting into, and, after drawing a tag, make no attempt at all to hunt during the seven-month season. On top of that, the majority of those who do try are unsuccessful in their efforts. In response, the state issues more permits than the actual number of buffalo that they want to be killed. Getting the proper ratio has been difficult, perhaps, as evidenced by the recent doubling of permits.

Thanks to one of those permits, I'm now looking for America's most iconic animal while crunching fine particles of glacial flour between my teeth. The wind has picked up since we left our camp near the mouth of the Dadina, about ten miles upriver, and now we're paddling the raft up to a large willow flat that stretches hundreds of yards along the river and almost a quarter mile deep. I climb to the bank and take a look around. The ground is littered with evidence of the buffalo—chips and tracks—commonly known to hunters as sign. I make a quick scan of the area, peering into the shaded underbrush for any animals. Nothing. I motion to the guys to tie up the raft. "It looks like a herd of buffalo took laxatives and had a hoedown up here," I whisper to Danny. We slip into the willows. Trails as wide as wheelbarrows course through the vegetation. The ground away from the trails is trampled with

Fresh buffalo sign above the Chetaslina.

hoofprints like a rototiller came through. The willows are browsed low, the stems frayed from the scraping action of the animals' teeth.

It all looks great, but after a more careful inspection I see that all of the sign is actually old and weathered. The smell of buffalo, sweet and musky like horses, does not linger in the air. The willow bark beneath the browsing marks has healed, and the most recent growth looks untouched. The trails are littered with leaves. There are no fresh squirts of urine in the dirt. A fresh buffalo track is a clean, palm-sized circle with a split-open crack down the center. But these tracks are rough and faded by drizzle. Some have undisturbed blades of grass growing at their centers. The buffalo shit looks old, too, partially decomposed and sodden. Some of it is capped by mosses and fungus.

Looking at the old evidence adds to the suspicions that I developed when I flew over this country a couple of days ago with Bushpilot Dave: that the bulk of the buffalo are still on their summer range up in the hills. Sure, I saw four buffalo within sight of the river the night before, but what's four buffalo out of a herd that might total two hundred animals? Maybe those four wandered off from the main group. Who knows?

We climb back into the raft and continue downriver. Rafferty and Jessen paddle just enough to keep us clear of trouble. On the river's straightaways they let the raft drift more or less as it wants. The headwind fights the raft, slows it down a bit. I lean back against a mound of gear with my feet up; my binoculars are stabilized against the chest of my life jacket. I can use the rotations of the raft to my advantage by training my binoculars on the bluffs ahead of us and then holding myself very still. As the raft slowly spins, the binoculars pan the country in a steady horizontal arc. They move down one bank of the river, then cross the water and work back up the other bank. I've been doing this for six or seven miles, ever since we made our foray into the willow flat, and I haven't seen anything promising outside of buffalo trails. There have been lots of those, plastered all over the steep bluffs to the east. They look like brown ribbons wrapped around the hillsides that are colored green with prairie sagewort. The trails are stacked like dirt rings in a bathtub. Some of them are cut so deep into the soil that they remind me of the rice terraces on the mountainsides of Vietnam. Here and there, short, diagonal trails connect the horizontal lines. All of the ground that contains the trails is legally off-limits, private property, but that hardly matters now because the trails don't have any buffalo standing on them.

It's nearly dark by the time we hear the Chetaslina River. It's a gentle gushing sound that grows louder and louder until we round a bend and there it is, spilling over the lip of a broad alluvial fan that ends in a sharp, clean edge where it intersects the fast-flowing channel of the Copper. The primary flow of the Chetaslina runs through a deep gravel-bottomed groove in the middle of the fan, and many shallower rivulets course along its edges like split ends coming off a hair. Danny and I jump out and drag the raft up a channel and beach it against the bank. I walk up to a mound of rocks that were stacked along the edge of the channel by floodwaters. The large rocks are cemented together by densely packed sediment that feels like coarsely cracked peppercorns in my bare hand. The light is falling, but from here I can see in all directions. There's not much to look at across the Copper, just a steep embankment, maybe two hundred feet high and nearly straight up. But our view up the Chetaslina valley is great. The valley runs northwest through a willow flat for a mile and then makes a gradual northward bend, like the curve in a hockey stick where the blade joins the handle. After the bend, ridges rise out of the valley and crowd in toward the river like collapsing waves. Judging from my map, there's a steep canyon above the bend. And above that canyon are hundreds of square miles of government-owned wilderness. Public land. It could be tough going to get up through the canyon; maybe tougher going to get back down. But this is the best plan we've got. The only plan we've got, actually. Based on everything I've heard, from Bush-pilot Dave and others, buffalo get to be few and far between, or else nonexistent, when you get below this valley. And our raft only goes one direction: downriver. If we can't get up this river, we're pretty much out of luck. The temperature has dropped again. I look at the sky. The clouds are dull gray and thick. Light snowflakes are crumbling away from them.

— 7 —

ONE OF MY FAVORITE buffalo-related stories begins on Thursday, August 27, 1908, with the destruction of the town of Folsom, New Mexico. That afternoon, about fifteen inches of rain fell on Johnson Mesa, in the northeast corner of the state. The rain came down so hard that it overfilled empty washtubs that were lying outside. The Dry Cimarron River, which drains much of the mesa, quickly overran its banks. A resident at the Crowfoot Ranch, in Colfax County, placed an urgent phone call to the telephone operator in Folsom, about ten miles away. The operator, Miss Sarah Rooke, made a series of frantic calls warning the residents of Folsom that a flash flood was bearing down on town. Her warnings were largely ignored, but she stayed at her switchboard, continuing her pleas. When the water hit, at about midnight, waves lifted Miss Rooke's home right off its foundation and carried her away.

Water swept through the town's streets in five-foot waves. The railroad bridge gave out. The Folsom newspaper later reported that John Young's house had remained intact because he'd nailed it to a fence post. Young's stable, "in which were tied three fine horses, was picked up like chaff, torn to pieces." Alcutt

McNaghten's mother survived the flood by clinging to her piano. Horses owned by the Stringfellow family were out to pasture when the flood carried them off. Rescuers traveled downstream at sunup. John Young's three fine horses were found downriver, all of them dead. The Stringfellows' horses were recovered seven miles downstream from town, all of them alive except for one colt. Alcutt McNaghten lost a saddle in the flood, and he found it among a pile of dead people on the north side of the river about a mile from town. The Wegner family was found dead as well; their house had been trapped in a whirlpool, and the biggest piece left was half of a door. In all, sixteen bodies were recovered in the following days. There was no sign of Sarah Rooke, the telephone operator, until the next spring, when Dan Harvey was burning driftwood about eight miles from town. He noticed a shoe in the pile of wood and upon further investigation saw that it was attached to Miss Rooke's body.

After the flood, a ranch hand named George McJunkin rode out to fix washed-out fences. McJunkin had been born a slave in the 1850s on a ranch near Midway, Texas, but some time after Lincoln's Emancipation Proclamation he joined a cattle drive headed to Dodge City. He eventually passed through New Mexico and liked the state because it had sided with the Union during the war. He found work tending cattle and breaking horses at the Crowfoot Ranch. He knew how to read and write and preferred books on archaeology, paleontology, and astronomy. While he was mending the washed-out fences, George noticed where the waters had gouged out the channel of Wild Horse Arroyo. It used to be just three feet deep, but now it was thirteen feet deep, and at the bottom a lot of buffalo bones were poking out of the ground. The bones, which were deeply buried and partially mineralized, caught McJunkin's attention because they were bigger than normal buffalo bones. He loaded some into his saddlebag, unaware that his discovery would set back the clock of human occupation in the New World by about ten thousand years, help launch a new scientific discipline, and cause a minor religious controversy.

I VISITED THE TOWN OF FOLSOM about five months shy of the flood's ninety-eighth anniversary. I was escorted by David Eck, an archaeologist with the New Mexico State Land Office, who was dressed with southwestern flair—boots, jeans, a Western shirt, a down vest, a ponytail, and a scattering of jewelry on his ears, neck, and fingers. When we arrived in town, I could see that the place had never really recovered from the travesty; after the flood, the town's population eventually dropped from eight hundred to sixty-five. Everything looked sleepy and brown, ready for spring. There were scatterings of occupied homes and disheveled barns and old stone buildings, all connected by busted-up fence lines. Cottonwoods bordered the streets and followed the river's course in scattered clumps. To the west, I could see Johnson Mesa, where the flash flood developed. Strands of snow, shaped like jigsaw puzzle pieces, clung to the shadows near the top. We drove up and down a couple roads a few times, until we found the local cemetery. The ground inside the fence was sand and gravel, overgrown with clumps of grass and tumbleweed. A lot of little bones lay here and there, some in small clusters of three or four. I pointed to one and David Eck said, "That's a finger bone. From a human." There were a lot of unmarked graves and little wooden crosses that had busted free from the ground. We located McJunkin's grave right away, though, just inside the gate. It was a simple and elegant granite slab that said "GEORGE McJUNKIN 1856–1922" and was decorated with pink and white plastic flowers that looked about as old as the finger bones.

I was glad that I'd come looking for McJunkin's grave, because the man is due a bit of recognition—he certainly didn't get very

*This granite tombstone replaced the original wooden
marker above George McJunkin's grave.*

much in his own lifetime. While he visited his "bone pit" often and
collected some of the buffalo remains, he could never talk anyone
into coming out and looking at it with him. He gave a sample of
the bones to the local blacksmith over in Raton. The blacksmith
showed the bones to the banker, who had once dug up a mammoth
skeleton. The two men agreed to head over there sometime, but
they didn't make the trip until December 1922, when McJunkin
was four months dead.* Still, the banker and the blacksmith were

---

*McJunkin's books, fossils, telescope, and an old Indian skull that he found were all
destroyed when a lightning bolt struck his shack and burned it down. He aged fast,
and when he started to slow down he moved into the Folsom Hotel. When he could no
longer get out of bed, he drank bootleg whiskey through a hose. He died broke.
Allegedly his final words were "I'm going where all good niggers go." His original
wooden tombstone was last known to reside in a small museum in Portales, New
Mexico. His current tombstone, the one I saw, was purchased by the kids who taught
him to read. (As is the case with just about everything having to do with old buffalo-
related stuff, these details are conjectural.)

smart enough to know that they were looking at something worth investigating. They shipped some sacks of the bones by railroad to the Colorado Museum of Natural History, in Denver. Museum officials recognized the bones as belonging to an extinct Ice Age buffalo. They wanted a complete skeleton for the museum, so they hired the blacksmith to dig the site. He and a small crew started working in May 1926. By June, they were hitting the bones of many different buffalo. Come July, things got very interesting.

Until that month, archaeology had been compromised by the Bible, much the way evolutionary biology is plagued by that same text today. Academic studies were heavily influenced, both implicitly and explicitly, by the Old Testament barrier; serious scientists threw around terms such as "antediluvian," which refers to things that occurred before the cataclysmic forty-day flood that Noah survived aboard an animal-laden ark. Back then, theories about human existence in the New World dovetailed somewhat perfectly with the biblical view—that man had only been on earth for six thousand years and only in the New World for two thousand years. It was assumed that Native Americans hadn't been in North America long enough (and weren't smart enough) to independently develop such technologies as agriculture and government, and so it was the job of science to determine how exactly those technologies were transferred across the oceans from Europe or Asia. To solve this puzzle, anthropologists relied on something called the direct historical approach. At the risk of grossly oversimplifying it, I will say that the approach involved looking at Native American tribal configurations at the time of European contact and then working backward in time from there. For instance, they knew that the Sioux Indians of the Great Plains had come westward from Minnesota and Wisconsin after the introduction of the horse. Using ethnographic and ethnohistorical approaches, such as oral history, linguistics, and written records, researchers hoped to piece together the answer to the next obvious question: Where did the Sioux live before they lived in the upper Midwest? If enough pieces of this puzzle could be assembled, researchers could gain a clear understanding of man's brief history in the Americas.

That approach was seriously compromised by McJunkin's find, because the bed of Ice Age buffalo remains happened to contain a number of intricately crafted, man-made stone projectile points that were clearly *in situ*, or "in place," within the context of the bones: buried between ribs, wedged into vertebrae, stuck into skulls. The points resembled the classic Indian arrowhead shape, except these points lacked the two lobes, or prongs, at the base. They were about the size of a human male's thumb, but only half as thick as a CD case. The most striking features on the points were the lateral channels, or "flutes," made by removing a long chip up the axis of the point, from the base forward, which gives each face of the point a concave surface. If one of these points were coming at your eye vertically, it would look like a less exaggerated version of this shape:)(.*

The news of a direct link between humans and the Pleistocene echoed loudly in the scientific community, and soon representatives from the American Museum of Natural History, the Smithsonian Institution, the Carnegie Institution, Harvard University, and the Bureau of American Ethnology had all journeyed to the Folsom site to weigh in on the evidence. They all agreed: human

---

*"Fluting" thinned the point and probably aided in the process of hafting it to a spear shaft. It is such an inefficient and technically demanding process that anthropologists believe it may have had religious as well as functional significance. The archaeologist Bruce Bradley has likened the fluting process to a football player crossing himself before a field goal attempt.

antiquity in the New World stretched back at least ten thousand years. From that day forward, the field of American archaeology, and the study of man's relationship to buffalo, became an issue of deeper and much more complex history.

I wanted to see the actual Folsom site, so David Eck drove us through a series of grazing pastures surrounded by fences and locked gates. We parked at a collection of old vacated ranch buildings and walked through a yard strewn with rusted, obsolete farm equipment. At an old log building with low ceilings and no door, David Eck said, "Allegedly, here's where McJunkin lived." I made him take a picture of me standing in the building, and then we walked across a dry riverbed and continued up a grassy slope that was peppered with elk tracks. We were directly beneath Johnson Mesa. We started down into another brushy draw. "This is Wild Horse Arroyo up ahead," David Eck said. The arroyo was deep, with steep walls. It was as if you'd ripped the roof off a house and

Thought to be George McJunkin's workshop.

stared down into a hallway from above. Attached to the hallway was something like a large, roofless bedroom where the arroyo widened out and bulged toward the south. A berm of excavated dirt lay above the arroyo, grown over in grass. Since the discovery of the site, it's been excavated several times by a number of experts, and they've managed to assemble a fairly complete picture of what happened all those years ago.

Wild Horse Arroyo, March 2006.

It was early winter, about 10,500 B.C. There were no cities on earth. When people nowadays think of those times, they conjure images of cavemen, but it seems as though these people did not like caves; rather, they slept in tents made of animal skin. They made their tools from cryptocrystalline rocks such as jasper, agate, chert, and obsidian.* The weather was generally cooler than today; New Mexico had glaciers. The human population on the western Great Plains was perhaps as low as a few thousand people, and even highly nomadic hunters could have feasibly gone a lifetime without encountering strangers. It's not unreasonable to suggest that they moved their camps fifty to a hundred times a

---

*Ancient quarries for tool-grade stones were sometimes quite large. Archaeologists have recorded pits measuring nine feet deep and trenches measuring six feet in width and eighty feet in length. Settlers in the American Southwest sometimes mistook these pits for the old gold-mining operations of wandering Spaniards, because only Europeans would have the work ethic to dig so much. One such flint quarry in Wyoming was named Spanish Point, even though the place was littered with bone and

year. Their preferred quarry, *Bison antiquus*, was less numerous and less predictable than the forms of buffalo encountered at the time of European contact. There was more water in the West, and grasslands were more verdant, so the movements of the animals were not as immediately constrained by the land's limiting factors.

A group of these hunters was likely migrating from their summer hunting grounds on the open plains of the Texas Panhandle to their winter habitats in the sheltered valleys of the Rockies when they passed near Johnson Mesa. The land in the region was low-quality habitat for game, but nonetheless the hunters encountered a group of *Bison antiquus*. The buffalo may have been completely unaware of humans, having never encountered them. Working together, the hunters herded at least thirty-two cows and calves into a steep-walled arroyo. They moved the buffalo uphill to where the arroyo ended, so that the animals were effectively corralled by dirt walls. The hunters predated the North American invention of the bow by as many as ten thousand years, and they probably killed the animals with spears thrown by an arm-powered contraption known as an atlatl. It was a bloodbath; the thirty-two cows and calves died in a tangled pile.

The hunters spent a couple days butchering their kill. They did not use the carcasses very thoroughly, but instead did something known to hunters today as "gourmet butchering." They removed only high-utility cuts, such as upper limbs, rib slabs, and vertebrae. They did not butcher all of the carcasses. It appears that they

---

antler digging tools. An interesting tidbit is that it's possible to tell whether a Folsom hunter was left- or right-handed. Sometimes the hunters would re-sharpen spear points that were mounted to the spear shaft. They'd only sharpen one face on each edge of the point; looking at re-sharpened points, you can tell whether the hunter was holding the spear shaft in his right or left hand. Folsom hunters were basically like us; about 30 percent were lefties.

removed the tailbones with the hides and took some of them away from the location, but not all of them. They cut out the tongues from the heads, but did not remove the brains or otherwise disturb the skulls. They did not break the bones for marrow. The anthropologist David Meltzer, of Southern Methodist University's anthropology department, examined fifteen hundred bones from the site and found definite evidence of knife work, such as cut marks, on only four bones. After the hunters left, the butchered buffalo lay at the surface for perhaps a year or so and were then covered up by silt from the walls of the arroyo. The bones did not see the light of day until the flash flood of 1908.

The discovery of the Folsom site captivated the American public. King Tut's tomb had recently been discovered in Egypt, and Americans were becoming increasingly intrigued by the deep human history of their own landscape. It was fortuitous timing that America's burgeoning interest in archaeology happened to coincide roughly with the Dirty Thirties; across much of the West, the Dust Bowl was stripping away the land's topsoil, and the drought was draining lakes and reservoirs. Denuded lands and dried-up lake beds revealed extinct mammal bones along with human-made projectile points that had been hidden from view for hundreds or thousands of years. Hunting for Indian arrowheads became a popular pursuit. In time, the U.S. map filled up with hundreds of kill sites where Ice Age Americans had camped or slaughtered prey.

Next to Folsom, the most interesting site to emerge was at a place called Blackwater Draw, on the western edge of the Staked Plains near the New Mexico–Texas line. During the Pleistocene, Blackwater Draw was a network of marshes and ponds amid vast and verdant grasslands, but nowadays it's a dry and dusty pit that holds the remains of a defunct gravel quarry. The wind blows strong there, and stepping down into the draw feels like leaving a noisy room. The site first came into the national spotlight in 1932, when an official from the Smithsonian Institution, E. B. Howard, came out to investigate various local reports of interesting bones coming up out of the ground. One such claim, perhaps more legend than fact, is that a schoolgirl on a field trip found a mammoth skull with a spear point embedded in its eye socket. Another claim had a boy finding a projectile point stuck into a mammoth tooth. Whatever the case, Howard found enough evidence suggesting a direct association between extinct mammals and humans that he began an excavation. Along with the remains of extinct animals such as camels, giant turtles, Pleistocene horses, short-faced bears, giant peccaries, dire wolves, and giant beavers, archaeologists found an abundance of evidence demonstrating human activity: campsites complete with fire rings, various stone implements, scraping tools made from the bones of extinct Ice Age mammals, and drinking ladles made from fire-hardened turtle shells. Most notably, they found an abundance of projectile points buried along with the skeletal remains of mammoths. The points, now known as Clovis points, were up to four inches long, almost twice the length of the points that were found with the buffalo bones at Folsom.* The Clovis points were less intricately

---

*Clovis points are extraordinarily valuable. Recently, a well-known collection of thirteen Clovis points, dubbed the Fenn Cache, was sold from one private collector to another for a rumored one-million-plus dollars. Single Clovis points fetch up to $60,000. Folsom points are significantly less valuable, but still nothing to laugh at. A broken Folsom point of uncertain authenticity and questionable provenance might sell for around $3,000. A pedigreed Folsom point, of undisputed authenticity, will fetch ten times that amount. As with all antiquities, though, the establishment of a projectile point's authenticity is troublesome. Today, an estimated five thousand recreational flint knappers produce 1.5 million arrowheads and flint tools annually. Through accident and ill intention, some of these points inevitably get circulated as authentic archaeological specimens.

shaped as well; whereas the Folsom points were fluted along the entire length, the Clovis points were fluted for only a third of the length.

Initially, the Blackwater Draw site was viewed as just another piece of evidence supporting the conclusions taken from the Folsom site, that man's history in the New World dates back to the late Pleistocene. The value of the site was amplified in the summer of 1949, when archaeologists working for the Texas Memorial Museum of the University of Texas began new excavations at Blackwater Draw. Their work focused on the stratigraphic and cultural sequences of the site, or in other words, the order by which the artifacts and bones were deposited in the sediments. The archaeologists discovered Folsom-type points and buffalo bones in the layers immediately above those containing Clovis-type points and mammoth bones. Over the next twenty years, through the 1950s and 1960s, emerging technologies in radiocarbon dating helped assign specific dates to the remains associated with specific projectile points. The Clovis-related artifacts were clustered around 13,300 years ago, and the Folsom-related sites proliferated less than a thousand years later. Subsequent discoveries at many other archaeological sites around the country buttressed these findings. A theory emerged: Ice Age hunters could be grouped into broad cultures with fairly rigid technologies that fit into some sort of time line.

These findings helped reveal something quite interesting: not only had human hunters been in the New World for much longer than previously suspected, but they were undergoing fairly rapid transitions at the termination of the Ice Age. The hunters' prey base was changing, and they responded to those changes by evolving their technological and cultural traditions. The term "Paleo-Indian" was adopted as an umbrella term to contain the various human cultures that existed during this period, including the makers of the Folsom and Clovis points.* Several questions about Paleo-Indian hunters began to nag anthropologists: Where did they come from? How did they get here? When did they get here? The root of those questions is found in a predicament: if humans entered the New World at the oldest known site of human occupation, that means they spontaneously generated in the American West about fourteen thousand years ago. Because that is highly improbable, people have put forth ample theories ranging from the outrageous (the first Americans came from outer space) to the semi-outrageous (the first Americans were Pacific Islanders blown astray).

Even the leading theory, that the first Americans were Siberian nomads who followed in the path of the buffalo, crossing from Asia to Alaska via the Bering Land Bridge, was plagued by a lack of proof. In a way, the mystery was fueled by one of the primary things that anthropologists understood about Paleo-Indians. Since they had evolving, codified systems for producing projectile points, there should be evidence of their technological evolution at their point of origination. There was nothing quite like that in Siberia, nothing like that in the Pacific Islands, and, as far as anyone knew, nothing like that in outer space. The closest Old World approximations to Clovis points were the spear points produced by the Solutrean Paleolithic cultures of western Europe that are best known for their cave paintings of Ice Age mammals.

---

*"Paleo-" is of Greek origin and means, simply, "old." My use of the word "cultures" in this context is imperfect, but it's the best word we've got to describe the various groups of Paleo-Indians. They were marked by different technological systems and the occupation of different habitats, and it's not unreasonable to think that they had varying lifestyles and belief systems. Whether they were actually "culturally distinct" by today's standards (whatever those are) is unknown.

The similarities led to a theory called the Solutrean connection, which was plagued by logistical problems. If the North American Paleo-Indian culture was born in western Europe, how did those peoples, or their technologies, get to the New World? A water route was highly improbable. And if the western Europeans migrated through Asia, why didn't they leave evidence of themselves?

A partial solution to these problems was discovered in the late 1970s when an archaeologist named Mike Kunz was wandering through the western Brooks Range of Arctic Alaska. Kunz worked at the Blackwater Draw site as a graduate student in the mid-1960s, and upon graduation he moved to Alaska to conduct archaeological surveys ahead of construction on the Trans-Alaska Pipeline. When the pipeline was completed, Kunz went to work for the U.S. Bureau of Land Management's Arctic Field Office, doing archaeological surveys on the National Petroleum Reserve–Alaska. At twenty-three million acres (think Indiana), the NPR-A is the largest undeveloped block of federally owned real estate in the United States, and it occupies land that was once the eastern foot of the Bering Land Bridge. In 1978, while working in the vicinity of the Ivotuk River, Kunz climbed atop a prominent mesa and was surprised by what he saw. "When I walked up there," he explained to me, "the first thing I saw, I said, 'This looks a lot like a Paleo-Indian point.' Then I found another one. And another one." Over the next twenty years Kunz and his crew excavated 450 stone tools, including 150 projectile points, from the top of the mesa. Many of the points were mixed in with campfire charcoal from forty hearths. The charcoal yielded calendar dates from 13,600 to 11,000 years ago. While the area was not the oldest known site in North America, Kunz was the first to find tangible proof of a connection between the Bering

Land Bridge and the Paleo-Indians of the mid-continental United States. In 1993, he published his findings in *Science,* and his discovery was covered by everyone from Sam Donaldson to the BBC.

I wanted to see the mesa for myself, and in the summer of 2006 I spent ten days getting there and back. First I flew from Anchorage to Fairbanks International Airport, and then I spent a night in town before catching an early morning cab to Fort Wainwright Army Base. I boarded a single-engine Cessna Caravan loaded with supplies and bound for "the Slope," as locals call that vast expanse of largely unpeopled tundra lying between the Brooks Range and the Arctic Ocean. After a three-hour flight, the airplane dropped through a purple-rimmed hole in the clouds to land at a gravel airstrip on the tundra marked by a collection of tents, a Bell JetRanger helicopter dubbed 4-Papa-Alpha, and a hand-painted sign reading "When you are here, you're still nowhere." I was 150 miles north of the Arctic Circle, 160 miles west of the nearest road (which was gravel), and 200 miles from Barrow, Alaska, the northernmost settlement on the North American mainland. I spent the next twenty-four hours holed up in a tent while waiting out a windstorm. The sun circled slowly overhead without ever setting. When the wind finally calmed, I flew out with Kunz and his helicopter pilot, Mad Mel Campbell, to have a look around.

Kunz and Mad Mel had matching white scraggly beards and severely weather-beaten faces. Mad Mel was an avid gum chewer, carried a .44 Magnum for bear protection, and was missing the end of his nose, which was hacked off during skin cancer surgery; Kunz carried a 12-gauge pump for grizzly protection and kept a toothpick locked between his teeth so tightly that I thought it must be holding something in place. About six miles out of camp,

Mad Mel began to circle a prominent mesa that sat on the tundra like a beached ship. It was about a hundred yards wide and maybe a little bit longer, rising 180 feet above the surrounding landscape. Kunz spoke to me through a helmet-mounted headset, loud enough to be heard over the whump-whump-whump of the chopper. "Except for some different plants down there, it looks basically the way it did fourteen thousand years ago," he said. He leaned forward from the helicopter's backseat and pointed to the crest of the mesa. "There's a 360-degree uninterrupted view of forty square miles from there. I've seen thousands of caribou pass below that mesa. I don't think these people actually camped on top; they probably camped along the creek, where there was cooking fuel and water. But they made fires and they sat up there and watched for game. They worked on their tools and points while they waited."

"What do you think they were hunting for?" I asked.

"My guess—and this is just a guess—is bison," said Kunz.

When I was hanging around with Kunz, I asked him what he thought was the absolute coolest thing that he could find in the Alaskan Arctic. He described for me an elaborate scenario by which a complete social unit of Paleo-Indian hunters was buried by a landslide twenty thousand years ago—"their clothes, their tools, their dogs, their food, everything"—and then encased in permafrost. Now, all of these thousands of years later, the earth's warming atmosphere melts some of the ice. "And I'm flying along in my helicopter," said Kunz, "and there's a goddamned hand sticking up out of the ground. That would answer a lot of questions."

Barring that rather stupendous development, work in the NPR-A comes down to the nuanced job of hunting arrowheads. I spent eight days doing such work with a sixty-two-year-old volunteer archaeologist named Tony Baker, a self-described "Indian arrow-head nut." While Baker can't remember how many states he's hunted arrowheads in, he's found them in over a dozen. His father, Ele Baker, found a flint knife at the actual Folsom site in 1936. His daughter, Traci, found a projectile point at the site in 1994—the last point to come out of the site. Together, Baker and I found dozens of artifacts. We found them on mesas, ridgelines, bluffs overlooking large river valleys—just about anywhere you could imagine yourself sitting and looking for animals. The artifacts were varied in their vintage and function: well-balanced knives that fit my hand as comfortably as a handshake; awls that could pass through my skin with the tiniest little push; and delicately crafted projectile points that seemed as though they were originally designed with the hope that they'd end up in a museum. Some of the stone tools we found were relatively new; Baker identified several as coming from an immediate cultural predecessor of the modern Eskimo. One day, while walking along a sharp ridge above an unnamed river, we found a style of projectile point that Baker described as a sluiceway. He believes such points could be very old, perhaps older than the points that Kunz found on the mesa. It was almost as long as my index finger; in cross section, it had a lenticular shape. I lay on the ground and stared at the point for fifteen minutes or so, turning it in my hands and thinking of all the things that will never be known. Was the person who made this point pleased with how it turned out? What did his clothes look like? How did he comprehend the scale of his landscape? What were his ideas of God? Was he often afraid? How did his people dispose of their dead? Which did he enjoy more, mammoth meat or buffalo meat?

I placed the point back into its divot in the ground as carefully as if it were a baby bird. The archaeologists in the NPR-A simply record and photograph their findings; the artifacts are left in place. If the archaeologists find an abundance of projectile points of an appropriate shape, they will dig in search of datable materials such as charcoal or bone. When and if that work begins, it could be big news. Mike Kunz believes that there could be ten thousand years' worth of missing human history in Arctic Alaska; man may have entered the New World as long as twenty-five thousand years ago, or ten thousand years earlier than any scientifically accepted dates for human occupation. "They've found a site in Siberia that's thirty thousand years old," explained Kunz. He was referring to the Yana site, where human hunters camped in the ice-free floodplain of Siberia's Yana River. They left behind the butchered remains of woolly rhinoceros, mammoth, wolf, bear, lion, hare, and Eurasian steppe bison. "Granted," Kunz went on, "those people didn't wake up one day and say, 'Fred, let's go to America.' But they were on their way, and they were close. There was a dryland passage between continents at the time. For thou-

Author lounging at the foot of what was once
the Bering Land Bridge. Western Brooks Range,
Alaska, July 2006.

sands of years there may have been only ten groups of twenty people in all of northern Alaska. That's a wild-ass guess, mind you. And there've been several thousand more years of history to wash the evidence away. But we could find them. I think we will find them. It's just a matter of time."

HERE'S A SLIGHTLY CONTROVERSIAL, fairly easily challenged version of events that just might be true: Humans first crossed into Alaska sometime around twenty thousand years ago, and the tools of these first immigrants did not readily resemble the projectile points that Folsom hunters used to kill buffalo, or that Clovis hunters used to kill mammoth. Instead, they hunted a similar suite of animals with projectile points that were certainly different, and perhaps more varied and less intricate. These first Americans were prevented from moving southward by the glacial ice sheets spanning central Canada—the same types of ice sheets that had prevented the southward migration of buffalo some hundred thousand years earlier. In the meantime, additional humans, with other technologies, continued to arrive from Siberia sporadically for thousands of years. Northern Alaska and portions of northern Canada became a cultural incubator, or a melting pot. As the climate changed, the hunters continued to develop a tool kit and hunting method that were specifically tailored to the conditions, raw materials, and animals of North America. Soon their projectile points looked like nothing found anywhere else in the world. They had evolved into what we now know as Paleo-Indians.

By fourteen thousand years ago, the Canadian ice sheets had receded enough to allow southward human migrations. As people moved south, they encountered more animals and perhaps the weather became nicer. The first people to arrive mid-continent might have followed the Pacific coast with the aid of boats made from wood and skin, but it's more likely that they traveled through an inland ice-free corridor that opened onto the Great Plains in the vicinity of Edmonton, Alberta, perhaps in the same general location where the buffalo first emerged. By the time of their arrival, they had assumed a cultural identity that we now know as the Clovis hunters.

The day that the Clovis hunters arrived was a very bad day for mammoths but, one could argue, a good day for buffalo. What happened stretches the limits of human imagination, but at the same time the evidence is utterly compelling. In short, what is known as the Rancholabrean Land Mammal Age came to a very sudden and dramatic close upon the arrival of man. The continent lost 50 percent of its large mammalian biodiversity. All existing species of land mammals weighing over four thousand pounds vanished; literally dozens of species between four hundred and four thousand pounds disappeared; all of the wonderful animals that we discussed earlier—the elephants, horses, saber-toothed cats, ground sloths, American lions, short-faced bears, camels, American cheetahs—all gone.*

Some people have argued—and continue to argue—that the preponderance of blame for these extinctions lies with global climate change. The earth entered the interglacial period that continues today, and it started to get very warm. Rain patterns changed and the land dried up. Mixed forests disappeared; large herbivores couldn't adapt and died out; predators and scavengers had nothing to eat, so they died, too. If man had anything to do

---

*This is assuming that the elephant seal is an aquatic mammal; it births on dry land but spends up to 80 percent of its life in the ocean.

with it, they argue, he was simply there in time to mop up the stragglers.

The climate change theory has problems. First and foremost, most of these vanishing species had already survived dozens of glacial and interglacial episodes, some as severe as (or more severe than) the one that coincided with their demise. What's more, the extinctions across North and South America followed a sequence that had already occurred across Europe, Asia, and Australia; that is, most of the large mammals on those continents vanished at a time that was contemporaneous with the arrival of man. In several cases, large mammals survived drastic climate change on remote islands where physical distance and isolation prevented colonization by man. While mammoths had vanished from North America and Siberia by twelve thousand years ago, they survived on Russia's Wrangell Island until thirty-seven hundred years ago—right about the time that the island's archaeological record begins. Ditto with a few Greek islands, where pygmy elephants survived until the arrival of man about four thousand years ago. Of course, Africa is a notable exception to this rule, because that is where man evolved and coexisted with large land mammals for millions of years. There was no *Surprise, we're here!* moment. In Africa, man and beast adapted to each other's presence.

In the 1970s, a statistician named James Mosimann and a paleoecologist named Paul Martin published a highly controversial set of ideas commonly known as the blitzkrieg hypothesis. Using complex statistical formulas, they argued that it was mathematically possible for a pioneering population of one hundred Clovis hunters to annihilate North America's megafauna. The hunters were killing large mammals that had no prior experience with humans, and they exploited this advantage with devastating precision. Well fed and healthy, and without internecine warfare, the Clovis hunters could have doubled their population every twenty years. As their populations grew, and as game was extirpated, the hunters expanded their range in arcs of ever-increasing size. The expansion and its accompanying mammal extinctions terminated in the southeastern United States. Within just three hundred years of their arrival, the Clovis hunters could have totaled 300,000 people hunting across three million square miles. Within that time frame, goes the blitzkrieg hypothesis, the Clovis hunters could have killed a hundred million large mammals.

Everyone from climatologists to biologists has attacked the credibility of the blitzkrieg hypothesis for a plethora of reasons, but it remains the most cohesive picture of what happened to all the animals at the end of the Pleistocene. Often, people have a knee-jerk reaction to the hypothesis because it suggests that early Native Americans were not the great land stewards that our modern mythology would have us believe. Though the hunters probably had no concept whatsoever of the finiteness of the land's resources, the archaeological record is replete with evidence of wastefulness and unsound game-management practices. At the Colby site in Wyoming's Bighorn Basin, Clovis hunters slaughtered at least seven mostly immature mammoths and left much of the meat behind. They stacked the unbutchered remains in mounds and topped the mounds with the mammoths' own skulls and tusks. The meat was never recovered. A couple summers ago I visited the Dent site along the South Platte River, just east of Colorado's Front Range. Clovis hunters downed thirteen mammoths there, ambushing the animals along a deeply cut path leading to the river. The elephants ranged in age from two years old to forty-three years old, and archaeological evidence suggests that it was the second time such a thing happened in that same place. If we use the contemporary population dynamics of African elephants as a point of reference, it's likely that the loss of thirteen mammoths from a single valley would have had major, long-term implications for the regional elephant population as a whole.

That the buffalo survived at all is something of a miracle, an ecological fluke. Many species that were smaller than the buffalo vanished with astonishing rapidity. Geneticists believe that buffalo went through a population bottleneck at or near the Pleistocene-Holocene transition; much of the animal's genetic diversity was lost. Buffalo disappeared from Victoria Island, British Columbia, and Orcas Island, Washington. They vanished from southern Ontario and northern California. They vanished from Massachusetts and parts of Florida. Isolated, remnant populations of buffalo did survive for a while in Alaska and the Canadian Yukon, but they were ultimately doomed for extinction as well; after an approximate 200,000-year presence, these northern animals were gone before the time of Christ.

The Great Plains and eastern foothills of the Rocky Mountains may be the only place on the continent where buffalo have existed in perpetuity since the arrival of man. The animals were probably helped along by a number of factors. Global climate change caused the expansion of arid grasslands into areas that had been mixed forest, which increased and improved available habitat. In addition, the disappearance of the massive herbivores, along with their accompanying hordes of gargantuan bears, cats, and lions, did for bison what getting rid of cats and rats would do for New York City's mice: the decreased load of competitors and predators provided an ecological windfall for buffalo. In terms of geologic time, you could say that the animal made an overnight transition

from just another moderate-sized grazer to the continent's dominant, largest land mammal. And with the disappearance of the
mammoth, it's a no-brainer that the ancestors of the Clovis
hunters would exploit this emerging resource. After all, you
wouldn't expect them to walk all the way back to Siberia.

— 8 —

EARLY THIS MORNING, when I wake up on the alluvial fan where the Chetaslina River flows into the Copper, I try to adjust the rocks beneath the tent that are poking into my back and hips. Our body heat has loosened the ground, and I'm able to pry them out with my thumb. Then I lie in the darkness listening. I can hear Danny, Jessen, and Rafferty breathing under the hoods of their sleeping bags, each in his own rhythm, and I think about how they are leaving tomorrow. The tent will be a lot colder with just one person in it. It's too windy to hear animals; a bear could be chewing on the tent zipper and I wouldn't know it. Instead, I listen to the weather. The tautly stretched nylon of a tent broadcasts changing conditions much more dramatically than any radio or TV announcer. High wind sounds like a passing train. Breezes ruffle like a distant, wind-whipped flag. Light, wind-borne drizzle is transmitted as a collection of clean popping noises. A hard rain is a drumroll. Sleet comes in little slaps, like a hundred bored students bouncing sharpened pencils on their desks. A heavy snowfall comes as a drowsy, peaceful hush.

Under the noise of the wind, I hear an unusual version of these noises. It sounds like precipitation, but not any sort that I'm accustomed to. I always sleep with the strap of my headlamp wrapped around my wrist like a bracelet, and I turn it on to make sure no water's coming in through the vent. Everything looks dry, and I doze off. When I wake up again an hour or so later, it's just getting light out. There's something in my mouth, and I realize that I'm unconsciously nibbling on glacial flour. My hair is gritty with the stuff. I wipe my hand against my nose and see that my snot has turned as black as graphite from breathing it in. A glance outside the tent's door verifies what I suspect. The ground is dry, and our tent is getting windblasted by dustlike particles that can crawl into places that an ant couldn't get to.

I was hoping to get an early start walking up the Chetaslina, but we decide to move our camp into a nearby willow patch that is sheltered from the wind by a stand of spruce trees. Danny and I clear a large area for the tent, removing any rocks bigger than a golf ball. The ground is too rocky to drive tent stakes into, so we anchor the tent in place by padding large rocks with life jackets and placing them in the inside corners. Then we run guylines from the corner grommets of the rain fly out to thick stubs of drift logs that we mound with rocks. It's stable enough that it will rip apart before blowing away. Once it's all set up, I walk over to the tent's original location and scatter the anchoring rocks so it looks like we were never there.

By the time our backpacks are

Buffalo tracks in Wrangell–St. Elias.

loaded and we're heading upriver, I can see wisps of clouds blowing between me and the spruce trees that are just a hundred yards away. Swirls of snowflakes fill the air. Unlike the banks of the Dadina River, the banks of the Chetaslina are wide open and parklike. I remark that you could push a baby stroller through here. We travel upriver about a half mile and then veer slightly inland on a well-used game trail that heads away from the river's course like the hand of a clock that's pointing at the two. I notice a few sets of buffalo tracks in the trail that seem much fresher than any we've seen so far. I point them out to the guys. "They aren't *fresh* fresh," I whisper, "but they aren't months old, either." Without discussing it, we move farther and farther away from the banks of the Chetaslina; soon we're a couple hundred yards inland from the high-water mark. We're trespassing now, plain and simple, but my curiosity about the buffalo tracks is getting the best of me. The trail passes through a thick stand of spruce. I can see an opening in the trees out ahead of us, and the trail goes toward it.

We emerge in a small meadow that has been trampled so thoroughly by buffalo hooves that it looks like it was tilled by a tractor. The ground is covered with red fescue, sedges, and prairie sagewort, all grazed down to a level that reminds me of a golf course putting green. The scattered willows are snipped back like bonsai trees. A traveler passing through Appalachia in 1784 compared such buffalo-grazed ground to land that had been ravaged by an invading army, and he compared the size of well-used buffalo trails to "public roads in a populous country." At first I think I'm looking at a place where a group of starving buffalo herded up for the winter, but there is evidence suggesting that the buffalo must have spent part of their summer here as well. There are buffalo wallows all over the place, big bowl-shaped excavations in the ground that look almost like birdbaths measuring eight to twelve feet across. Buffalo scratch the wallows into the ground with their horns and hooves, turning the soil into a fine powder. They roll in the dry dirt or, if it's wet, the mud. No one knows for sure why buffalo use wallows, though they do so most often in the summer. Maybe the dirt helps them keep cool; maybe it repels bugs. During breeding season, a rutting bull will piss in a wallow and then coat himself in the piss-wet dirt before challenging another bull to a fight.

I lose the tracks in the meadow, so I cut a couple half circles to pick them back up again. I'm looking around for the tracks when Danny says, "You hear that? An airplane." Once I stop to listen I hear it as well, the distant drone of a single-engine aircraft. It comes into view, flying low beneath the clouds along the Copper River. It's about a mile off. "That might be Bushpilot Dave's Super Cub," I say. Danny finds the plane in his binoculars. "No, that's not Dave's." It would be almost impossible for the pilot to see us, but we each step beneath a tree to hide until the plane passes from view.

Author lying in buffalo wallow near the confluence of Chetaslina and Copper rivers.

We pick the fresh tracks up where the trail passes from the meadow and goes through a thick stand of spruce. I start down the trail until I can see another meadow ahead of me. I turn to Danny. "Instead of busting through here and spooking something," I say, "we should try to get up on that ridge and look down into this stuff." I motion to Jessen and Rafferty to turn around. We follow another buffalo trail back to the river and resume our upstream course.

The ridge we want climbs out of the valley floor at an angle as steep as a staircase. It's like we're climbing up the pointy end of a piece of pie, with the bottom of the left side of the piece being the Chetaslina River and the bottom of the right side being the Copper. A heavily used buffalo trail caps the spine of the ridge. There are no fresh tracks on it. A tree has fallen over the trail, and a two-foot section of the trunk is barkless and dented from getting hit by buffalo hooves as the animals scrambled over. A five-minute walk up the ridge puts us high enough above the

Looking up the Chetaslina valley toward
the Wrangell Mountains.

valley that we can look down into the surrounding trees that we just came out of. We can see the meadows, but there are no buffalo in them.

As we scan the area with our binoculars, Danny says, "There's a black bear up there." I look to where he's looking, up on a distant hillside a bit higher than where we're now standing. A small jet-black blob is messing around in a patch of reddish plants. I put my binoculars up.

"It's eating juniper berries," I say.

"It's just a little one," Danny says.

We move farther up the ridge until we're standing on the crest of the Chetaslina River's eastern rim and looking down toward the tumbling water. The drop is so severe that I'm careful not to get too close to the edge; I can picture the dirt crumbling away and sending me plunging down the hillside to break my neck. Far below us, at the bottom of the valley, the river's channel is bordered by thick stands of conifers intermixed with patches of alder and willow. The valley climbs toward the glaciers in an almost straight line. In the distance, I can see where the trees end in the higher elevations. Beyond that, there is no valley at all, just enormous blocks of snow and ice vanishing upward into gray clouds. Just beyond the clouds and out of view, there are mountains so high that only microorganisms can live on them.

Directly across from me, the valley's western wall rises out of the river bottom at a much more gradual pitch than the eastern wall. The slopes are mostly treeless, with vibrant growths of low shrubs and grasses. The crest of the ridge is flat and broad, and capped by birch trees and mountain ash. Small springs have cut deep, gash-like drainages into the hillside. Thin bands of spruce trees grow in the drainages, like privacy curtains between sections of meadow. The bands of spruce are spaced a couple hundred yards apart; looking at the long hillside, I am reminded of marks on a ruler. A dusting of snow has collected on the well-worn game trails traveling between the stands of spruce. If you were stalking an animal on that hillside, I think, those trails and the bands of trees would come in handy as travel routes and protective cover.

The vast majority of the ground that we're now looking at is public land, open to hunting, and a lot of animals could be hidden out there in the mazes of meadows and timber. I sit down to begin picking the landscape apart with my eyes. Danny, Rafferty, and Jessen sit down next to me; our feet are dangling over the edge of the cliff, and we're each holding a set of binoculars. Taken out of the wilderness context, we'd look like a bunch of guys watching a football game from a bleacher in the nosebleed section. Waiting and watching for animals is one of the most important parts of hunting. It's not always fun, but I'll sit for hours in anticipation of an animal revealing itself. While I wait, I'll see strange and subtle things that I'd never notice if I was walking around: a coyote searching the debris field at the base of an avalanche chute and then stopping to scratch his muzzle with his rear foot; a grouse chasing a low-flying moth; a deer with a sore on its leg.

My eyes scan the opposite ridge, and I blurt out, "Holy shit, there's some buffalo. Four of 'em, straight across and passing left to right." The bulls are passing out from behind a band of spruce trees. They're walking in single file, with about a buffalo's length between them. They seem very deliberate in their travels, as though they're going somewhere that is well known to them. The animal in front is clearly the biggest, an old bull. I pull out my spotting scope and center the bull in the lens. The animal is well beyond rifle range, just under a mile away. Still, I can see the details of the animal, the small characteristics that make it an individual creature rather than just a representative of a species. Its mane is chocolate brown, tangled, and curled. Its rump is darker. William Hornaday described the color of a buffalo's flank as "between a dark umber and liver-shining brown." Several characteristics, beyond sheer size, distinguish the appearances of male and female buffalo. The base of a cow's horn, where it comes out of her head, is about the size of her eye socket; a bull's horn has a much greater circumference than his eye socket. Another thing is the penis sheath that extends downward at a forward angle from the bull's belly. The penis hangs in the bottom of the sheath like a roll of quarters in a Ziploc bag. The tip of the sheath is adorned with a long tuft of hair, which probably protects the tip of the bull's penis from freezing temperatures. The tufts are usually clumped into a single strand from frequent wettings by urine. When erect, the reddish pink penis extends out of the sheath like what happens when you turn the base of a lipstick tube.

The buffalo's slowness reminds me of an old man crossing rough ground. The animal moves methodically, placing each foot as though unsure whether its legs will hold up or not. Of course, this slowness is deceptive. A buffalo is perfectly capable of moving with great agility when it needs to. A buffalo can clear six feet in a standing high jump and fourteen feet in a standing long jump. At a run, buffalo can hit thirty miles per hour, and there are reports of them clocking out at forty miles per hour. A good horse can outsprint a buffalo, but just about any buffalo could beat any horse in an endurance run. The animal's oversized trachea, which plays a role in heat regulation, also helps it during periods of extreme exertion. A buffalo's tongue moves forward when it runs, opening the passage to increase the amount of oxygen that can come into the lungs. Also, when you look at a buffalo, you'll notice that it has a knee-like joint about one-third of the way up its leg. That's actually the heel of its foot; the hoof is the toe. The long, incredibly strong tendons between the heel and the toe stretch every time the buffalo's foot hits the ground, and the springlike retraction of that tendon allows the animal to recover 40 percent of its running energy. I sometimes think of buffalo as souped-up hot rods that are hidden inside minivan shells.

A few months earlier, in the late summer, the four bulls that I'm now watching were probably busy knocking the shit out of each other. Bull buffalo hit sexual maturity at age three, but they usually are not successful in breeding until their sixth year. (Females mature between the ages of two and four.) During their peak breeding season, usually a span of two weeks in midsummer, they engage in vicious bouts of head-butting and pushing contests as they compete to breed with as many females as possible. In any given day during breeding season, there will be scores of fights among a herd, and 5–6 percent of the bulls will die each year from battle wounds sustained from horn goring. One in three mature bulls can expect to have at least one rib broken in fights during its lifetime. When a male buffalo ejaculates during intercourse, his abdominal muscles flex so violently that his back hooves lift off the ground and the entirety of his two thousand pounds comes to rest on the haunches of the one-thousand-pound female. Females carry their fetuses for approximately 285 days and give birth from mid-April to May. The calves are bright reddish tan.

The walking distance between me and these bulls is much greater than the actual linear expanse separating us, because a river and a lot of rugged ground lie between them and me. I use my compass to take a bearing on their location, at 280 degrees. It's going to take me about an hour to get over there. They'll be long gone by then, but at least I'll have a point of reference as well as an idea of where I might pick up their tracks in the dusting of snow on the trails.

Dropping down off the ridge is the easy part; we pick our way down an eight-foot-high ledge by climbing down backward and hooking our boots and hands into crevices of rock. From there gravity takes over, and we slide down a rocky slope on our asses while using our boot heels for brakes. We land in a grove of young cottonwoods along the Chetaslina. The river is roaring so loud that we have to raise our voices to hear each other talk.

Now is the part I've been dreading all morning. The Chetaslina moves about a thousand cubic feet of glacial runoff per second and drops seven hundred feet in its final eighteen miles. That's as much elevation as the Colorado River loses through the entire 229-mile stretch of the Grand Canyon. In short, the river is really cold, about 32 degrees, and really turbulent. Still, Rafferty removes his boots, drops his pants and socks, and then puts his boots back on his bare feet. He picks up a walking stick and steps into the current. He uses the stick to probe the river's bottom ahead and downstream of him, trying to wedge it into gaps between large rocks. With the stick anchored on the bottom, he leans into it and trudges forward. In just about two minutes he's across the river, wet to his waist and doing jumping jacks to warm back up. I

Matt Rafferty crossing the Chetaslina.

don't want to look like a candyass, so I climb in alongside Danny and Jessen and we start across. My berries shrivel up into my groin the minute they hit the water, and I scoot across while silently begging various divinities that I be spared from stumbling and dunking myself and all my gear. Once across, I remove my outer shirt and dry my legs, then put my clothes back on and drain out my boots as best as possible.

I check my compass again and pick a landmark on the hill before plowing into the alder-choked hellhole bordering the river. It's so thick that I have to drag my pack behind me on the ground. I use my other hand to cradle my rifle in a safe position so the barrel and scope don't get clogged with debris. I remind myself that I need to put a piece of tape across the barrel once the air warms enough for the tape to stick well. The ground rises up abruptly when we hit an old riverbank. The alders give way to grass, and there's a buffalo trail following the edge. I see a wolf track in there, and then some old buffalo tracks and a couple of fresh sets. Crystals of ice are forming in pools of water collected in the deeper tracks. I point at the ice. "Temperature's coming down again," I whisper. We cross the trail and plunge into the spruce trees, which are interspersed with an abundance of wild rose. The thorns on the stems scratch across our clothes like the sound of Velcro coming undone. Downed trees are everywhere, so we have to climb from one log to the next, often going twenty or thirty yards without actually hitting the ground.

"There's gotta be a buffalo path through here that goes in the right direction," I say.

"You'd think," says Danny.

"I don't know how they'd get through here if there wasn't," I say. "Let's back up to that trail and see if there's a fork somewhere that goes back into here."

We back up and follow the trail northward about fifty yards, and there's a buffalo path headed in the right direction. The path zigzags in an erratic pattern, dodging logs and thick brush and sometimes veering off for no apparent reason at all. I realize that we're probably covering three times as much ground as we would going in a straight line, but we do it three times quicker than if we were bushwhacking. As the path approaches the slopes of the valley's western wall, the trees become sparser and the ground evens out. A few small trails split off the main path, which grows thin and hard to discern, and then it vanishes altogether as it enters an opening. We stack dead limbs against the base of a tree to mark the location of the trail in case we have to come back in the dark.

Once we're high enough up the hill to see over the trees in the valley floor, I can look across and see the exact spot where we were sitting when we first spotted the bulls about two hours ago. The dusting of snow has melted in that time, and now there's nothing to show fresh tracks. I check my compass; the spot is at about 90 degrees. Despite the trail's crookedness, we're only 10 degrees off from where we wanted to be. The four bulls were moving north, so they should definitely be somewhere upstream from us. If they stayed on the slope, they'll be fairly easy to find. There's virtually no chance that we'll locate them if they dropped into the timber at the bottom of the valley or crested the ridge and dropped down the other side.

I whisper to Rafferty and Jessen that we're going to move along through the meadows very slowly, angling uphill and up valley. "Stay back a bit," I say. "But not too far back, you know? Keep your eyes and ears open. If you see something, make a little bird whistle. We do this noise, like this." I make the noise. It's more of a people noise than a bird noise, but it does the trick.

I work the bolt of my rifle. It snags the top of a shell in the magazine and slides it forward into the chamber. It's a .300 Magnum, locked and loaded. With Danny behind me, I angle up the hillside toward the crest. We cross a number of small buffalo trails, and then we reach a major buffalo hangout at the top of the ridge. The ground is spotted with buffalo wallows as though someone lobbed some artillery rounds up here. The trail along the crest is as wide as a pickup truck in places, though it squeezes down to a buffalo's width when pinched between trees.

The spruce trees just into the woods from the trail have been de-limbed and rubbed bare by the animals' back scratching. Dead, broken limbs are scattered about, and the dried needles have dropped from the limbs. Each rubbed tree has a little trough around its perimeter from where the animals walked in circles as they scratched. Some of the trees have been toppled over; others are snapped off. The toppled trees make me think of an oft-repeated story, about how early efforts to connect the eastern and the western United States with telegraph lines were hampered by buffalo. The animals that wandered the treeless plains couldn't resist the chance to scratch themselves against the poles that supported the telegraph lines, and they'd keep at it until the poles were knocked over. An official in the East wrote to suggest driving spikes into the poles to protect them from buffalo. His plan was executed, but the buffalo only began scratching themselves even more.

I start moving slowly along the trail, stopping every ten or so steps to look and listen. There are three problems that face a hunter who's stalking a big-game animal. (I'm speaking of wilderness mammals that have continued to evolve with historic, long-term human predation, mind you, and not those animals that you see chewing their cuds next to national park gift shops.) At the top of the list is human odor. If an animal smells me before I see it, it's likely that I never will see it. Wild animals live and die by their noses; they might question their eyes and ears, but their nostrils don't lie. Right now I'm okay as far as odor goes; the wind on this ridgeline is just right, with the thermal currents carrying my scent back down the valley and away from where I think the buffalo might be.

I do have to worry about the next two concerns, sight and sound. Of the two, sight is most important. While an animal might not immediately run off when it sees me, it certainly will not forget that I'm here. Usually an animal will spot me by detecting the movement of my body. If you look at a large herbivore such as a buffalo, you'll see that its eyes are laterally positioned, or placed on opposite sides of the head. This type of eye placement allows for panoramic vision; a buffalo can see almost 90 percent of its surroundings without turning its head (obscured, however, by wisps of hair). Lateral positioning is superb for the detection of predators that are lurking to the sides and rear of an animal, though it does leave the animal with a compromised ability to see visual detail. Predators, such as owls, humans, and lions, have eyes that are frontally positioned, allowing for narrower, more binocular vision. (Humans see a little less than half of their surroundings at any given moment.) Frontal positioning is superb for depth perception, which enables predators to calculate the proper timing and trajectory for effective strikes and to concentrate on a specific target. This is essential, because a 150-pound mountain lion needs to have a very precise strike if it's going to take down a 300-pound yearling elk.*

---

*The world of humans is much more colorful in the daytime and much darker at night than the world of buffalo. The retina of an eye contains two types of photoreceptors, rods and cones. Rods are more sensitive than cones, and much better in low-light conditions, but they don't detect colors. Perhaps because buffalo are active at night (and because their predators are active at night), they have a much higher percentage of rods to cones than humans. As for low-light vision, human eyeballs have a density of cones in the center and a greater abundance of rods toward the periphery. When you're messing around with something in the dark and can't quite see it, try looking at it out of the corner of your eye. You'll see it more clearly.

Sound is last in the sensory hierarchy. Wild animals do not always associate human sounds with immediate trouble, though they most certainly pay attention to our noises. Out of curiosity, I've hidden from distant herds of buffalo and yelled at them. They'll sometimes stare in the direction of the noise for several minutes before going back to whatever they were doing. Then, once they resume their activities, they will periodically snap their heads up to take a fresh "listen" in the area of the earlier noise. Buffalo ears are small and hidden inside the thick hair on their heads, but if you watch a buffalo's ears carefully, you can see that they swivel in a slow back-and-forth motion that reminds me of a submarine's periscope. If nothing reveals itself, they may even walk toward the noise. It's almost as if they're checking up on unresolved business, as if they're thinking, "What the heck *was* that?"

We work our way along the ridge, stopping, looking, listening. I find a dry buffalo chip tucked under an overhanging spruce where it was shielded from the weather, and I add it to some others in my pack's water bottle pocket in case I need to make a fire later. An hour goes by, then two hours. We see no trace of the four buffalo. They have simply vanished. When I had looked at this ridge from the opposite side of the river, I thought it ran in a straight line. Now that I'm up here, though, I see that there is a slight curve to it, facing inward toward the river. Imagine being perched on the rim of a coffee cup. You'd be able to see the interior wall of the cup curving away to both your left and your right. Though the curvature of the ridge is much less severe than a coffee cup's rim, the effect is similar; it allows me to see a greater stretch of the slope from any given position. I tell the guys that we should sit and wait. We spread out a bit on the ridge, so we each have a different perspective on the surrounding land. I go down the slope about twenty yards and climb out onto an outcropping of rocks that gives me a little better view upstream. I get all nestled in among some boulders that will break up my outline and conceal my movements in case a buffalo appears out of the timber at close range. I take off my backpack and pull out my extra clothes and some food. I put the pack against a rock and lean against it. One time, a friend of mine was nestled among some rocks like this down in Montana while he hunted coyotes. He felt something sharp under his ass and lifted up to see a large Paleo-Indian projectile point. He wasn't the first hunter to sit in those rocks.

I lay out my food and water to my right side and then check my rifle's scope and barrel to make sure they're clear of dust and debris. If water or snow gets into the barrel and freezes, it can cause the barrel to rupture when you pull the trigger. I remember that I need to put some tape over the barrel to keep it clean. I dig into my pack for my hunting kit and pull out a small roll of duct tape. I peel off a strip that's about a half inch wide and four inches long and place half of it over the end of the barrel. The sticky part isn't very sticky in the cold, so I rub the tape's backing in order to heat the adhesive and get it to work better. Then I wrap the second half of the tape around the barrel's end to hold the first half in place, the way you would bandage the tip of your finger. When a cartridge is fired, the expansion of the gases is what drives the bullet out. Some of those gases escape ahead of the bullet, and they rip the tape away before the bullet gets there.

Up the hill from me, in a mountain ash, there is a small flock of Bohemian waxwings stripping fruit from the tree. That's the only thing moving. I pull on my hat and gloves. Either those buffalo will come out of that timber on the valley floor, or they won't. It's entirely up to them. I can't see the sun through the clouds, but I can tell where it is by looking around until my eyes hurt. I track the sun across the sky until it's close to the horizon. It takes hours. Then the sun ducks down below the clouds and lays out a nice sunset, just as smooth as if it were throwing out a picnic blanket. My fingers get cold. Then my toes get cold. I burrow into my jacket, but it doesn't really help. I sit like that until it's almost too dark to see my brother, just fifty yards away. The buffalo never show up.

— 9 —

WHEN WE'RE DOZING OFF in our tent at night, Rafferty usually announces that we'll probably be dead in the morning from a buffalo stampede. "It's been nice knowing you boys, all the same," he says. At first it was only a half joke, because buffalo are known to kill people on occasion. The most vicious attack ever reported is a completely unsubstantiated tale passed down by the early-twentieth-century folklorist and historian Henry W. Shoemaker. He wrote about a giant Pennsylvania bull named Old Logan that led his herd of "brutes" into a cabin occupied by a woman and her three small children; the victims were "crushed deep into the mud of the earthen floor by the cruel hoofs."

More truthful stories come out of Yellowstone National Park, where you've got more of a chance of being mauled by a buffalo than you do a bear. Between 1980 and 1999, sixty-one park visitors were injured by buffalo. That's over twice the number injured by bears during the same time span. While Colonel Richard Irving Dodge claimed to personally know five hunters who were killed by buffalo in the Kansas Territory of the mid-nineteenth century, Yellowstone's buffalo seem to have something against photographers. Two men, one in 1971 and the other in 1983, were killed by buffalo while closing in for snapshots. The most common buffalo-related injury in the park is a puncture wound to the legs, though a dozen or so of the victims have been thrown into the air by the swift swing of a buffalo's head. One man turned a somersault in the air and ended up in a tree. In 1984, a sixty-three-year-old Texan named Gladys Hoffman was attacked by a buffalo in a Yellowstone campground while she posed for a photo. The animal punched one hole below her ribs and another hole into the cheek of her ass and then threw her about fifteen feet through the air. Besides her puncture wounds, she suffered fractures in her ribs, back, and wrist. She lived to sue about it.

Unfortunately, Rafferty's not here to repeat his joke. He, Danny, and Jessen took off this morning in the raft. They got an early start, figuring that they'd make it downriver to the village of Chitina by nightfall and then back to Anchorage in time for work on Monday. When they left, Jessen assured me that he'd come back down and look for me next weekend. When the guys shoved off and the current scooted them away, Danny turned in the raft and waved back at me. "Nice knowing you," he said.

Now I feel like I'm inside one of those horror movie trailers where the announcer warns, "There's no one to hear you scream." Not only that, but I have no way of getting to a place where they could hear me scream. A big, cold river separates me from any feasible route out of here. I boil water for oatmeal and coffee, and then I'm distracted when I feel something like a busted-up pack of ramen noodles inside my backpack. I stick my hand in and remember that I've been filling the pocket with buffalo chips. I select the two biggest remaining pieces, which are the size and thickness of my hand if I were to cut my fingers off. I place the pieces on the fire, and they're gone within a minute. It's like watching toilet paper burn. I walk into the willow patch and col-

A woman and child gather cooking fuel on the Great Plains.

lect some larger chips that have the opposite characteristics of what I've just burned. These are twelve-inch disks that are dense and thick. But when I put them on the fire, they refuse to burn and instead let off a gag-inducing smoke. What the hell? I think. The Smithsonian's William Hornaday loved a good buffalo chip fire. He was especially impressed by the buffalo's tendency to shit in sheltered valleys and draws—just the places where man liked to camp. When pioneers were crossing the Great Plains on their way to the goldfields of California or the farmlands of Oregon, it's said that they would cook a couple hundred meals over buffalo chip fires.* If these things were such a pain, how did they manage

---

*Pioneers crossing the Great Plains would string blankets beneath their Conestoga wagons and fill the blankets with buffalo chips as they traveled along. Conestoga wagons were manufactured in the Conestoga River valley of Pennsylvania. People used to call the wagons Stogies for short. Nowadays, people call cigars stogies. If you read about this sort of thing much, you'll come across a lot of reasons why: that cigars look

to pull that off? Flustered, I gather up some moderately dense chips from the willow patch and prop them on twigs next to the fire. I put some rocks behind the chips to reflect heat and help them dry out.

As I'm messing around with the chips, a single wolf lets out a long howl toward the southwest. It's the first howl I've heard so far this trip. Wolves howl for all kinds of reasons that are difficult to decipher, but a single howl from a lone wolf is usually understood to be a form of communication between the wolf and his pack. It's like a wolf saying, "Hey, I'm over here," or, "Where are you guys?"† I've heard a number of lone-wolf howls before, but it occurs to me that I've never heard a lone-wolf howl while I was alone. This feels different, as if the wolf were teasing me.

My map shows a large network of lowlands about a half mile down the Copper River from my camp. There are braids of river channels drawn on the map, along with symbols for marshland, so I figure that the area is below the average high-water mark and therefore public land. I load up my pack and grab my rifle and start heading downstream. I pick my way over large piles of driftwood tangled on the bank. After walking for about fifteen minutes, I come to several dry stream channels coursing out of a large willow flat. I follow the largest channel away from the river. The

---

like wagon spokes; that the drivers of Conestoga wagons liked to breathe through lit cigars to filter out trail dust; that tobacco farmers in Virginia used Conestoga wagons to haul their crops to market. None of those reasons are true. Instead, stogies are stogies because the first cigar producer in Pennsylvania set up shop in the Conestoga valley and he produced good, cheap cigars. The name stuck.

†Sometimes a whole pack will howl together, on and on. Biologists believe that this type of group howling could be a form of entertainment, or a moment of bonding. But the dominant wolves in a pack will often bite less-dominant wolves if they join in the chorus. If the howling doesn't mean anything, I wonder, why would they care?

willows and alders are thick on either side of me, so that I can't see more than ten or twenty yards in any direction. I find a game trail that comes out of the willows and intersects the stream channel. Along with old buffalo tracks, there are prints from grizzly, fox, coyote, moose, and wolf. The wolf was going in the same direction that I am. The tracks are fresh, and I think about the wolf howl from earlier. Is this where that howl came from? No, it was more to the north. And farther off.

In the late winter, Bushpilot Dave flies over this country looking for carcasses from moose that starved or were killed by wolves over the winter. When Dave finds a carcass, he watches it for grizzly bears throughout the spring. A bear coming out of hibernation will camp out on a moose carcass for days on end. If it's a big bear, Dave might try to land a client within the vicinity of the carcass so he can try to stalk the bear.

"You ever see bears on buffalo carcasses?" I asked him.

"No, I never have," said Dave.

"You think the wolves around here will kill buffalo?"

"I've never seen any evidence of it."

Bushpilot Dave told me about a time when he was flying up the Chetaslina valley, near the glaciers, and saw something that caught his attention. A small herd of buffalo was lying in a patch of willows while three or four wolves pranced through the middle of the group. "The bison didn't even stand up," said Bushpilot Dave. "They just looked at those wolves like 'What you going to do about it?' "

When Europeans showed up in North America, they found wolves throughout Mexico and Canada and in every state except Hawaii. Wolves were most abundant on the Great Plains, which was home to maybe one and a half million. The wolves followed Indians, scavenging the buffalo carcasses that they left behind.

When the Lewis and Clark expedition was traveling up the Missouri River in 1805, they found a hundred rotting buffalo carcasses left over in a place where Indians had made a large kill. "We saw a great many wolves in the neighborhood of these mangled carcasses," wrote Lewis. The wolves were so overstuffed that Captain Clark walked up to one and killed it with his spontoon, a sort of walking staff tipped with a blade.

Wolves certainly did not need humans to kill buffalo for them. The wolves hunted by feeling the herd out, so to speak; they'd hang around, checking for crippled or sick animals, or calves that might be separated from the herd. It was a perfectly efficient method, especially when one considers that among a herd of five thousand or ten thousand buffalo, there's bound to be an animal or two that's in no condition to mount a serious defense. All in all, it's estimated that wolves killed 33 percent of all buffalo calves annually. Maybe one million to two million buffalo died at the teeth of wolves every year.

Nowadays, wolves occur in numbers that remind me of my monthly checking account balances: Northern Michigan and Wisconsin share about 400. Minnesota has 2,500. Idaho has 200. Wyoming and Montana have about 250 wolves between them, which are generally confined to the mountainous regions dominated by federally owned wilderness areas and national parkland. Any wolf in Montana or Wyoming that strays eastward into the Plains is going to find a lack of buffalo and elk and an abundance of sheep and cattle. And as soon as it lays a tooth to a piece of livestock, it becomes fair game for government-paid predator control officers. Canada has somewhere between 52,000 and 60,000 wolves, which occupy 90 percent of their historic range in that country. (My checking account analogy stops with Canada.) The 10 percent of Canada that is missing wolves is largely that portion of the country which lies within the Great Plains—the same portion that used to have the most wolves and buffalo.

In Alaska, which has a healthy and stable population of six thousand or seven thousand wolves, the predators still occupy their entire historic range. On average, Alaskan wolves weigh eighty to ninety pounds and eat seven pounds of meat a day—that means that one wolf could eat five mature buffalo a year. If every wolf in Alaska had to rely on buffalo meat, Alaska's entire supply would be used up in less than a month. But, as Bushpilot Dave suggested, the wolves in Alaska do not seem to target buffalo. The reason is that the wolves haven't yet "learned" how to kill them. Wolves are educated by their pack leaders, who were educated by the pack leaders before them. The wolves in Alaska haven't had much time to learn how to handle buffalo, which weren't introduced to the state until the late 1920s (they didn't show up along the Copper River until even later, in the 1950s). Biologists also believe that wolves haven't bothered to learn how to hunt buffalo because it's not worth their time to do so. There are only a few buffalo herds in Alaska, and those herds are smallish, with just a hundred or so animals per herd. For wolves, the value of the resource does not justify the danger and energy that would go into exploiting it. Wes Olson, a ranger at Elk Island National Park, near Edmonton, Alberta, told me that "it takes a herd of about a thousand bison to get wolves interested." At that point, he explained, "there's a greater chance that the herd will contain unhealthy animals, or an abundance of calves."

The three thousand to four thousand buffalo that live in Yellowstone National Park share the land with a couple hundred wolves. Those wolves are monitored, studied, pestered, and photographed more than any other population of predators on earth, and all that attention has yielded some compelling observations about wolf-buffalo interactions. As of 2003, park biologists had documented fifty-seven predatory interactions between buffalo and wolves. Most of those interactions took place in late winter and occurred in areas marked by a scarcity of elk, which usually provide the bulk of the Yellowstone wolves' diets.

To kill large prey, wolves usually start by biting the rear of the fleeing animal's legs until it is "hamstrung," or can no longer run. The biologists in Yellowstone found that the wolves would quickly lose interest in a herd of buffalo if the buffalo refused to run. Of those fifty-seven observed interactions, the wolves could only get the buffalo to run on fourteen occasions. Even then, the buffalo proved to be formidable prey, as the buffalo's herding tendencies worked to their advantage. All those whirring, kicking, tightly interwoven hooves presented the wolves with a dangerous situation. In fourteen attempts made against herds of fleeing buffalo, the wolves made a kill only four times. On those occasions, the wolves either isolated a buffalo or else chased the herd into deep snow. On average, the battles that ended in a buffalo's death lasted about nine hours.

In the mid- to late nineteenth century, during the great buffalo slaughter of the Euro-American hide hunters, there was such an abundance of unused buffalo flesh strewn across the landscape that wolves grew fat and plentiful. Indians talked of running overfed wolves down on horseback to kill them with knives, and Euro-American explorers described "tamed" wolves lurking near the camps of hide hunters. When the hide hunters began to run low on buffalo, they sought alternative ways to supplement their incomes. Some expanded into the wolf hide business. When a wolfer killed a buffalo, he'd lace its carcass with strychnine. In the morning, all he had to do was collect the dead wolves. Some wolfers would wait until they had a wounded buffalo on the ground and then open a vein with a sharp knife and give the buffalo a mainline of strychnine. The buffalo's circulatory system would carry the poison all through the carcass, saving poison and increasing the wolf kill. It's commonly said that the wolf hunters were some of the only white people who were disappointed to see the buffalo vanish. They suspected that wolves would vanish right along with them, and they were ultimately right.

AS I FOLLOW THE STREAM CHANNEL, I realize that I've lost the set of wolf tracks. Maybe the wolf smelled me and took off. I follow the channel for another half hour, taking it very slowly, and it begins to split into many other smaller channels. I stay to the middle branch, and the surrounding hills close in. I reach the back end of the willow flat without noticing any fresh buffalo tracks. So much for this plan, I think. I check out my map and compass. If I walk to the northeast, I'll hit the eastern bank of the Chetaslina River at a point that is much higher up the valley than I went yesterday. I should go up there and find a good lookout, I think, where I can see across to the other side of the valley where those four bulls were hanging around.

To get there, I have to cut through a couple miles of land owned by Ahtna, Inc., or else go all the way back to the mouth of the Chetaslina and then follow the river up. This presents an unsavory dilemma, because I hate looking at the same ground twice even more than I hate trespassing. So with a nagging feeling of guilt I follow a small game trail into the spruce forest, and once again I'm a reluctant violator of the laws of private property. Also, I'm once again struggling through alders, rose hips, and downed spruce trees. I step over a log and snag the leg of my wool pants on a broken limb. It rips a hole just big enough to accommodate my thumb. I always carry a travel-sized spool of dental floss in my pack along with a curved needle designed for stitching people up. I think about stopping to stitch the tear, but for some reason I don't. After ten more minutes of fighting through the brush, I look down and see that the small rip has expanded from the back of my knee clear down to my ankle, offering a vivid validation of the old saying "a stitch in time saves nine."

In fact, a stitch in time would have saved about seventy. For a half hour I sit on a wet log in a thin pair of underwear while I sew my pants back together. Once I'm on my way again, I run into a well-trodden buffalo trail that seems to be going more or less where I want to be. The trail is stamped through the mosses and lichens on the forest floor, right down to bare dirt and rock. When I stand on the bottom of the trail, the normal level of the forest floor is at my shins. Like many of the buffalo trails I've found, this one seems perfectly errant in its patterns. In truth, though, there's a system to its direction. Buffalo select their trails in order to travel over the path of least resistance, even if that involves taking a few extra steps. But there's a limit to how far a buffalo will detour. Following their trails, I can almost understand their thinking. If the trail intersects a nasty swath of tangled and downed timber that would take a long time to go around, they'll opt to plow on through like bulldozers. In some places, the trail breaks into several routes through the obstacles, as though different buffalo have different opinions about how to handle travel annoyances.

A few hundred years ago, Euro-American explorers who traveled through buffalo country thought that the animals were incapable of walking straight lines. Buffalo have a thick mat of hair between their eyes that resembles souped-up pubic hair in its texture. People assumed that buffalo trails were crooked because the animals had to walk sideways in order to see where they were headed. Other people thought this was ridiculous. They figured that buffalo walked in crooked lines because their eyes were too far off to the sides of their heads; buffalo, they explained, couldn't see forward or backward at all, hair or no hair. "Not being good travelers sideways," one man said, "they look ahead with one eye and to the rear with the other, deflecting to the right and then to the left for a distance of two or three hundred yards."

In the early 1830s, when engineers were laying out the route for the Baltimore and Ohio Railroad, it's said that they had to follow buffalo trails through West Virginia. In two places where the railroad was run through tunnels, along the eighty-three-mile stretch between Grafton and Parkersburg, the buffalo trails are supposedly directly overhead. There are many such stories across the eastern United States. The passage through the Cumberland Gap is said to have started out as a buffalo trail. Indians in Kentucky used a 225-mile path between Big Bone Lick and Maysville that they called, simply, "the Buffalo Path." When Euro-American settlers started coming into the first "far west" of Ohio, Kentucky, and Tennessee, they often used buffalo trails instead of Indian trails because they were hoping to run into the one and not the other. Their movements and settlements were influenced by the buffalo paths, which led them to things that they needed: meat, water, salt licks, meadows, and good places to cross rivers. Later, they widened the paths into wagon trails and, later still, roads.

One man who did not think that buffalo made good engineers when it came to the routing of roads was George Washington. The buffalo had minor cameo roles throughout Washington's life. He killed a buffalo in the Ohio Territory back in 1770. A year before the Declaration of Independence, Washington asked a friend to catch some buffalo calves for him because he was kicking around the idea of raising a herd and marketing cloth made from the wool. During the Revolutionary War, Washington corresponded with his officers about killing buffalo in order to feed troops. In the winter of 1780–81, officer Daniel Brodhead wrote to Washington about the lack of game in the vicinity of Fort Pitt. He warned Washington, "I have risked the sending of a party of hunters to kill buffalo at Little Kanawha," an Ohio River tributary that flows through western West Virginia, "and to lay in the meat until I can detach a party to bring it in, which cannot be done before spring."

After the war, in 1784, Washington made a westward trip to check on his Pennsylvania landholdings. He was a surveyor by training, and on his way home he cut through western Maryland to scout out possible routes for a canal system that could connect the Virginia coast with the Ohio River. (It was never built.) He got lost on an obscure trail called McCulloch's Pack Horse Path, which, Washington wrote in his diary, "owes its origen to Buffaloes, being no other than their tracks from one lick to another & consequently crooked and not well chosen."

The trail is especially obscure nowadays, because no one knows where it began or ended, or how exactly it got its name. Generally, it's accepted that the buffalo trail passed close to Gorman, West Virginia, and then snaked its way north and west across Garrett County, Maryland, before passing back into West Virginia and heading off toward the Ohio River. I wanted to see it, but I knew I didn't stand a chance of finding it without some help. The Garrett County Historical Society put me in touch with the Reverend John A. Grant, who wrote an unsigned article about the path in 1948. Grant was now eighty-four years old, a clergyman for the Episcopal Church. I made arrangements to meet him at a crossroads in two weeks, and when I called on the morning of our appointment to make sure he remembered, he acted as though it was the most superfluous phone call that he'd ever received in his entire life.

Grant drives a Buick and wears a style of hat commonly worn

by churchgoing old men, with a bill that snaps to the body of the hat. His skin looked as pale and thin as wax paper, and was textured like wax paper that had been wadded up and then smoothed back out again. He was born and raised in Oakland, Maryland. "I had the most fortunate childhood," he told me. His father took him hiking and taught him a lot about history. He liked to be outside as a kid, so he slept on his porch in the summertime and the birds woke him up very early in the morning, before his family was stirring. "That's how I became a voracious reader," he said. Under his mattress, he kept books about ancient Hebrew, Egyptian hieroglyphics, and Scandinavian runes. When World War II started, he enlisted for pilot school. He was nearby when the first atomic bomb was tested in New Mexico, and he heard a rumor that the explosion was from a munitions train blowing up.

Grant appreciates the small coincidences of history, the places where the past and the present collide with some sort of tangible, visible result. Outside of Oakland, he showed me a dipping well where George Washington once drank water. Grant dipped up a handful and tasted it. "That's good water," he said. "No wonder Washington drank that." In downtown Oakland he showed me some railroad tracks and the exact location of a train depot used by Confederate agents to move contraband during the Civil War. Whenever the Confederate sympathizers were loading supplies, they'd send beautiful women out to urinate in the bushes in order to distract the attention of Union agents.

Next he showed me a place along a road where Henry Ford, Thomas Edison, Harvey Firestone, and the writer and conservationist John Burroughs got stuck in the mud in Edison's Packard. A local man pulled them out with his Model T, and he advised Henry Ford to "get yourself a Ford." Down that same road we passed a red log cabin with a late-model Chevy 4x4 in the driveway. Grant said that his friend lived there and drove that truck. Before he retired, this friend was deputized as a "federal agent" by the late Bobby Kennedy. Later, the friend was invited to the White House to receive an award. He shook hands with President John F. Kennedy, who asked him where he was from. "Western Maryland," answered Grant's friend.

"Where in western Maryland?" asked the president.

"Oakland," said the friend.

"I know Oakland," said the president. "I ate buckwheat cakes next to the church."

Our final destination was the Herrington Manor State Park. Of the female rangers at the park's entrance, Grant said, "They're pretty tough hombres." We drove down a park road that was shaded by thick timber. Grant stopped the Buick at a very arbitrary-looking place, stepped from the car, and invited me to inspect a piece of rock that he had picked up. I hadn't really thought about how old he was until I saw his palm. "This rock we're standing on," Grant said, "was crushed with sledgehammers by workers with the Civilian Conservation Corps, a program founded by President Franklin Delano Roosevelt. Those workers lived in a camp here. We would come here to swim and watch them work."

He looked into the woods. There were many kinds of trees growing in the forest, including several that I was unfamiliar with. And there was the faintest trail coming through the trees. "I believe your trail, the trail that Washington followed, crossed this road here." I walked up and down the road a few steps and looked around. I picked up one of the hand-crushed rocks and put it into my pocket. Birds chirped. I became worried that I'd someday lose the rock, and so I picked up another and put it into a different pocket. I looked back into the woods. It was hard to imagine a line

A shedding bull buffalo near Yellowstone National Park.

of buffalo plodding single file through the undergrowth with George Washington coming behind them, but I stared until I could see them crystal clear.

AS I'M WALKING DOWN the buffalo trail, I notice that the spruce limbs hanging over the trail hold strands of tangled and bleached buffalo wool. The tufts look like someone dragged a brownish cotton ball across the bristles of a wire brush. Some of the tufts are as high as my own head, and the individual strands are several inches long. Those tufts probably came from the humps of big bulls shedding their winter coats. Travelers on the Great Plains reported walking through cottonwood groves where the ground was covered ankle deep in shed buffalo hair. Settlers who crossed the Great Plains without seeing a single buffalo would still find enough wool hanging on sagebrush and hawthorn bushes to experiment with weaving it. I was thinking about this as I walked along, and I worked a few tufts of wool into a twisted piece of thread about two inches long. The thread felt nice in my fingers, and I started grabbing whatever tufts of hair I passed. My hand was nearly full by the time the trail climbed out of the spruce forest and entered a large network of meadows punctuated by thin stands of aspen. In areas that now contain buffalo, researchers have found that one-third of all nesting birds use buffalo wool to line their nests. The wool is also hoarded by rodents such as mice and voles. I think about this, then wad the wool into a small ball and hang it from a low stem on an aspen tree.

I come to a hill, and I guess that it's the backside of the ridge paralleling the Chetaslina valley. As it gets steeper and steeper, I start switchbacking my way up. When I'm a quarter of the way up the hill, I start to feel intensely hot. I drop my pack and pull off my hat and jacket just in time for a wave of nausea that forces me to sit down. I haven't felt right all day long, but this is ridiculous. My head's pounding. I feel under my shirt, and my skin feels like the inside of a wet plastic bag full of mushrooms.

"Damn," I say aloud. I go through the events of the last few days in my mind, trying to pick out moments when I might have drunk contaminated river water and picked up some kind of waterborne parasite such as giardia or cryptosporidium. I've had beaver fever twice, once in Colorado and once in Michigan, and each time it started out with uncontrollable pants messing followed by a nasty load of flu-like symptoms. But I can't think of when I might have drunk bad water without treating it first, either with iodine, boiling, or filtering. Plus, I don't have any diarrhea going on. If it's not beaver fever, I don't know what's happening. It must be some other kind of fever. Is there such a thing as buffalo fever?

I'm still hotter than hell, so I pull off my outer shirt. Then I strip off another layer. I finally start to cool down, and I lie back against the slope of the hill. It feels good. I close my eyes and place my hat across my lids to block out the light. I start to doze, but then I jerk myself to an upright position. Grizzly bears can be scary and having buffalo fever would suck, but neither of those things will kill you as smoothly as hypothermia. An average of 689 people die from hypothermia every year in the United States, in all fifty states and during every month. The annual incidence rate for hypothermia fluctuates between 2 and 4 deaths per million citizens, and it seems perfectly intuitive that Alaska is the nation's hypothermia capital. Here, there are over 4 annual deaths per 100,000 citizens. That's over ten times the national average and twice the rate of the state's nearest two competitors, Montana and Wyoming, which average 1.58 and 1.57 per 100,000 people, respectively.

The really spooky thing about hypothermia is the phenomenon called "paradoxical undressing." People suffering from hypothermia often shed their clothes. The reasons for this are somewhat murky, but it probably has to do with the behavior of blood vessels. When your body gets really cold, the blood vessels near the skin contract to prevent the flow of blood to the body's surface. This keeps more blood near the body's core, where it can stay warm. But the blood vessels don't want to be contracted, and it takes a lot of energy to keep them that way. Eventually they tire out and dilate. The warm blood rushes back to the surface, and you get a sensation of intense heat.

I look around at my discarded clothing, and I think of those news descriptions you see whenever someone dies of hypothermia out in the woods. In 2003, the dead and hypothermic body of a thirty-five-year-old Alaskan hiker was "not clothed from the waist up and was missing a shoe." In 2004, when a hypothermia victim's body was recovered in northwestern New Mexico, "his jacket and neck chain were recovered a short distance away." In 2005, a man in Wyoming was found "partially dressed in a pullover, T-shirt, pants, and one sock." I envision an article about my own death, and think about how the police will never realize that I had undressed because of buffalo fever. My buddies would read the article and say, "What an idiot! Steve should've known better than to paradoxically undress. The dumb ass!"

I force myself to get up and put my hat and shirt back on. If I'm going to take a nap, I'll have to do it in my sleeping bag. To get back to camp, I have to reach the crest of the ridge, or else I'll have to traipse back through the spruce bottom. I take a few steps, feeling totally nauseous, and then rest a moment. I take a few more steps, get nauseous again, then rest again. I do this a few more times, wondering all the while whether or not grizzlies are attracted to the smell of human vomit. I'll bet they are; they'd probably love it. I start picking my way down the ridgeline. I make it back to my camp before dark. I get a fire going and boil some pasta, but I can only get a couple of bites down. I put the food back in the box and rig the lid shut with straps. Then I put some pebbles in the cooking pot and set that on the lid so it'll make a noise if a bear messes with it. It's below freezing and I can hear slush flowing in the Chetaslina. I chamber a round in my rifle and place it next to my sleeping bag. I'm shivering as I undress and climb in. Danny left behind an extra sleeping bag, and I pull it over my own. Sleep comes folding over me before I can zip it up.

— 10 —

JUDITH COOPER, a graduate student in anthropology at Southern Methodist University, in Dallas, Texas, does not immediately come across as the sort of person who'd spend a lot of time hanging around in places where Indians once killed massive amounts of buffalo by chasing them off cliffs. She is slight and shy, with intelligent eyes, and on the day I met her, she was dressed in stylish jeans and black boots and had on makeup. When asked how she ended up in her line of work, though, she was quick and certain with her answer. "Every kid is interested in archaeology," she told me. "For me, that interest never went away." With that, we spent a couple of hours talking about the business of falling buffalo.

The Blackfoot term for a buffalo jump is *pishkun*, which translates roughly to "deep blood kettle." Most known buffalo jumps—they number in the hundreds—are located along major river valleys on the northern Great Plains. At the Vore Buffalo Jump, near Sundance, Wyoming, volumetric calculations taken from a bone bed that is a hundred feet in diameter and twenty-five feet deep suggest that perhaps twenty thousand buffalo were killed there over a great many years. The pile of buffalo bones beneath the Ulm Pishkun Buffalo Jump, outside of Great Falls, Montana, is one mile long. Head-Smashed-In Buffalo Jump, along the eastern face of the Rocky Mountains in Alberta, Canada, has a bone bed that is thirty feet thick—or well over half as deep as the cliff is tall. The great mass of buffalo bones at these jump sites attests to their productive tenures, but it also opens up a small mystery. As anyone with experience moving sheep or cattle can verify, it's a real pain in the ass to get large animals moving in a direction that they don't want to go, especially when the animals have to put their hooves down on unfamiliar surfaces. Since buffalo can't fly, open air certainly qualifies as just such a surface. So what would compel a buffalo to commit suicide? I was hoping that Judith could help explain.

In 2005, Judith co-authored a paper in *American Antiquity* that included a detailed assessment of the topography surrounding Bonfire Shelter, the southernmost (and perhaps oldest) buffalo jump in the United States. The site is at the head of Mile Canyon, a Rio Grande tributary near the Texas-Mexico border. The cliff's face is eighty-five feet high. At that elevation, the buffalo would be falling at forty-seven miles per hour when they smacked the ground. (It seems that hunters didn't like their cliffs to be much taller than that, probably because the buffalo would be too smashed up to do any good.) There is a conspicuous V-shaped notch eroded into the cliff's rim; it looks like a pour spout on a water pitcher. Beneath the notch is a fifteen-foot-tall cone-shaped mound of rubble that contains several distinct layers of buffalo bones along with human artifacts. The uppermost layer has the remains of at least eight hundred buffalo; during decomposition, the carcasses built up gases and burst into an inferno that turned most of the bone to ash. That's how Bonfire Shelter got its name.

The ground at the top of the cliff at Bonfire Shelter is typical of most buffalo jumps, with ample grassland and nearby access to water. These features were probably reliable attractants to buffalo, but evidence from other buffalo jumps suggests that Indians sometimes sweetened the deal for buffalo, so to speak, by luring them into position. There are historical accounts describing hunters who were so skilled in the ways of buffalo that they could dress up in a buffalo hide and lead a curious herd into the region of the trap.* At the Madison Buffalo Jump, in western Montana, archaeological evidence suggests that groups of as many as one hundred hunters may have gently herded the buffalo to the plain above the precipice.

The next step was to get the buffalo moving. Indians used a variety of techniques to instigate the stampede, and then to control the motion and energy of it once it started. They let the wind carry their human odor to the buffalo; they lit wildfires; they waved torches; they hid in depressions in the ground and jumped up just in time; they built rock cairns in the shapes of humans; and they simply chased after the buffalo while waving their arms. But still, there's the burning question: How would you scare a buffalo herd so much that it would stampede off a cliff rather than turning to face an inferior number of adversaries that each weighed less than a tenth of an individual buffalo's weight?

To be fair, the word "jump" is not particularly suitable for describing how buffalo jumps worked. The animals did not plunge off the cliffs in a suicidal flight, like so many versions of *Thelma*

---

*These hunters, variously called "buffalo callers," "bringers-in," or "bringers of plenty," held a position of religious significance in their clans and tribes. One bringer-in refused to eat any buffalo that he lured to its death, for fear that he'd lose his abilities. Instead, he ate buffalo that were killed by others out on the open ground.

and Louise. Rather, as Judith explained, they were the victims of subterfuge, or a sort of grassland hall of mirrors. Working with colleagues, Judith used GIS, or geographic information systems, to create a digital, three-dimensional topographical map of Bonfire Shelter. Judith described the creation of the Bonfire maps as "taking a systematic approach to something that is very mundane" (a description of the actual process includes the phrase "inverse distance weighted spatial interpolation"), but the outcome is extraordinary. The map is capable of yielding a buffalo's-eye view of the animal's own impending death—all on compact disc.

There is no archaeological evidence of man-made obstacles in the area of Bonfire Shelter, and Judith believes that the natural landscape offered all the essential physical components for an effective stampede. The routes, or "drive lines," had an obvious termination, the V-shaped wedge, but could have begun just about anywhere on the surrounding prairie. To select a theoretical route for a stampeding herd, the researchers chose sixteen arbitrary points along a circle radiating two and a half miles from the jump-off point. They rated each of these routes based on a number of factors, such as the loss and gain of elevation, physical obstacles, and visibility. From there, they narrowed it down to five possible routes that the hunters could have feasibly utilized to deliver the buffalo to the location of their death. Of those, drive line No. 4 seemed the best candidate.

Judith turned on her laptop. The screen was filled with what looked like a video game. I was standing on a rolling plain beneath the big Texas sky. "Your eyes are 1.7 meters off the ground," Judith said, "and you'll be running at almost top speed for a bison—we calculated fifty kilometers per hour." She clicked the computer's mouse, and suddenly I was running away from some unseen threat, traveling at a buffalo's speed and seeing the ground from a buffalo's level. Everything looked all right. All I saw was ground, rolling ahead of me. A distant horizon, swells of land, slight rises and drops in elevation. I sought out paths of least resistance as I was channeled by the landscape. My decisions seemed logical. Knowing what was supposedly behind me—a bunch of guys with sharp sticks—I continued to run toward what seemed like an unbroken expanse of open ground. But then, suddenly, something happened. The land that looked continuous was in fact an optical illusion; the plain was interrupted by a deep chasm. At my height, it wasn't possible for me to see the chasm until I was seventy-six feet away. Traveling at thirty miles per hour, I crossed that expanse of ground in less than two seconds. To stop would be like slamming down your car brakes on an L.A. freeway with a line of Mack trucks riding your bumper—just because you stop doesn't mean you're going to stop.

Anyone whose sensitivities are disturbed by modern slaughterhouse practices would be utterly repulsed by the mayhem at the foot of a buffalo jump. In the fall, buffalo suffered compound fractures. Splintered femurs were driven far enough into bodies to puncture stomachs and spill contents. Buffalo landed on other buffalo. Their horns and hooves ripped into each other's hides and flesh. The backs of the buffalo's eyes turned red with blood. Unhurt animals were trapped under the weight of their herd members. Calves wandered about in a daze, bellowing for their mothers. Severely injured buffalo regurgitated food and choked on their tongues. Animals with rib-punctured lungs drowned in their own blood.

There were many survivors, wounded but alive. Near Emigrant, Montana, over fifteen hundred arrowheads have come out of the ground beneath a buffalo jump, suggesting that such kills required a lot of mop-up. The Indians usually constructed obstacles to help contain the wounded animals. Using buffalo ribs and broken mandibles, they'd dig postholes for juniper posts that they cut down to size with fire. The posts supported the walls of sturdy corrals. They'd sharpen sticks on both ends and drive them into the ground, angled toward the fall zone like some medieval defense mechanism. Or they'd build fences out of sticks and brush covered with hides, or latticeworks of lodgepoles, or leg bones left over from older kills, or even whole frozen carcasses.

When it was all said and done, a successful buffalo jump must have been a thing of beauty. I like to think about the breathless Indians who wandered among the raw carnage, knives drawn and ready for the work ahead. I suspect that they experienced feelings of awe, gratitude, happiness, relief, and accomplishment. To understand their emotions, imagine that everything you've owned and worked for—house, clothes, furniture, jewelry, artwork, luggage, cookware, bedding, food—was thrown off a cliff and dashed to smithereens. If that happened, you would lose all of the things that the Indians gained from the smashed-up buffalo at the foot of the cliff. Their entire lives were contained within the steaming pile of blood, meat, and fur; all they had to do was pick out the parts, rearrange them, and put them back together again in useful ways.

INDIAN HUNTERS had many clever ways of killing buffalo. They'd dress in wolf hides and crawl up close enough to sink projectile points into the rib cages of the unsuspecting grazers. A hunter might kill several buffalo this way before the herd took flight. Early in the spring, buffalo calves were so dependent on their mothers that they wouldn't run off even when the mother fell dead. Indians would snatch these calves by the back legs and bring them home so that their children could practice archery and spear throwing on live targets. Then the hunter could skin the calf and climb into its fresh hide and waddle back into another buffalo herd to make a kill.

In the wintertime, Indians would herd buffalo into snow-drifts; while the animals floundered on their spindly legs, the hunters would walk across the drifts on snowshoes and kill the animals with knives. If the ice on a lake was slick, Indians would chase buffalo out there and spear the animals when they fell down. On the Missouri River in the winter of 1805–6, the fur trader Charles McKenzie watched the Mandan Indians use another trick to kill buffalo on the ice. They would drive herds "to the banks of the Missouri and, by gradual approaches, confine them into a narrow space where the ice was weakened, until, by their weight and pressure, large squares of ice . . . would give way and vast numbers of animals were plunged into the river and carried by the current under the solid ice to a 'mare' a little below, where they again emerged, floated and were received by crowds of women and children."

In the summer and fall months they'd kill buffalo with fire and water. Along the Mississippi and Missouri rivers, Indians would torch vast tracts of land next to the river and then wait for the buffalo to jump into the water to escape. While swimming, the animals were so slow that hunters could grab on to their hair and slit their throats while they swam. The explorer and missionary Father Louis Hennepin described how the Indians would set large fires that encircled entire herds "except some passage which they leave on purpose, and where they take post with their bows and arrows. The buffalo . . . are thus compelled to pass near these Indians, who sometimes kill as many as a hundred and twenty in a day." Sometimes Indians would use nothing beyond their own bodies to corral buffalo. A group of hunters would surround small buffalo herds and then close in until the animals were contained in a circle. The Indians would kill the buffalo as they tried to escape, often so close that the hunter could pluck out his used arrow from the side of the animal before it fell over and broke it.

Despite the ingenuity of these methods, anthropologists seem to be most interested in the large-scale, industrial slaughter of buffalo that is typified by the use of buffalo jumps. While it seems as though buffalo jumps were in isolated, scattered usage for much of the time since the end of the Pleistocene, they came into their heyday at about the time of Christ. Their widespread usage marks the advent of large tribal alliances that gathered together on a seasonal basis to trade, socialize, and conduct religious practices. Feeding these big groups of people required large-scale buffalo hunting; likewise, large-scale buffalo hunting required big groups of people. The use of buffalo jumps dropped off precipitously with the introduction of the horse; with beasts of burden, the Indians could kill just as many buffalo without having to rely on luck to put the animals in the proper position. From then on, the most common hunting method was the one that we know from movies: bare-chested, brightly painted Indians who daringly rode into running buffalo herds while firing arrows and bullets into the animals at point-blank range.

One could make a cogent argument that the widespread advent of buffalo jumps marked the beginning of the end for buffalo. It seems as though the massive, wholesale slaughter of complete buffalo herds was like an addictive drug. North Americans had long viewed the buffalo as a giver of everything, but buffalo jumps may have helped create the fallacy that the buffalo was the giver of *lots* of everything—so much so, in fact, that tribes who used buffalo jumps were able to operate trade networks that distributed buffalo hides to tribes who lived outside of the buffalo's range.

Some of the largest buffalo jumps are on the plains of northern Montana and southern Canada, and perhaps it's no coincidence that those landscapes were the first to produce buffalo slaughters big enough to clear out entire geographic regions. The hunters who first managed to pull this off were the Métis, a people of mixed French-Canadian and Indian ancestry who lived in settlements along the Red River of Manitoba, Canada. By 1820 they had perfected the industrial slaughter of buffalo, and they made a lot of money selling the meat and hides. On what became known as the Red River hunts, the Métis brought along chaplains to conduct Mass and police-like officials who enforced organizational rules. In June 1840, a typical year, the Métis organized a hunting party of 1,630 people, 1,210 two-wheeled "Red River carts," 1,644 horses and oxen, 542 dogs, and 1,240 skinning knives. They returned in mid-August with over one million pounds of dried meat and buffalo hides. Estimates vary, but the total kill for such a year may have amounted to fifty thousand buffalo. For the Métis, the commercial value of the kill was around a quarter-million dollars. It was enough money to push the Métis toward ever distant horizons to find untouched herds of buffalo. They were hunting well into Montana and the Dakotas before they finally ran out of animals and the famed Red River hunts ground to a halt.

A buffalo "robe" is a tanned hide with the hair still on it; the animal was usually killed in the fall or winter when it has prime fur. From 1830 to 1870, when the Red River hunts flourished, robes were the driving factor of the buffalo trade. They were fashionable in the eastern United States and Europe, and they were a necessity in the West. People used buffalo robes for mattresses, blankets, coats, or just about any application for which you needed something warm and soft. The market absorbed as many as 200,000 buffalo robes every year, and these were supplied almost exclusively by Native American and Métis hunters of the Great Plains. Prices for robes varied depending on the region and how dishonest the purchaser was, but one buffalo robe might fetch a hand-sized wad of tobacco, or three cups of sugar and a cup of coffee beans, or one quart of watered-down whiskey, or twelve steel arrowheads. Three robes could get a bracelet. Twenty robes, a gun. One of the robes would retail for anywhere from $5 to $50 in the East.

The Indians may have gone on selling small numbers of buffalo hides for decades longer without running out of buffalo if it hadn't been for a perfect storm of factors that struck the buffalo herds in around 1870. Perhaps most important, cheap transportation came to the Great Plains. The Union Pacific Railroad began in Omaha in 1865 and reached Utah in 1869, where it joined another line to become the nation's first transcontinental railroad. At that point, the great western herd was said to be divided into the "northern herd" and the "southern herd." Obviously buffalo continued to cross the line, and many were killed by trains and train passengers, but it was generally recognized that the tracks created a buffalo-free zone across the center of the animal's range. Subsequently, the southern herd's range was punctured and divided again and again by the Santa Fe Railroad and the Kansas Pacific branch of the Union Pacific. Besides fragmenting the buffalo's habitat and providing an efficient way to transport massive amounts of buffalo hides to the East, the railroads delivered guns and people to buffalo country.

The second phase of the perfect storm began when commercial tanneries in the eastern United States and Europe made some discoveries about buffalo hides. They'd been experimenting with the skins for years, but the hides were difficult to work with (too thick), and the end product was too porous. Eventually, though, they struck on a system by which they could produce high-quality buffalo leather with elastic tendencies that was perfectly suited for industrial belting and footwear. Orders for "flint hides"—air-dried, untanned buffalo skins—started to come in. And because the tanneries were producing hairless leather, it didn't matter which time of year the buffalo were killed.

One of the first large requests for flint hides came in 1871, when a merchant in Dodge City named W. C. Lobenstein took an order for 500 from a tannery in England that was producing leather goods for the British army. Lobenstein hired two suppliers to procure the hides, and the suppliers turned to a young man named J. Wright Mooar. Born in Vermont in 1851, Mooar headed west shortly after the Civil War and got started in the buffalo business by hunting meat to feed troops at Fort Hays, Kansas. After moving to Dodge City, he found work selling buffalo meat to track-laying crews working on the Santa Fe Railroad. He was a respected and polished buffalo hunter when he started hunting for flint hides, and in short order he had 557 of them. Mooar sent the surplus of 57 hides to his brother in New York City. The brother sold the hides to a local tannery, which tampered with the new tanning processes and then placed an order for 2,000 more. Soon, other tanneries were placing standing orders for "as many as we can get." The price of buffalo hides jumped up, until they were fetching $3 apiece. Mooar immediately established a buffalo-killing "firm"; by the time the buffalo were all gone, about ten years later, he had personally killed twenty-five thousand.

By the summer of 1872, literally thousands of buffalo hunters had converged on the Great Plains. They had (or would soon earn) names like Buffalo Bill Comstock, Buffalo Bill Cody, Cross-Eyed Joe, Apache Bill, Buffalo Curley, Wyatt Earp, Pat Garrett,

Tom Nixon, Limpy Jim Smith, Buckshot Roberts, Squirrel Eye Emery, Mr. Hickey, Prairie Dog Dave, and California Joe.* As their names suggest, these fellows were not stay-at-home-dad types. They were Confederate soldiers escaping the shame of Reconstruction. They were Union soldiers escaping the boredom of victory. They were orphans. They were wanted alive for fraud here, wanted dead for murder there. They were men like Wild Bill Hickok, who killed a man after an argument about who could kill whom the fastest. They were men like Lonesome Charley Reynolds, who turned to buffalo hunting after he shot the arm off an army officer at Fort McPherson, Georgia.† They were men like Crooked Nose Jack McCall, who was hanged for shooting Wild Bill Hickok in the back of the head.††

Different hide hunters worked in different ways, but the ones with a head for business started their own outfits. An outfit was usually managed by the shooter. He'd hire a couple of skinners and a camp tender. A six-man outfit might depart civilization

---

*Earp was a participant in the shoot-out at the OK Corral. The actuality of his career as a buffalo hunter is sometimes challenged. A man by his name was arrested several times on prostitution charges in Peoria, Illinois, at a time that Wyatt Earp later claimed to be buffalo hunting in Kansas. Pat Garrett killed Billy the Kid, a.k.a. Henry McCarty, William Antrim, and William Harrison Bonney. Tom Nixon was killed by Deputy Sheriff Mysterious Dave Mather, a sometime buffalo hunter who was rumored to be an ancestor of the Puritan writer Cotton Mather, who played an influential role in the Salem witch trials. Buckshot Roberts was killed by Billy the Kid's gang, the Regulators. California Joe was killed by the Sioux.

†Lonesome Charley died with Custer at the Battle of the Little Bighorn. Legend has it, he had a premonition of his own death the night before he was killed and gave away all of his belongings.

††Jack McCall sometimes went by Billy Sutherland and Billy Barnes. Oddly, Billy Barnes was a name used on occasion by both Wild Bill Hickok and his brother. After Wild Bill's death, there was confusion about who killed whom. Some thought he'd been gunned down by his own kin.

with two or three ox-drawn carts loaded with barrels of coffee, salt, sugar, flour, camp equipment, skinning equipment, and bullet-making materials: five twenty-five-pound kegs of Du Pont gunpowder, eight hundred pounds of lead, hundreds of brass casings, and thousands of cartridge primers.

Heading into dangerous country, a hide-hunting outfit might travel with another outfit or two for safety's sake. While the wagons headed toward a general area where buffalo herds were expected to be hanging around, the shooters would cut broad circles on horseback scouting for buffalo sign. The scouts might be gone from the wagons for several days at a time, returning to their rendezvous point only when they found a herd or cut a good trail. When they did find buffalo, they didn't storm into the herd with their guns ablaze. They were more calculated than that. First they'd check the lay of the land and find a good campsite, preferably in a deep gully or canyon where they were hidden from Indians. They also needed a water source and plenty of buffalo chips or wood for cooking fuel. With the camp set up and everything ready, the shooter would get some sleep and then ride out early in the morning. They liked .44-, .45-, and .50-caliber rifles manufactured by Sharps and Springfield, and they carried hundreds of cartridges. Most shooters liked cartridge belts that they could wear around their waist; such a belt held about forty-two rounds. A shooter might wear two, or else put his ammo into a bandolier worn across his chest.

A shooter would tether or hobble his horse somewhere close to the herd but well out of sight and downwind. Then he'd study the herd. Which way was the wind blowing? Were they feeding or sleeping? Holding still or walking? Preferably, the buffalo would be still. If there were thousands of the animals, the shooter would select a particular band off to the side of the main bunch. A group of about fifty was a good number. Then he'd use creek beds or sagebrush clumps or stands of cottonwoods to stalk within a couple hundred yards. If he got too close, he'd risk spooking the herd. If he was too far off, he'd risk making bad hits and wounding buffalo.

He'd get his gear all set and ready before he started shooting. He needed a solid rest, someplace to steady the barrel of his gun. He might use a wadded-up jacket, crossed sticks stuck into the ground, mounds of packed snow, or mounds of buffalo chips. He'd take off his ammo belt and lay it next to him. Then he would try to determine the herd's leader. Usually an older cow, the leader might be out in front of the herd and setting the pace of movement. That's the one he wanted to hit first. If the buffalo were bedded down, the shooter might not know who the leader was. If that was the case, he'd pick a buffalo on the outer, distant edge of the herd.

The shooter would send his bullet through the target's lungs, which were called "lights." A lung-hit buffalo usually wouldn't run but would just take a few steps before sinking to its haunches and tipping over. It would kick for a second and then be still. The fallen buffalo's herd mates could respond in a number of ways: the buffalo might walk up and smell the blood pouring from the animal's nose; they might act very aggressively toward the downed animal and gore it; they might ignore it; they might slowly walk away; or they might take off in a wild stampede. The shooter was hoping for any reaction but the latter. The goal was to have the herd milling about in complete confusion—no idea where to go, no idea where the danger was coming from. As soon as one of the buffalo showed any initiative toward leaving, the shooter would put a bullet in its lungs. If the buffalo seemed to want to travel in a particular direction, the shooter would drop an animal or two in its path and change its mind. If a buffalo ran, the shooter would try to knock it down in a hurry. If he fired more than a round or two a minute, his rifle barrel would get too hot. J. Wright Mooar cooled his barrel by pissing on it. Snow came in handy for this purpose.

When a herd started moving away from a shooter, it was said to be "adrift." The shooter would follow along, going from downed body to downed body so he could use the carcasses as rifle rests and hiding places. He had to be careful, because half-dead or stunned buffalo might get up and charge him. Sometimes he'd prop his gun on a downed buffalo, and it would be breathing or twitching too much for him to get a solid rest. The buffalo might lift its head and stare at him, wild-eyed.

There are documented reports of shooters killing one hundred or two hundred buffalo within an hour or two, but thirty or forty was usually considered a good day's shooting.* A shooter didn't want to go too far over that number, because he was limited by how many hides his skinners could remove. Left overnight, buffalo bloated too much, and the hides got tight and hard to pull off. Or wolves ripped them up. Or the carcasses froze.

In really good hunting, skinners might make upwards of $20 a day. They usually got twenty-five or thirty cents per hide, though skinners from Mexico would do it for twenty cents. Skinners fol-

---

*Tom Nixon used two rifles to kill 120 buffalo in forty minutes. In Montana, a hundred miles northeast of Miles City, Vic Smith killed 107 without moving. A Dodge City resident "known for his truthfulness" killed 250 in a single day by making several consecutive stands. Colonel Dodge saw where a hunter killed 112 buffalo in forty-five minutes, dropping the animals within a semicircle of two hundred yards. Charlie Hart, a survivor of the Confederate prison at Andersonville, had several such days. He once killed 63 in two hours; another time he killed 171 in a single day; yet another time he downed 203 on ten acres of ground. Brick Bond killed 250 in a single day. A hunter named John R. Cook once killed 88 in a stand, and later admitted that the sight of them made him feel sick.

lowed along in the shooter's path with a wagon. Some skinners drove a big steel rod through the buffalo's head, anchoring it to the ground. Then they'd make the skinning cuts and pull the hide free with a draft team. Other skinners didn't like this method, because it left too much meat on the hide. They'd just skin the animal slice by slice with a knife. In skinning females, the entire skin was removed except for the forehead and nose. The hide on the head of a bull was too tough to skin, so they left the whole thing from the ears forward. The historian Mari Sandoz said that these bull buffalo, when covered in white fat, looked at a distance like maggots with black heads.

The hides had to be pegged out to dry, meat side up and fur side down. In wet weather, the skinner flip-flopped the hides back and forth until dry. The skinners would either do the hide-staking right where the buffalo fell or else haul the hides back to camp and do it there. If the ground was soft, they'd use wooden pegs. If the ground was frozen, they might use rocks, or just stretch the hide as best as they could and hope that the bunchgrasses and cacti held it in place. A skinner might carve his initials in the subcutaneous tissue. When the hides were dried out, usually after a week or so, they'd stack them into piles that were eight feet high. They'd cut leather cords from fresh hides and then run the cords through holes cut in the bottom and top hides, so they could cinch the stack down tight. Now the hides were ready to be hauled to a railroad depot. After a few months out, or "a season," a hunting outfit could have upwards of four thousand or five thousand hides. Prices varied. When the hides were really flooding in, they sometimes dropped down to $1.00 or less.* Toward the end of the

---

*Buffalo tongues were prepared for shipment in a variety of ways. They were packed fresh into wooden barrels between layers of salt; they were brined in a mixture of water, sugar, and salt, then smoked like bacon and packed into barrels; and they were air-dried with salt and then submerged in barrels full of brine. A popular brine recipe, for

hide-hunting era, when the only buffalo left were in Montana, hunters were getting $3.50 for cows, $2.50 for bulls, $1.50 for yearlings, and seventy-five cents for calves. Maybe a thousandth of that meat went to market. Beyond the occasional load of brined tongues (twenty-five cents apiece) or smoked hams (three cents a pound) it simply wasn't profitable to handle meat.* If it had been, the hunters would have gladly buried the railroad tracks in the stuff.

In 1870, a pound of butter cost fifteen cents. Eight pounds of coffee cost $1. Land was usually bought and sold in 160-acre parcels, at about $5 an acre. A two-room house, measuring sixteen by twenty-two feet, could be built for $300. A very good monthly wage for dangerous, professional work on the frontier, such as a sheriff or hired gun, was around $150 to $250. A cowboy made from $20 to $40 a month. A good prostitute could take in $200 a month, at upwards of $5 a client. (Thus, when prices peaked, a good buffalo hide could buy a hunter an hour's worth of intimate female company.)

Hide hunters were some of the grubbiest people on the face of the earth. As it was for the hippies of the late 1960s, long hair was

---

a nineteen-gallon barrel, was water, two pounds of sugar, and a tablespoon of saltpeter, or potassium nitrate. As a food additive, saltpeter inhibits some bacterial growth and gives meat a reddish color. (It is also a principal component of gunpowder.) In the days of eating buffalo tongues, saltpeter was produced from various forms of decomposing organic matter, such as stale urine, pigeon shit, or bat guano. Now it's produced through the Haber process, which uses atmospheric nitrogen to produce ammonia and, in turn, saltpeter. Despite its more appetizing modern production method, the use of saltpeter in food has waned in recent decades thanks to health concerns—it's been linked to kidney disease, anemia, and heart problems. I only recently quit adding the substance to my own home-smoked hams and tongues, and then only because I learned that it diminishes the male libido. There's no direct proof of this particular health effect, though prison officials used to add saltpeter to prison food in order to chill the inmates' sexual frustrations.

a fad among them. Their blankets would get so full of lice and bedbugs that they'd lay them on anthills so that ants could carry away the larvae. The hunters would often eat little else besides buffalo. Beginners, or "tenderfeet," would start out eating prime cuts, but within months they suffered nutrient deficiencies that caused their tongues to break out in lesions. After a while they learned to be more like the Indians and eat the buffalos' internal organs and bodily fluids as well. They'd eat liver, kidney, and glands, and they'd dribble bile on red meat. Some hunters seasoned meat with gunpowder for a peppery effect. If they were away from water, they'd open a dead buffalo's stomach and use their fingers to filter out the bits of vegetation while they slurped the watery ooze.

Often, the stench of rotting carcasses around their camps would prevent them from eating. Flies would get bad enough to run off their horses. Hunters would sprinkle their hides with strychnine, but flies and maggots still ruined many. In wet weather the hides would rot. In hot weather the hides would rot. When there was snow on the ground, the hunters would smear mixtures of gunpowder and buffalo grease under their eyes to help cut the glare. In blizzards, they would gut out freshly killed buffalo carcasses and spend the night inside, like in the *Star Wars* movie. They waterproofed their boots and clothes with raw buffalo fat and sat in the smoke of fires that were burning pound-sized globs of the stuff. They greased their lips with it as well. When they were thirsty, they'd suck on rocks. The canvas and buckskin material of their clothes would get so stiff from dry blood that it would crackle when they moved.

The job had its dangers. Hide hunters sometimes died from rabies after being bitten by skunks lured into camp by the carnage. Along the Yellowstone River near Glendive, Montana, a buffalo hunter was killed by a buffalo that woke up after the hunter had already cut out its tongue for dinner. Three hide hunters were killed in a prairie fire so intense that it stripped the wooden stocks off their rifles. In 1871, two hide hunters from Wisconsin froze to death in Nebraska. Their companion lost both feet. In the Easter blizzard of 1873, upward of a hundred hide hunters froze to death on the southern Great Plains. A man's carcass was found frozen to a set of railroad tracks. Seventy amputations were performed in Dodge City after the blizzard; one man lost both of his arms and both of his legs.

The U.S. government made a mockery of its vow to protect Indian land from white encroachment, so the Indians attempted to do the job on their own. The Comanche were particularly vigilant against buffalo hunters. They killed scores of hide hunters, including well-known ones such as Marshall Sewall, John Sharp, and Joe Jackson. They'd scalp their heads and mutilate their bodies.* Sometimes they'd stake the bodies to the ground and pepper them full of arrows and bullet holes. At least once they left behind an eerie drawing of dead white men, showing the exact locations of the wounds on the bodies. If the Indians were hungry, they'd shoot the hunters' draft animals. Other hide hunters would come along and find legless mules and oxen still harnessed to the carts. If a hide hunter was killed by Indians, his colleagues would band together to drive the Indians back out of the hunting grounds. They sometimes took vigilante justice to such extremes that the U.S. Army would threaten to declare them illegal militias. Now

---

*Marshall Sewall carried a three-pronged tripod, or "rest stick," to support the barrel of his rifle while he shot buffalo. His killers poked two of the tripod's prongs into his temples, the third in his navel. Other hunters had their heads opened and their brains scooped out. Indians also liked to move the dead hunters' scrotums from their groins to the insides of their mouths. Sometimes the hunters' abdomens were opened and packed with hot coals.

and then, inexpertly scalped hide hunters and stolen hides would generate paranoia among other hunters, fearful that the killing was an inside job and that a murderer was in their ranks.

THE HIDE BOOM only lasted a dozen years before the buffalo ran out. The first big hunting push was in the vicinity of Dodge City. In 1871, the first big year, the hide hunters killed so many animals so close to town that residents complained about the stench of rotting carcasses. That winter, a half-million buffalo hides were shipped out of Dodge. The hunters spread out from there, organizing their hunts along the eastward-flowing rivers of the Great Plains. They hunted out the Republican River, near the Nebraska-Kansas line. Along the south fork of the Platte River, hundreds of buffalo hunters lined fifty miles of riverbank and used fires to keep the buffalo from getting to the water at night. In four daytime periods, they gunned down fifty thousand of the thirst-crazed animals. Within a year or two the hunters had cleaned out the regions immediately to the north of the Arkansas River, and then they hunted out the watersheds of the Cimarron, Canadian, and Red rivers. The hide hunters pushed south into the Texas Panhandle and southwest Oklahoma. Soon, hunters who outfitted in Dodge were straying so far from home that their hides were shipping out of Fort Worth, Texas. By 1878, there weren't enough buffalo on the southern plains to warrant the chase.

The Texas hunt was followed by a brief lull in the action while a new railroad, the Northern Pacific, cut into the northern range. Once the railroad made it to Miles City, Montana, in 1881, word spread that the core of the last great herd had been tapped. Hide dealers calculated that 500,000 buffalo ranged within 150 miles of town. Soon there were five thousand hide hunters killing the animals. A herd that was estimated at seventy-five thousand head crossed the Yellowstone River three miles outside of Miles City, moving north as a great mass. Hunters stayed with the buffalo like sheepdogs, pushing them along. Accounts vary, but anywhere from zero to five thousand buffalo were all that was left by the time the herd reached Canada. By 1883, the one remaining large herd had moved into the Black Hills. It started out as ten thousand buffalo and was quickly reduced to one thousand by white hide hunters. Then the Sioux warrior Sitting Bull and a thousand of his men fell on the herd and killed the rest. A man who took part in the slaughter said that "there was not a hoof left."

When the hide hunters were done, the skinned-out carcasses that they left behind rotted down, and green grasses sprang up in the places where the juices oozed. Then the green grass turned brown in the fall, and the carcasses were picked down to the bone by scavengers. The bones turned white in the sun. At that moment it might have seemed as though there was nothing more that we could get out of the buffalo, but there was. Makers of fine bone china began to purchase the best of the bones, those that weren't too dry or weathered. Burned to ash and added to ceramics formulas, the bones gave American- and English-produced porcelains a translucency and whiteness that could compete with imported Oriental china. Other big consumers of quality buffalo bones were the sugar, wine, and vinegar industries; they had been using wood ash to neutralize acids and clarify liquids, but in the early nineteenth century they found that bone ash did a better job of making sugar more shiny and wine less cloudy. Industries also used buffalo bone ash in fine-grained polishing agents and baking powders. Metallurgists found that bone ash was useful in the process of refining minerals.

By far, the biggest consumer of buffalo bones was the fertilizer industry. It didn't care so much about quality; cracked, dried-out, dirty bones were just fine. Workers would grind them into a coarse powder known as bonemeal, which can be tilled into nutrient-poor or acidic soils. Firms that produced buffalo bonemeal fertilizer managed to sell a lot of the product to homesteaders on the Great Plains who were trying to produce corn and wheat on lands recently abandoned by buffalo.

The homesteaders who bought buffalo bonemeal were often the same people who'd been picking the buffalo bones up. Upon their arrival in the wake of the hide hunters, homesteaders burned whatever buffalo chips were lying about, and then they were forced to burn buffalo bones as heating and cooking fuel. The smoke from these fires smelled just like burning hair. Some men found the buffalo bones to be an encumbrance to tilling and working the soil. A homesteader arrived in Nebraska and cursed

Remains of a hide hunter slaughter somewhere in Canada.

the bones. "Buffalo bones was laying around on the ground as thick as cones under a big fir tree," he said, "and we had to pick them up, and pile them up, and work around them until we was blamed sick of ever hearing the name buffalo." Settlers stacked the bones in great heaps and torched the stacks. When the bone market developed, or when railroad spurs reached their "neighborhood," the settlers took to selling bones. For many, buffalo bones were the first cash crop to rise up out of their newly acquired dirt. An advertisement on the front page of the July 23, 1885, edition of North Dakota's *Grafton News and Times* read: "Notice to Farmers: I will pay cash for buffalo bones. Bring them in by the ton or hundred. I will give fifty pounds of the best twine for one ton of bones, for this month only, or a $40 sewing machine for forty tons. I want 5000 tons this month."

A train car could haul the bones from approximately 850 buffalo. Stacked alongside the railroad tracks, bones fetched $8 a ton. It took about a hundred buffalo skeletons to make a ton of bones, so each animal's skeleton was worth eight cents. If the bones were wet, it might take only about seventy-five skeletons, so a burst of rain on a pile of dried bones was considered a good thing by bone pickers. In all, the money was good enough to inspire many bone pickers to go full-time instead of just cleaning up their own land. A man named George Beck and his brother hunted bones outside of Dodge City. The Beck brothers operated with two wagons and two teams of oxen. They camped under the stars and cooked bread, bacon, and sweet potatoes over buffalo chip fires. When their wagons were filled, they hauled them to the wagon trails connecting Dodge City to peripheral military forts out on the wild prairie. They would dump their load and paint their mark on a prominently displayed skull. Government freighters who supplied goods to the forts would fill their empty wagons with the

Becks' bones on the way back to Dodge City and then drop the bones at the railroad tracks.

On the northern Great Plains, a group of Indians gathered 2,550 tons of buffalo bones in anticipation of a railroad coming through. In Kansas, bone pickers accumulated a pile of bones along the Santa Fe Railroad that was ten feet high, twenty feet wide, and a quarter mile long. The Santa Fe was greeted outside Granada, Colorado, with a mound of bones that was ten feet by twenty feet and a half mile long. Railroads would build spurs from the main line just for the sake of collecting stacks of buffalo bones. It was good business for them. The Empire Carbon Works, in St. Louis, processed 1.25 million tons of buffalo bones during the buffalo bone era. It paid on average $22.50 a ton. That's over $28 million paid out for buffalo bones, which came from perhaps 125 million skeletons—or more than four times the number of buffalo that ever existed at any one time.

Before the buffalo bones were all picked up, people traveling through buffalo country reported bones so thick on the ground that they looked like fallen snow. If you could have watched the bone pickers' progress in time-lapse photography taken from outer space, it would have looked like the snow was melting ahead of a great westward-moving heat wave. The wave traveled fast, pushing up river valleys and railroads first and then spreading outward until there was hardly a bone left anywhere. By 1890 it was hard to find a buffalo bone south of the Union Pacific Railroad. As the skeletons petered out, the fertilizer and carbon industries announced a "bone crisis." Prices shot up. Indians began digging bones with shovels and picks beneath buffalo jumps that dated to the birth of Christ. They once believed that these bones were capable of rising back up into brand-new buffalo, but times had changed.

What locals refer to as "Boneville,"
along Rouge River, Detroit, Michigan, late 1800s.

The Detroit Public Library houses a famous photo from around the time of the bone crisis. It shows a mountain of stacked buffalo skulls that's thirty feet high at the crest and hundreds of feet long. The photo was taken in a rail yard at the Michigan Carbon Works in Detroit, a place that locals called "Boneville." I've driven past there several times—crossing the Rouge River on the I-75 bridge, you can look down and see the exact place. It would require an involved feat of extrapolation to calculate just how many thousands of skulls were in that heap. The most interesting thing about the photo is the man standing at the top. Wearing a suit and top hat, a large buffalo skull propped against his leg, he resembles an exclamation point standing at the top of a very long sentence about death and destruction.

Since the end of the buffalo bone days, the Michigan Carbon Works has downsized dramatically. The agricultural industry turned away from bones and began using pulverized phosphate rock as a source for phosphorous fertilizer. Many old markets for bone carbon are now satisfied by carbon black, a by-product of fossil fuel combustion that is otherwise known as soot. Today, what's left of the Michigan Carbon Works is a small company called Ebonex, located on South Wabash Street in Melvindale, Michigan. They burn cattle bones to create ash that is used as dye in colored plastics, coated paper, wood stains, and paints. The Food and Drug Administration has given bone ash GRAS status, or generally regarded as safe. It's used to treat water on fish farms, and it's used in water filters for household aquariums. They also sell a lot of bone ash to movie production companies that want to replicate oil spills. Mixed with vegetable oil, bone ash makes a biodegradable dead ringer for Texas tea. If you've seen *The Beverly Hillbillies, Die Hard 3, Men in Black, Fear and Loathing in Las Vegas,* or *Jarhead,* you've seen the contemporary products of a company that once produced about 650 tons of buffalo bone ash every year.

— 11 —

WHATEVER BUFFALO FEVER IS, it doesn't last long. When I wake up just before daylight, I feel perfectly fine. I kick my legs inside my sleeping bag for a minute. Still fine, no nausea. I'm using a plastic Popov vodka bottle as a water bottle, and the contents are frozen almost completely solid. The temperature must have dropped in the night. The expanding ice has forced the bottle into a bulbous, gourd-like shape. There's a pocket of open water in the center of the ice, so I reach through the neck of the bottle with the blade of my Leatherman and auger a hole toward it. Everything outside the tent is crusted in a thin hard layer of frost. The cooking pot is so cold that my fingertips stick to it. I go over to the river, kick away some ice, and dip the pot into the water. My fingertips are immediately released. The river's flowing with slush. The thawing of the glacier at the head of the Chetaslina River must have slowed considerably because the water level has dropped nearly a foot. I scrub the pot with fine gravel and then fill it with water.

Rather than messing with the buffalo chips or looking for wood, I try to get my gas-powered stove lit. When I remove the fuel tank, my thumb sticks to the metal. I blow some warm air on there to get my thumb back, and then I open the filler cap on the tank. I don't have a funnel with me, so I use a short stick to guide the gas from the fuel can into the small port on the tank. I tighten the filler cap, slide the tank into place, and then turn the pump plunger a half crank counterclockwise. After a dozen pumps the tank is pressurized. When I open the valve wheel on the generator, the stove lets off a sound like a can of shook-up beer getting opened. After four flicks of my lighter the stove hasn't lit and the tank quits hissing. The stove's too cold.

"Son of a bitch," I say.

I close the valve wheel and pump the plunger a couple more times. Then I pour a dab of gas on the master burner and light it. The metal clinks and clacks as it heats up. With the flame burned out and the metal good and hot, I dip a twig into the fuel can and then light it with the lighter. A turn of the valve wheel and a touch of the twig to the hot burner bring the stove to life. I wave my fingers over the flame until the feeling returns.

I want to get going early, so instead of a regular breakfast I eat a couple of mini-sized candy bars and some half-frozen pasta chased down with a cup of coffee. When I'm done, I rinse the cup in the river and pack it into a nylon sack with a couple days' worth of food and some other odds and ends that I'll need. The tent's on top of a small tarp to help keep the floor's fabric dry; I yank the tarp out from under the tent like a magician pulling a tablecloth from under plates and glasses. There's a layer of glacial flour frozen to the tarp like sandpaper, so I shake it out and brush it off before rolling it up and fastening it to the outside of my pack. I stuff my sleeping bag into its sack and stuff that into the bottom of my pack.

My dry suit is frozen like a rock, and I can't even get my legs into the openings. I turn the stove back on and stand over it, exposing a little bit of the material at a time until the suit is limber enough to climb into. I don't want my boot liners getting all wet, so I pull them out of the boots and tuck them under the lid of the pack. I put the boots on over the feet of the dry suit and tie them up enough to prevent me from tripping on the laces. I strap my rifle to my pack with a bungee cord and then find a good walking stick to help me across the Chetaslina River. I step into the water, taking it slow, and I ease across by using the stick as a point of resistance against the current. Once I'm on the other bank, I take off the suit and shake out the boots as best as I can. The boots start to freeze almost instantly, and I have to walk around for a couple of minutes before they're loose enough to lace them up. I stick a smooth rock into each leg of the dry suit so it doesn't blow away while I'm gone, and then I hang it over a patch of willow. My toes are so cold they ache.

I barely go two hundred yards and a wolf's standing in front me. He's so close that I could spit a cherry pit and hit him if I wanted to. He doesn't see me, but he knows something's not right. I hold dead still. The wolf swipes his nose through the air as fast as a waving hand. He looks through me before looking at me, like I'm just another clump of willow standing here. He licks his upper lip, in a quick flash of the tongue that goes from his left to his right. Then his eyes pass over me again and he seems to see what I am, or maybe what I am not, and his body shrinks down into the ground as though suddenly supporting a great weight from above. When the wolf springs into a run, headed upstream, his head and front shoulders are scrunched low to the ground as if he's preparing to duck under a fence. I jog ahead to catch another glimpse, but there's nothing to see but willows and rocks.

My plan is to follow the Chetaslina upstream until I get clear of the Ahtna land and then make my way up to the crest of the ridge where I'd seen the four bulls a couple days before. In my mind, I've come to think of the ridge as "Buffalo Ridge." I'm going to start sleeping up there so I won't have to waste daylight hours hauling myself back and forth to my main camp.

As I work my way upstream, I notice some wet splashes on the rocks ahead of me. Something came out of the river dripping wet. I follow the splashes across the river rocks and come to a fresh set of buffalo tracks stamped into the frozen crust of ground. The tracks are huge, the biggest set I've seen by far. Buffalo hunters used to swap tales about giant buffalo that were one and a half times taller than regular buffalo. They called them buffalo oxen. In livestock terminology, oxen are adult castrated bulls used as draft animals. They're thinner in the neck and get taller than bulls that are allowed to keep their nuts, so when hunters saw particularly big buffalo on the Great Plains, they assumed that the same processes were at play except that it was wolves doing the castrating. Maybe the wolf that I just saw was licking his lips over the thought of getting himself a set of buffalo balls for lunch.

The sudden appearance of the tracks kind of depresses me. I'm not feeling very good about my prospects of finding a buffalo, and for some reason this encounter with the tracks makes me feel even worse. The tracks seem so purely random in their occurrence— just a single animal cutting through hundreds of square miles of wilderness with no apparent aim. The tracks aren't in any of the places where I've been concentrating my energies: they aren't on a trail; they aren't in a meadow; they aren't on a ridge. This might be the closest I've gotten to a buffalo, and the only reason I know it was here is because of a few droplets of water on some rocks. Indians used to find buffalo in lots of ways beyond actually seeing the animals. On the Great Plains, clouds of stirred-up dirt often gave buffalo herds away. The animals would kick up the dirt while they ran or wallowed, creating what one explorer described as "vast clouds of dust rising and circling in the air as though a tornado or whirlwind were sweeping over the earth." In hot weather, people could see clouds of water vapor coming off large herds that were hidden from view behind hills. When it was cold, a cloud of frost sometimes hung over large herds. The nature of the frost could tell a skilled hunter how large the group was and how compactly they were herded together. Birds gave buffalo away, too. Some birds followed the herds in order to pick grass seeds out of their fresh droppings or to hunt for insects kicked up by the buffalo's feet. One of these species of birds used to be called a buffalo bird, but now it's known as a cowbird. A small flock of these birds flying over the distant prairie could tell a hunter that it might be worthwhile to walk over there and see what was up.

I try to follow the buffalo, but I lose its trail. In the trees, the crust of frost on the ground is not thick enough to show animal tracks. Sometimes, I'll lose an animal's trail and then find it again by looking for likely routes. Then I'll jump ahead to see if I can find fresh tracks that validate my guess. I try this a few times but don't find anything. Instead, I continue along, staying on the west bank of the Chetaslina. I follow the river's course through alder snags and across gravel bars. Sometimes the river cuts so close to the spruce forest that I'm forced into the woods to bushwhack. I start crossing intermittent sets of buffalo tracks on the softer ground. Some are old and some are fresh, and I can see places where the animals have been milling around and feeding on patches of willow. I move very slowly, scanning the land in front of me and taking only a few steps at a time. I'm a little over four miles upstream from my campsite at the confluence of the Copper and the Chetaslina. Here, the east fork of the Chetaslina flows into the river's main channel. The rivers collide at an angle similar to how your fingers come together when you make a peace sign with your hand. The land between the two branches is filled by a ridge that collapses sharply into the valley floor. Like every ridge around here, it's capped by a worn buffalo trail. I should go over and check that for fresh sign, I think. I take a few steps that way and then come into a small opening amid the spruce trees, and I get hit by a breeze that's carrying the smell of buffalo. It's a lot like the smell of horses—not the smell of horses standing in a stable amid their own filth, but that of horses out in the open, on green pasture. I slowly drop down to my haunches, then inch my way over to a spruce tree so that my profile is broken up. I start looking ahead through the brush and trees with my binoculars. I don't see anything yet. I've often found elk like this, just by smelling them. I can usually tell the difference between the smell of elk that are there and the smell of elk that *used* to be there. This odor I smell now has a strange touch of warmth to it, like they either are here or have just left.

I slip my rifle down from my shoulder and lay it quietly across my knee. I'm breathing slowly as I concentrate on the smells and the sounds of the woods. I move ahead a little more, picking my path very carefully to not make noise. I hear nothing but a distant chickadee and the gurgle of flowing water. The frozen ground is quiet against the knees of my wool pants. I move a little more and then stop. Away from the river, the forest is an impenetrable tangle of young spruce. The odor of the animals is no longer on the breeze. Just as I'm hoping that the buffalo didn't head into the tangle, I hear it. A snapping twig. Then I hear another. I raise my rifle and glance through the scope, but I can't find anything. I stand and take a few quick steps forward, and sure enough there's a well-worn trail. I slide the rifle's safety lever forward and place my finger through the trigger guard. The trigger finds its place inside the first joint of my finger. I take a few slow steps down the trail, my rifle raised, but the sound of snapping brush is moving away from me at too fast a clip. I don't want to bust through the brush and take a running-away shot at a buffalo's ass, especially if I can't tell whether I'm looking at a cow or bull or calf or what. I back up and move downwind of the animals until I'm a couple hundred feet away from their trail. Then I start moving parallel to their route, picking my way through thickets of spruce and head-high alder. It's slow going, but the last thing I want is to spook a herd of buffalo out of the area.

If it was in fact a group of buffalo that I heard, I have no way of knowing how fast they are moving. My only real hope is that I'll pass ahead of them in the valley floor and then be ready and waiting in case they move into the open meadows along the valley's western wall. It takes me about forty minutes to get to the edge of the valley's floor. I move slowly uphill on a very long and steep incline. I stop every few steps to look back behind me, down into the timber, to see if I can glimpse any movements. I watch for dark patches of fur, and I watch for shaking brush and moving treetops that might give a buffalo away. My field of view expands as I climb higher and higher, until I'm at the crest of the ridge and I can see down into many of the small meadows and willow patches that are scattered around the valley floor. I can see meadows along the hillside to my left and right. Scanning the surrounding country, I know that I'm *looking* at buffalo. I just can't *see* them.

When I take off my pack, the sweat on my back evaporates and cools my skin so quickly that I shiver. I position myself so that I've got a good view of most everything around me. Then I wait. A couple of hours go by, and nothing stirs except birds. It occurs to me again just how much activity you could miss out here in this timber. Hell, I just had at least one buffalo walking through the woods not seventy-five yards away and I never even caught a glimpse of it. At least I *think* it was a buffalo, I remind myself. I never actually saw it. But what else smells like that?

COLONEL RICHARD IRVING DODGE wrote a book in 1877 titled *The Plains of the Great West and Their Inhabitants*. In it, he closes his treatise on buffalo with a discussion of what he calls "mountain" or "wood" buffalo. "These animals are by no means plentiful," Dodge writes, "and are moreover excessively shy, inhabiting the deepest, darkest defiles, or the craggy, almost precipitous, sides of mountains, inaccessible to any but the most practiced mountaineers. Unlike their plains relative, there is no stupid staring at an intruder. At the first symptom of danger they disappear like magic in the thicket, and never stop until far removed from even the apprehension of pursuit. I have many times come upon their fresh tracks, upon the beds from which they had first sprung in alarm, but I have never even seen one."

There are, in fact, two classifications of North American buffalo that are recognized (by some) today: there's the wood buffalo of the Canadian boreal forests, and the plains buffalo of the Great Plains. The animals are separated by some minor variations; most notably, the hump of the wood buffalo is squarer in profile, and the wood buffalo's hair is longer, darker, and straighter. Taxonomists once described the wood buffalo as a separate species altogether, with its own name. While the plains buffalo was *Bison bison*, the wood buffalo was *Bison athabascae*. However, modern genetic research has revealed essentially no difference between the two.

Still, the apparent morphological differences between the two are exploited for good cause by those who would like to expand the range of buffalo in northern North America. Bob Stephenson, a biologist with the Alaska Department of Fish and Game, has been working on a decades-long project to introduce wood buffalo from Canada into the Yukon Flats region north of Fairbanks. Stephenson prefers to call it a reintroduction, arguing that the buffalo was extirpated from that region by human hunting. Opponents to the plan argue that historical evidence of wood buffalo in that area is scant and that there's no concrete evidence that they were killed off by humans. To put them back would be to tamper with Mother Nature's grand, inscrutable plan. To be honest, I don't think it really matters where these buffalo actually lived or how they died. The Yukon Flats are capable of supporting what might become America's largest herd of free-ranging buffalo; the sooner that happens, the better.

Of course, when Colonel Dodge talked about wily buffalo living in the mountains, he didn't know about genetics and he didn't know about Bob Stephenson. What he did know was that buffalo tended to behave in different ways depending on where they lived, and his theories about this were repeated and fortified by many other writers and observers who were infinitely familiar with the animals. Buffalo were sometimes excessively shy in the presence of humans, taking off at the slightest whiff of man, or else they could be tame enough to let a person walk up in plain sight and shoot them with an arrow. Generally, buffalo living in a mountainous or wooded habitat, be it Pennsylvania or Canada's Northwest Territories, were much warier of humans than buffalo living in the open country of western Kansas or eastern Montana.

Often, people discuss various animals' responses to humans in terms of intelligence. Big white-tailed bucks are "smart" because they're so wary of humans, but buffalo are "dumb" because they're not. This is a flawed way of thinking about animal behavior, because it operates on the assumption that animals evolved with the sole concern of avoiding human predation—the smart ones figured it out, the dumb ones didn't. In fact, many animals put a much greater emphasis on energy preservation and territorial defense than they do on avoiding predators. It doesn't necessarily suit an animal's needs to burn precious calories by running like hell every time a predator appears, especially if the animal encounters a lot of predators that are unable to make successful attempts at killing it.

Also, keep in mind that before man arrived in the New World, buffalo probably didn't use running away as a defense mechanism, and in any case running away would have been a bad idea for a few reasons: first, many of their predators, such as cheetahs, lions, short-faced bears, and dire wolves, were ridiculously fast and probably couldn't be outrun; second, a herd can only run as fast as its weakest members, and fleeing would have exposed the calves and pregnant females at the most vulnerable rearward position; third, they weren't built for running. Remember, the bodies of North American buffalo were much larger before the arrival of man. Their horns were well over twice as long and quite a bit thicker. Instead of sweeping upward and backward, the horns had a more forward orientation. Such heavy headgear was suitable for facing off predators, and it wouldn't do much good for a buffalo to turn its horns away in order to expose its bare, clumsy ass to a large predator with long teeth and sharp claws.

When approached by the earliest human hunters, such as Clovis hunters, buffalo probably behaved in the same way that they do when encountered by wolves today. They gathered in defensive positions, often with mature males toward the periphery and females and calves toward the center. With their heads down and their sharp horns exposed, a pack of these giant buffalo would not have presented an inviting target for a bear or lion. But humans rendered that defense strategy obsolete—a human hunter just had to walk up and start hurtling spears into the group. Buffalo slowly wised up to the risk, as is demonstrated by the gradual advancement in technology among buffalo-hunting people. It's likely that buffalo initially developed a safety zone for humans that accounted for the distance that a man could hurl a spear. Then came the bow and arrow, and the buffalo probably increased the size of their safety zone. It was like a game of tit for tat that stretched on for millennia.

The arrival of firearms eventually tipped the scales wholly in the humans' favor. Think of a space alien movie, the kind where extraterrestrial invaders come to earth and use weapons of ridiculous potency to lay waste to humanity. In those movies, are the human protagonists portrayed as stupid? No, they're portrayed as surprised and defenseless. By the end of such movies, the humans have usually wised up and learned how to avoid ray guns or expandable tongues, and in the end they turn the tides and survive. In most places, the buffalo weren't given enough time for this happy ending. They were wiped out so quickly that they had no time to adjust to the risk of a predator that could kill them from five hundred yards away.

In places, though, the buffalo did survive just long enough to learn how to avoid human predation: accounts of "wise," "skittish," "shy," "wary," and "smart" buffalo came out of such regions as central Canada, the high mountains of Montana, the Dakota badlands, and the remotest, most arid regions of the Texas Panhandle. These remnant and increasingly wild populations of buffalo may have survived and multiplied if they hadn't been cursed by their own value—even when a regional population of buffalo was reduced to nearly nothing, it continued to make economic sense for human hunters to pursue them. The payoff warranted almost any amount of exertion. While a white-tailed deer might give a hunter fifty pounds of meat, a buffalo would yield ten times that amount or more. And the hides became all the more valuable as the animals disappeared. When there were still millions of buffalo in North America, hides were selling for a dollar or two. But when there were just a thousand or so left, in the late 1880s and early 1890s, the hides increased in value to hundreds of dollars on the souvenir market—or the equivalent of a month's wages for a common laborer. No amount of wariness or intelligence on the part of the buffalo was going to save them so long as they had a price like that on their heads.

Thanks to the modern conservation movement, which was in many ways initiated by attempts to save the buffalo in the early 1900s, the animals have protections that go beyond their own abilities to hide. You can no longer sell the meat of wild game animals, and the trafficking of hides is closely monitored by federal and state wildlife agencies. Would-be buffalo hunters are limited by the available number of permits issued for any given herd, which is usually a minuscule amount compared with herd size. The methodologies of those hunters are also limited, usually by dozens of laws that are meant to even out the playing field. Now, in the handful of areas where limited numbers of human hunters have been allowed to hunt wild herds of buffalo over the course of several years—Alaska, portions of central Canada, Utah's Henry Mountains, the North Rim of Arizona's Grand Canyon—both hunters and state wildlife agencies are seeing that buffalo are quite capable of getting smart.

I can certainly attest to that, especially as I sit here with two freezing feet and six or seven numb fingers. I'm still watching over the timbered valley where, I believe, a suspected herd of buffalo has vanished into what Colonel Dodge referred to as one of those "deepest, darkest" defiles. I've been moving my eyes slowly across the land, and I feel as though the world has shrunk down to these few square miles that are below me. I've been sensing a change in the weather for an hour or so. The dry, cold air is becoming a little warmer, and there's an increasing heaviness to it. It seems that the birds are more fidgety. Gray jays have been moving down valley. I'm looking down on them at a very slight angle, and their flight patterns form series of arcs across the backdrop of spruce.

Earlier, the cloud cover was high and loosely packed, but it seems to have grown thick and dense. The clouds come to an abrupt end toward the northern horizon. As I watch them, something rather surreal happens; the sky to the north becomes completely clear, and for the briefest moment, just seconds, I can see the entire southern exposure of the mountain peaks. I've known that they were there, could even feel that they were there, but it's stunning to actually see them for once. They stand like enormous paperweights whose job it is to anchor the world in place. There's a beautiful sunset sprayed across their icy faces, which makes them seem even more vital. The wilderness seems to stretch out like it's releasing a great breath. And then the clouds drop down again and hide the mountains, and it feels as if the world has inhaled until there's nothing left but this small section of valley. The brevity of the view reminds me of times when I've spotted a cool seashell exposed for a glimpse in the reaches of a receding wave, only to have the next wave swallow it up.

I'm still kind of stunned by the mountains when I catch a quick movement. A patch of brown. It's almost at eye level on the hill that separates the Chetaslina River's two branches. It's maybe a half mile away, but still I lurch forward and grab at my rifle. Before I have time to get excited about what I think I see—a buffalo—I realize that I'm looking at not just one grizzly bear but two. They're on an open avalanche slide, feeding on scattered clumps of rose hips. The slope is so steep that each of their steps sends down a small cascade of dirt and gravel. As I watch the bears, I see the first flakes of snow come falling down from the clouds. They're big wet flakes, and within a few minutes I can't see anything except the thirty yards of ground at my feet.

I figure that I should find a place to spend the night. If the snow lets up, I'll come back here and wait until it's too dark to see. I take my backpack and move into the timber. I only have to go a stone's throw and I'm sheltered by thick trees. Even back here away from the trail there's a lot of buffalo sign. I look around for a smooth flat place to lay out my sleeping bag, and I find the perfect spot in the bottom of a wallow. The wallow is sheltered beneath a large spruce and the snow hasn't even begun to collect in the smooth dirt of the bowl. I kick away a few buffalo chips whose density suggests that they might be good fuel.

I get a strong smell of buffalo when I drop to my knees to unload my pack. In the dust on the bottom of the wallow I can see the perfect imprint of a buffalo's knee, and also the smoothly pressed soil where its flank rested.* On the Texas plains, a white hide hunter was shot to death in the bottom of a wallow in the

---

*Buffalo wallows often collect standing water in the spring, providing a valuable type of wildlife habitat known to ecologists as ephemeral aquatic ecosystems. Because they eventually dry up, fish cannot live in them. This makes buffalo wallows popular places for frogs and aquatic insects to lay their eggs, because there's nothing in them that can eat their tadpoles and larvae. When the buffalo were removed from the West and replaced by people, the people weren't as happy with the wallows as the frogs had been. In fact, homesteaders thought that wallows were a tremendous nuisance because cattle didn't use them and no grass grew there. The farmers struggled to get rid of them. The mud in the wallows was loaded with water-soluble salts, and they called it alkali mud. It dried like concrete. People who lived in sod houses would collect the mud from the wallows and use it to cover their roofs, and then they'd fill the wallows with sand, dirt, or manure until they started to sprout grass. Now ecologists have begun to wonder what we lost when we destroyed thousands upon thousands of small ephemeral ponds. For instance, researchers studying western chorus frogs in Kansas

Author's camp on "Buffalo Ridge," above the Chetaslina River, October 2005.

1870s. Comanche Indians caught him on flat ground, and he apparently tried to sink into the wallow for shelter while defending his position. It wasn't quite deep enough. The Indians probably gave no more thought to killing him than cowboys would give to killing cattle rustlers.

I empty out my pack, putting everything up against the base of the spruce where it's sheltered from the falling snow. I pull out the buffalo chips that I've been carrying around and stack them with the chips that were already beneath the spruce. I've got a nice pile

---

have been trying to understand the frog's historic relationship to buffalo wallows. One thing they've found is that tadpoles hatched in buffalo wallows will develop differently from tadpoles hatched in streams. Also, they'll have different responses to environmental variables such as water acidity and ammonium concentrations. This is particularly interesting at a time when frogs are vanishing from North America at an alarming rate.

of about a dozen good ones, plus there are plenty of dry sticks lying about. My tarp is rectangular, six feet by eight feet, with grommets in each corner. I use two short pieces of cord to stretch one end tight up against the trunk of the tree about waist high. I tie the opposite corners to the bases of small saplings so that the tarp is pitched sharply with the low end facing the wind. That's the end where I'll put my feet; my head will go at the high end so that the condensation from my breath doesn't collect on the tarp and drip back down on me. I cut a long pole with my Leatherman and rig it under the tarp like a ridgeline so the snow runs off to the sides instead of sagging down in the middle.

As soon as the tarp is up, I clear the snow out from underneath its edges and stretch out my sleeping bag. Toward dusk the air seems to get a little warmer again; the snow is wetter and heavier than before. I wonder where those bears are now. I've got an old bird's nest in my pocket and a cardboard tube that I saved from inside a used-up roll of toilet paper. I shred them up and top them with dry spruce twigs. The fire takes off, and I lean a couple of my primo buffalo chips against the burning twigs. The chips catch quickly, and I'm surprised to see them burn beautifully like coal. It's my first good buffalo chip fire, and I feel that I'm learning something out here. I can't say that there's some higher power in this world that doles out justice and penance, but, at least in the wilderness, good things do seem to come to those who wait. As I slink down into my sleeping bag and watch the deeply glowing embers of my fire, I feel like I'm fulfilling my part in some sort of cosmic agreement. I'm happily waiting. And tomorrow's going to be a big day, I just know it.

— 12 —

WHEN I WAKE UP, the first and only thing I see is snow. It's all around me in the half-light of the morning, hanging from trees and carpeting the ground in an ankle-deep layer. I reach up out of my sleeping bag and smack the tarp on either side of the pole. Snow slides down in wettish clumps that fall and crumple into the perimeter of my dry patch of ground. I reach out of my bag and use my pan to scrape the snow away. The air's cold and wet, and I pull my arm back into the warmth of the bag. This snow is the best thing that could happen. If I can cut a buffalo track in this stuff, I'll be able to follow the animal no matter where it goes or what it does; it would have better luck losing its own tail than losing me. There's a heavy fog in the air, the kind that doesn't break up until the sun comes. I slide out of my sleeping bag and lace up my boots. Before making any noise or starting a fire, I creep over to the edge of the bluff to have a look around and make sure there aren't any fresh tracks from animals that passed nearby in the night. It's reasonable to think that buffalo hanging around in the higher elevations might be moving out, headed away from the mountains and toward the lower elevations along the Copper River. This is the first major snow of the year, a sudden reminder of what's in store for the next six or seven months. I look toward where I saw the grizzlies last night, but the fog's too thick to see that far.

I go back to my camp and kindle a small fire. When the fire takes, I snap a couple of leftover buffalo chips in half and stack those on along with some more twigs. I don't think that animals readily equate smoke with humans. I put a pan of snow over the fire and then keep adding more snow as it melts. It takes about six pans mounded with snow in order to get one pan of water. As it comes to a boil, I pour two envelopes of instant oatmeal into my cup and tip in the steaming liquid. I throw a handful of coffee into the water left in the pan. When I'm done with my oatmeal, I pour the coffee into my cup while using my fingers as a sieve to keep out the grounds. I'm not sure where I'll sleep tonight, so after gulping the coffee, I stuff my sleeping bag into my pack and roll up the tarp, careful not to make too much noise.

I haul my pack back to the edge of the bluff and crouch in the gray rising light, watching and waiting. It's exciting to see the fog lift, as though something wonderful will be revealed. As I'm thinking about what route I should travel, I notice that the hill beneath me is so steep that I can't see the entirety of the slope; I can see the base of the hill, and the ground beneath my feet, but I can't see the middle portion. Something prompts me to step forward and lean out and look down.

The thing that happens next occurs in just a few seconds, but those seconds drag along in a sort of crystal clear eternity. The moment I step forward, I'm washed over by the realization that I will now have to kill a buffalo. I seem to think this before I actually see the animals, as though my thoughts are faster than my eyes. There are around twenty of them, cows and calves, emerging one by one from a small band of timber that stretches up the hillside from the valley floor. Most of the buffalo are traveling single file along a deeply cut trail, headed down the valley. Other buffalo are spread out to either side of the main line, grabbing passing bites from the prairie sagewort plants that are sticking up out of the snow. Their breath is steaming in the air, and it hangs like a cloud around them.

They have no idea that I'm here. From their perspective, only my eyes are showing above the crest of the hill. The thermal currents are wisping up the slope, into my face. I scan across the herd and pick a large, thickly furred cow, second back from the front. There are several yearling buffalo behind her, but no calves. She may be dry or may have lost her calf in the summertime. I sense a slight nervousness wash over me. There's a year's worth of food contained within that animal, but also a life. The seriousness of what I'm about to do feels like a great weight, but the weight has an inertia that carries itself forward. I raise my rifle, just as so many people before me have raised spears and atlatls, bows and muskets. I slip the safety forward with my thumb and lift the rifle until my eye is looking through the scope. Under magnification, the buffalo seems to be drawn closer to me. The buffalo's side is smooth and muscled, the ribs hidden from view by a layer of fat. The shoulder moves slowly underneath the hide, like a human body stirring beneath a blanket. I position the crosshairs of the scope just below the halfway point between the buffalo's brisket and back, about five inches behind the rear edge of the shoulder blade. I don't want to hit anything but lung. This is how food is made. I touch the trigger. As the rifle recoils, I glimpse the buffalo's body through the scope as it lurches downward first and then quickly upward—a lung shot. The next thing I see is a great confusion of hooves and brown hair. My buffalo tips downhill and rolls to its back. It starts sliding across the snow, slowly at first, hooves whirling in the air. It picks up speed as it goes, and almost immediately the carcass is careening downhill across the slick snow. I have this sudden sense that I'll lose it, but it's leaving a trail that's as clean and wide as the path of a snowplow. The other buffalo kick and buck nervously and chase the sliding buffalo for twenty or thirty yards. I feel the ground shake. Clods of frozen dirt and snow fly in all directions. The herd swings around in one great pivoting mass and charges back toward the direction they came from. They cross the thin band of timber in a flash and veer downhill toward the valley floor. I turn back to the downed buffalo in time to see it crash into a stand of aspen trees at the base of the hill. Sticks and snow go flying every which way. The body hits the base of a dead tree and snaps it off at ground level. The trunk shoots downhill and out from under the tree. As the buffalo disappears, the body of the tree comes down with a cracking thud, aiming uphill and spitting dead limbs into the fresh snow.

And then there's just pure quiet. My ears buzz in the stillness of it. I eject the spent shell and chamber a fresh round. With my pack on my back, I start sliding down the hill, trying to stay on my feet, but I fall to my hip and slide the rest of the way down. The path is streaked with two long runs of red blood, the thick streak from where the bullet passed into the buffalo's side and the thinner streak from blood pouring out of its nostrils. It's both gruesome and relieving—the gore of a clean, quick kill.

I see the giant lump of the animal before I get to the stand of trees that it crashed into. I dig my heels into the ground to slow my slide down, and the inertia of my movement puts me right back on my feet. I approach the body with my rifle in both hands, ready in case it stands back up. The buffalo is on its back, its head pointing uphill, its chin to the sky. Its legs are jutting here and there, wedged behind trees and pinned beneath logs. The large fallen tree is lying across its belly. The buffalo's rib cage is perfectly still, with no sign of breathing. I come a little closer and jiggle its horn with my boot. Nothing. Its eye is already glassing over. Stone dead.

Killing a large animal inevitably gives me a sense of sorrow. I know it will hit me before it does, the way you go to bed drunk knowing you'll be hungover in the morning. It hits as I run my fingers through the tangled mane of the buffalo's neck. The animal

The hafl-skinned carcasss at the foot of "Buffalo Ridge."

feels so solid, so substantive. I feel compelled to question what I've done, to compare the merits of its life with the merits of my own. It's not so much a feeling of guilt. There's no moment when I want the buffalo to stand back up and walk away, no moment when I wish that the bullet would retreat back into the barrel. It's more complicated than guilt. Seeing the dead buffalo, I feel an amalgamation of many things: thankfulness for the meat, an appreciation for the animal's beauty, a regard for the history of its species, and, yes, a touch of guilt. Any one of those feelings would be a passing sensation, but together they make me feel emotionally swollen. The swelling is tender, a little bit painful. This is the curse of the human predator, I think. When a long-tailed weasel snakes its way into a rabbit's den and devours the blind and hairless young, it doesn't have to think or feel a thing. Watching a weasel, you get the sense that a complete lack of morality is the only path to moral clarity.

Within minutes, my contemplation is broken by the immensity of the chore ahead of me. I walk around the buffalo's body, and I'm surprised by how many steps it takes. It's like circumnavigating a rowboat. One thousand or so pounds. The buffalo doesn't **care** who gets its meat, wolves or birds or bacteria, but right now that decision does not belong to the buffalo. It's up to me, and brooding over my actions isn't going to help. The buffalo is in a horrible position for skinning and butchering. In the cold air, the carcass will lock up with rigor mortis almost immediately. I can already feel its legs tightening. It would be much better if I could get it over on one side. I grab one of the horns and try to turn the front of the buffalo, the way a rodeo cowboy twists a calf's head to topple it. It won't budge. The head feels like it's fastened to the ground by a hidden section of cable. I grab the buffalo's front leg and try to twist it free from a tree trunk. There's no way. I take my saw and cut through the wrist-sized piece of wood. Before I can finish the cut, the tree snaps under pressure, and the carcass slumps down the hill and comes to rest against another tree. Below me is a steep pitch of large boulders. If I do cut the animal loose, it's going to land in a worse place than here.

I lay my rifle against the carcass before getting started. I want it handy. Then I unroll my tarp and lay it across the ground so that I can empty out my pack without losing gear in the snow. First I take my small ripping knife and make a ventral incision that starts at the anus and ends at the chin. The cut is a little over seven feet long. I go just deep enough to cut through the hide, but not so deep that I puncture the abdominal lining. Beneath the cut is a layer of shiny, orange-tinted fat. When I cut up the center of the brisket, where the ribs meet, I can see the ivory color of bone. With my large skinning knife, I start to peel the hide away from the left side. I skin the left side down to the armpit on the front leg and down to the base of the back leg.

I don't have an open pathway by which I can drag the organs clear of the body, so I want to get one of the back legs out of the way before I gut the buffalo. I straddle the rear left leg and hold it between my knees. I use my small knife to cut through the hide in a complete circle around the ankle. I start peeling the hide back, sort of like unbuttoning a shirtsleeve and rolling it up. I poke a hole between the Achilles tendon and the leg bone and slip a cord through it and tie a bowline. I throw the other end of the cord over a limb and hoist the leg so that it's stretched out and suspended in the air.

I make an incision up the inside of the leg. The cut meets the ventral incision just about where the testicles would be on a male. It takes about twenty more minutes to skin the whole leg. When I'm done, it looks as if the buffalo has one leg in a pair of pants and the other leg out. I cut into the meat where the leg joins the torso, following the outer edge of the pelvis. The work has been blood-less so far, but I have to sever a major artery and it leaks a few ounces. The blade hits bone, and I jiggle the leg to locate the ball joint. There's a powerful tendon at the core of the joint. I slip the tip of the knife between the ball and the socket as delicately as picking a lock; the tendon cuts with an audible pop. The leg loosens on its mooring, and I take up the slack with the rope. A few more slices and the ham drops away from the body. The hoof end is hanging from the tree, and the ball joint is resting on the toe of my boot. It's heavy—it feels as if someone has set the leg of his chair on my toe. When I'm standing upright, the leg is just a little shorter than I am, and I'm six feet. I hug the ham around the knee and lean back to lift it off the ground. With the weight of the rope I can use my teeth to undo the knot around the Achilles tendon. I'll let it stiffen up in the cool air before I do any more work on it.

At the base of the ventral incision, right where a human's belly button would be, I poke a small hole through the abdominal lining. I do this with the blade pointing upward, so it doesn't go through and puncture the vegetation-filled stomach. Once I'm through, I can peek in there and see the purplish coils of intestines. I slip my middle and index fingers inside the incision and lift up, pulling the abdominal lining away from the body and creating air space between the thin layer of muscle and the organs. Slipping the knife blade between my fingers, I run the incision all the way to the brisket. The sharp bright purple edge of the liver is wrapped around the dull gray stomach like a hand. With the incoming gush of cold air, the large and small intestines contract and curl like stirred-up snakes. The diaphragm is holding back a few quarts of blood that spilled from the lungs.

Plains Indian tribes used to eat more raw meat than Indians in the eastern United States. They'd be digging in right now. They liked raw liver, warm and fresh from the carcass. They liked the juice squeezed from the bile sac. They liked raw kidney. They liked the warm, shiny fat around the intestines. They liked the coagulated slugs of blood in the ventricles of the heart. They would slice into the mammary glands of lactating females and lap the milk that dripped out. When they killed young calves, they would drink out the curdled mother's milk. While I've tried a few of these tricks over the years, my curiosity has been sated. I'll wait until I get a fire going.

I've never wasted my time arguing with vegetarians who are opposed to hunting. They're obviously serious about their convictions, and I respect their beliefs. On the other hand, I used to be endlessly troubled by meat-eating people who were uneasy with hunters and hunting. The glaring hypocrisy of their stance made me almost blind with rage. How can someone suggest that paying for the slaughter of animals is more justifiable than taking the responsibility for one's food into one's own hands? At moments like this, though, I understand their perspective much better. It takes a strong stomach and a lot of dedication to do this job properly. You need to be able to visualize the end result—high-quality food—at a time when your sensory perceptions are seeing everything but that. Civilization is a mechanism that allows us to avoid the necessary but ugly aspects of life; most of us do not euthanize our own pets, we don't unplug the life support on our own ailing grandparents, we don't repair our own cars, and we don't process our own raw sewage. Instead, the delegation of our less-pleasant responsibilities is so widespread that taking these things on is almost like trying to swim upriver. It's easier *not* to do them, and those who insist on doing so are bound to look a little odd.

I'm thinking about this as I get ready for the next step. I slice through the flesh that lies over the pelvis until I've exposed the fused, cartilaginous joint where the left and right sides join together. (If you press your hand firmly against your lower stomach, below your navel, and move your hand downward toward your crotch, that's the bone you feel.) Then I reach deep inside the buffalo, putting my arm inside the gutting incision and following the abdominal wall with my hand all the way back until I'm inside the pelvis. I can't see, but I can feel what I'm doing. I locate the bladder and the colon and pull them away from the pelvis while pressing down. I want them out of the way so that I can saw through the pelvis without cutting into them and spilling their contents on the meat. I spend the next few minutes with one arm up to the bicep in the buffalo's body and my other arm working the saw. Archaeological evidence suggests that Folsom hunters simply shattered the pelvis with a big rock.

I cut through the pelvis twice, once on each side. The bone lifts right out. I can reach in there and detach the connective tissues holding the colon in place. I cut a complete circle around the anus and sex organs, so that they are connected to the colon rather than the hide. Then I take my bone saw and cut through the sternum. The meat over the bones is heavy and coarse; already it looks like its most delicious final product, pastrami.

Opening the rib cage allows a fresh gust of cold air into the chest cavity. Steam pours out. I use my small knife to cut the diaphragm all the way to the inside middle of the back. The blood from the ruptured lungs pours out of the chest cavity and floods through the canal that I opened by removing the anal tract. Next I sever the aorta, esophagus, and windpipe inside the chest cavity, right at the base of the neck. The internal organs are lying loose inside the buffalo like soup in a bowl. I make a slit in the pericardium, and I pluck out the buffalo's heart. It's the size of a cantaloupe. Now, grabbing two firm handfuls of the guts, I pull with all my might. I have to bounce my weight against the resistance, until the whole package starts to peel free. I readjust my grip, wrapping a hand around the stomach, and soon everything comes slipping backward through the open path that I cleared by removing the leg. I guide the bladder and colon around the sharp edges of the split pelvis, and with one last yank the buffalo is completely gutted. Over one hundred pounds of offal are lying at my feet. My hands steam when I wipe them with snow.

I used to cut firewood for money when I was in college, and I tweaked my lower back. It hurts when I have to bend over for extended periods of time. The rough ground and slippery snow don't help. I stand and stretch, and while I'm up, I take a careful look around. The wind has switched again; it's now blowing downhill toward the Chetaslina. I concentrate on the dark swath of timber in that direction, because that's the way that trouble will come from. I know for a fact that there's at least a pair of grizzly bears in the area. Last night, they were less than a mile from me. Now I'm even closer to where they were. With these guts out and the smell blowing around, I'll be surprised if they don't find out about this. They were not big—they looked to be under four hundred pounds apiece, a pair of subadult siblings, which makes them even scarier. They're young and dumb, and probably desperate. It's mid-October, the salmon runs have petered out, and they should be going down for hibernation soon. The fact that they haven't means they're hungry, and the fact that they're hungry is what makes me edgy.

Grizzlies can handily kill buffalo calves, but they encounter serious problems when they try to attack adults. First off, there's the matter of speed. A grizzly can hit top speeds of over forty miles per hour, which is faster than a buffalo, but they can't sustain that speed long enough to wear a buffalo down. Another issue is a buffalo's horns. Grizzlies are not as agile and wiry as wolves, and it seems as though they can't effectively avoid a buffalo's defense mechanism. There's a documented case from Yellowstone in which a buffalo managed to kill a sow grizzly by punching a pair of holes through its belly and busting every rib in its side.

This hardly keeps grizzlies from getting buffalo meat, because they make much better thieves than killers. In one study, researchers found that grizzly bears kill only 5 percent of the meat that they consume. They get the remaining 95 percent from carrion. In Yellowstone National Park, rangers once recorded the visits of twenty-three separate grizzlies to one dead buffalo. That should not, however, be taken as a suggestion that they prefer rancid carcasses. Grizzlies will spend days following in the wakes of hunting wolf packs. In 2000, in the Lamar valley of Yellowstone National Park, a grizzly bear trailed a pack of wolves so closely that it was able to steal a buffalo calf from them before they finished killing it. When a grizzly gets its paws on a large animal, it will usually rip open the belly and eat the liver first. Grizzlies also like lungs and other organ meats. It's probably because they can force down a lot of soft tissue in a hurry; they want to maximize their caloric intake before a bigger bear comes along and steals what they stole.

Knowing that the guts will be of primary interest to the bears, I decide to haul them in a downwind direction. That way a bear that is following the odor will hit the guts before he hits me. I pull out the liver for my own use and set it on a log. At first I think I'll drag the whole pile a couple hundred yards through the trees, but once I get started, I can see that this isn't going to happen. I can barely budge it, even with the help of the slippery snow. I could lighten the load by cutting the stomach free, but I don't want to spill everything out and create even more odor. I break into a sweat after tugging the guts only about fifty yards. I give it a few more yanks and then snag the stomach on a sharp stick. It rips open and out spills a load of food that looks almost exactly like a bag of lawn-mower trimmings. That'll have to be far enough. I look up the hill at my rifle, next to the carcass, and think that I should have taken it with me.

My absence from the buffalo is an invitation to the six or seven gray jays that have been gathering in the treetops. They're about the size of robins, with much stronger beaks and more curiosity. They have this way of cocking their heads back and forth while assessing the safety of a situation. It makes them seem like something out of a Disney cartoon. Old-timers call them camp robbers. They like to hang around any kind of activity involving predators—bears, humans, foxes—figuring that food is bound to make an appearance. They smell meat from great distances above the ground, probably as the odor wafts on the upward air currents. If there's blood on the snow, they find it even faster, as red only means one thing in the wilderness. I wouldn't be surprised to learn that jays automatically cue in on rifle shots in heavily hunted areas. I don't want them shitting all over the meat as they peck at the buffalo, so I start a little gray jay bait pile about thirty yards off to the side. As long as they can eat something, they'll stay over there and leave me alone. I give them a few wads of kidney fat, because I like the way they wipe their beaks on twigs after eating it. They do this with a quick, back-and-forth action that reminds me of sharpening a knife.

The carcass is significantly lighter now, and I can rock it back and forth. It's still ungainly enough that it might slide and roll into an unworkable position, so I kick a few boulders free from the ground and position them to form a retaining wall. I also manage to twist the head around and jab a horn into the ground so that it's acting as a support on the downhill side. Sitting against a tree, I place my feet on the buffalo's ribs and heave against it with my feet. It slowly tips. I rock it a few more times, giving more pressure each time, and then it rolls. The side I've been working on— the side where I removed the back ham—is facing toward the sky.

The front shoulder will come off easier than the back. There's no ball joint to deal with. I cut the hide around the ankle, just below the shank, and then saw it off with my bone saw. Then I take my ripping knife and make a cut up the inside of the leg. I start at the ankle, go just behind the armpit, and meet up with the ventral incision. The hide peels off the leg quickly, and severing it from the body is almost effortless. With my back arched and the weight resting on my belly, I waddle over to a tree and lean the shoulder against the trunk.

I'm ready for a lunch break, but first I take my skinning knife and work the hide back to the backbone on the upward-facing side. There's some bright orange fat encasing the loins along the spine. I cut some of the fat away for cooking and then pull the hide back into place like I'm tucking the buffalo in for the night. That will help keep it from freezing too solid overnight, and also keep the birds off. I've got half of the legs removed and half of the carcass skinned. Seems like a good place to stop.

There's a wad of game bags stuffed into the bottom of my pack. The bags are made of stretchy, breathable material that is almost unrippable. It's as thin as cheesecloth; you could cover your whole body with the amount that you could fit in your mouth. I work a bag around the buffalo's shoulder. The bag will keep the leg from getting dirty, and it makes it easier to grip. I tip the leg over in the snow and then slide it into my backpack, shoulder first with the ankle sticking out. Only a little more than half fits into the backpack, but at least it's the heavy end. I tie my sleeping bag to the outside of the pack and load up a few more things that I'll need for the night. I roll the rest of my gear into my food bag and then wedge the package into the limbs of a small spruce tree. I wish there were some trees big enough to hang the buffalo's meat out of a bear's reach, but there's nothing nearly thick enough.

It's going to be dark in a couple of hours. I sit down next to my pack in order to wiggle into the shoulder straps. Once the pack is on, I struggle to my knees. From there I can stand up and lift the weight of the leg, which is severely off balance. I figure that the pack weighs a bit less than one hundred pounds. I get a compass reading, shoulder my rifle, and then start toward the Chetaslina. It's about one mile away. I've got my bone saw in my hand because I'll need to clear a trail through the brush. It will take me probably seven trips like this to get the meat down to the Chetaslina. From there it's still three miles to my main camp along the Copper. I'm not sure how I'll get the meat down that far. I'll figure that out later.

When I get away from the carcass, I start to think that I'm being paranoid about the grizzlies. They were headed upriver, away from here. Plus, the carcass is brand-new. What are the chances they'll find it before I get it to my base camp? And besides that, I lit a fire and spent the whole day there, spreading around plenty of human odor. I tell myself that I've probably got a couple days before I run into any trouble. I continue along, hacking my way through the brush. I beat a trail over logs and under logs, through thickets and around them. If I keep tromping through the same place, I'll eventually work up a good trail. I use my knife to shave thin strips of bark from the sides of trees to mark my path in case the snow melts. In places it's impossible to proceed, and I have to back out and try a new route. When this happens, I put a scratch across the bark peelings so that I don't get confused in the dark.

My wishful thinking about the bears vanishes when I return to the bank of the Chetaslina. There are tracks all over the riverbank, pacing back and forth. I'm just about downwind of the carcass. I'll bet they were walking the riverbanks when they picked up the odor. Shit. I drop my pack and unload the buffalo's leg. There aren't any trees around here that are big enough to tie the leg out of reach of a grizzly. Instead, I hang my sweaty face mask from a tree limb and drape my jacket over the meat. To add a little extra human odor, I drape my sleeping bag over the leg and light a small fire. Then I fill my bottle with water and drop in a crushed iodine tablet before I start to walk back up toward the kill site. You're supposed to give iodine a half hour or so to work its magic, but I chug the bottle after ten minutes in hopes that I can produce some urine.

When I get back to the buffalo, I strip out of my long under-wear and drape the bottoms over the meat. I make a scarecrow with the top. If I were braver, I'd sleep here tonight and make sure nothing messes with the buffalo. But I'm too chickenshit for that. Rather than heading back down with an empty pack, I pull the hide back from the buffalo and carve off the entire loin. It runs from the hip all the way to the base of the neck, like a loaf of French bread as long as a human leg. I have to cut it in half just to fit it in my pack. There's still a little extra room in my pack, so I remove the tenderloin from inside the cavity and put that in the top of the pack. I pull the hide back over the buffalo and start down toward the Chetaslina.

When I get near the river, I pick up a set of grizzly tracks that are walking on top of the boot prints that I'd just made an hour ago. I get a tingly sensation of fear, a warm upward rush from my stomach. I peer through the underbrush, looking for dark shapes. Nothing. The bear tracks are headed both ways, as if it walked toward the carcass and then turned around. After a few more minutes of walking, I find the place where one of the bears entered and exited the trail. I don't see any tracks from the other bear.

The leg is untouched, and there aren't any tracks in the snow next to it. The bears were apparently afraid to approach, but still, I don't relish the idea of sleeping here tonight. Besides, I'm missing a layer of clothes. I'd probably freeze my ass off. I stand for a moment, staring at the river and trying to decide what to do. I've got the buffalo's highest-quality cuts of meat in my pack, the loin and tenderloin, and I figure that I might as well haul them back to the Copper and spend the night in my tent. It's three miles away and on the other side of the river. If I hurry, I'll get there before dark.

— 13 —

IDREAMED ABOUT BEARS LAST NIGHT. They looked at me, spoke to me, turned into people that I've known. I have dreams like that often, dreams in which the animal and human worlds morph together in bizarre ways; I believe the dreams are the result of being a hunter, because the animals that appear to me are creatures that I've stalked and eaten in real life. The dreams started in my teens, back when I used to trap hundreds of muskrats every year to sell their pelts. Muskrats live in swamps, lakes, and rivers, and one of the most reliable ways to catch them is to set foothold traps on their floating feed beds, which are dinner-plate-sized mats of food and vegetation that the muskrats collect and store for later use. You run four feet of bailing wire from the trap chain and anchor it beneath the water's surface. In the morning, if the trap's gone, you know that a muskrat got caught and pulled the trap into the water and drowned. I'd reach down into the water up to my shoulder and feel around for the wire and then follow that wire with my hand until I felt the fur. In my dreams, though, I'd find the hair of a human.

Bears are the worst animal to dream about, because they sometimes act like people even outside of my dreams. They rise to their hind feet with such fluidity and ease that it's startling to watch. I can't help but think of human behaviors that correspond to their activities. I remember one time in early May when I was hunting black bears at the base of an avalanche slide in the Bitterroot Mountains of western Montana. A female bear and her two cubs were grazing on vegetation that was springing out of ground tilled by avalanches. I was watching the bear through my rifle scope when she caught my odor. She stood up and looked right at me, reminding me of the way you might stand to greet someone who just walked into the room. I felt rude for having a rifle trained on her chest.

The Chetaslina is running like a frozen daiquiri. I listen from my tent as the slushy water makes a tingling noise against the rocks. My back is a little sore from bending over and butchering all day yesterday. I do some stretches while lying in my sleeping bag and then unzip the tent door and crawl outside into the cold to make a fire. I stand in the smoke until my boots are thawed enough to get my feet inside. When I cross the river in my dry suit and step onto the other bank, the drips of water running down my legs freeze into little beads of ice. I pull off the suit as quickly as possible and put the liners and boots back on before they freeze solid again. I start the walk up toward the carcass. Being on my feet and getting warmed up makes my back feel better.

Speaking of bears, the two grizzlies must have continued to hang around the area during the night. I cut the first set of tracks when I'm still a quarter mile away from where I left the buffalo's front leg. I can see where one of the bears came downriver toward my camp along the Copper and then turned around and walked back. It's unnerving, the way these bears will pace back and forth, testing and exploring. It reminds me of a burglar casing out a job.

I continue along, taking it slow and easy, walking in the same path that the bear took. I've got my rifle down off my shoulder with the butt plate tucked up against my hip. My binoculars are in my other hand; I'm using them to study the brush up ahead of me for dark shapes or movement. I know I left the meat on the edge of the river, on this side, but I don't have an exact fix on the location. If a grizzly took the leg, he'd probably drag it off somewhere. That somewhere might be here.

Once I can see the face mask that I left hanging from the tree limb, I stop to listen. I can hear the croak of ravens off toward the carcass. They make a noise that sounds like ripping an empty beer can in half. I move closer and see that the leg is undisturbed. Surprisingly, the ground all around the leg is plastered with grizzly tracks. Some of the prints would have put the bear into easy reach of the meat—the closest prints are just thirty inches away. I can't believe that it would have come that close and then lost its nerve. Unless I happened to just come along and scare it off.

I take a piss next to the leg and start up my path leading toward the kill site. There are a couple of fresh sets of grizzly tracks over my boots, but after a few minutes of walking there's nothing but my own prints. Bright little splotches of red and blue in the snow mark where I stepped on remnant crowberries and blueberries left over from the summer. Soon I can see the general area of the carcass and the blood-streaked path that it cut in the snow. I'd be smart to move upwind and let my smell blow down through the area, but I want to get a good look at whatever's happening. I move in a half circle downwind until I'm on the hillside above the carcass and looking down into the tangle of aspens where it crashed. I don't see anything except birds, and I haven't hit any new grizzly tracks. The gray jays lift off the gut pile as I approach. I lean my rifle against the rib cage and unload my gear.

When I initially drew this tag, the world up here along the Copper River seemed so huge and unknowable. All of my questions were questions of space: Where can I go? How can I get there? Now the world is shrunk down to this small patch of snow and ground, hide and flesh. I like the way it feels here; my own little hangout. After collecting some wood, I get a fire going down in the spruce trees below the buffalo. My goal is to give the bears one more reason to stay away, but it also amplifies the homey feel of the kill site. Looking up the hill, I think again about the blood streaks from where the buffalo slid down the hillside. Low-flying aircraft would see that for sure, and they'd see the smoke from the fire. I'm on public land, totally legal, but someone might wonder how I got up here. They might wonder if I was trespassing or if I actually came up the river channel the way I'm supposed to. If they were curious enough, they could buzz circles overhead and look for my boot prints. I can't tell if I'm being paranoid or not. Thinking about bears is making me jumpy.

The hide is partially frozen, and it crinkles as I pull it back away from the meat. The body is starting to freeze up, too. If the massive neck and head freeze solid, it will be really difficult to remove the skull and clean it of flesh. I'd have to haul the whole thing out of here in one big, meaty piece. Grabbing the buffalo by the horns, I can twist its head into slightly different positions. The buffalo's body is stiff enough that it stays in whatever position I put it, like one of those wire-bodied Gumby dolls. With the head tipped to the side, I make two long slits with my knife, each starting where you touch your throat to see if your lymph nodes are swollen. I extend each of those cuts along the inside edges of the jawbone until they meet at the point of the chin. Then I pull back the triangle-shaped flap of hide, slicing it as it comes, until I can access and sever the base of the tongue. It spills out like a giant two-and-a-half-pound slug backing away from a wet, toothy sac. To eat it, you just boil it until the outside coating starts to peel away.

The simple, perfect ease of extracting the tongue is satisfying. I think of a day when I passed through Fort Pierre, South Dakota, in order to look at an area along the Missouri River where several hundred Sioux hunters slaughtered fourteen hundred buffalo and cut out the tongues. This was in the summer of 1830. They did the killing and cutting in the morning and then hauled the tongues into a trading post and swapped them for liquor. The remaining 1.5 million pounds of untouched buffalo parts were left on the prairie to rot. Since then, historians have used that anecdote for many purposes that have suited their own needs of the moment: to demonstrate the evils of alcohol; to prove the corrupting nature of capitalism; to argue that Indians were not parsimonious conservationists; and to show that Indians were practical about getting what they needed from the buffalo.

I think about this last point often as I butcher the buffalo. Every schoolboy knows that the Indians used every part of the buffalo, which is true. But they did not use every part of every buffalo. Their relationship with buffalo reminds me of my own relationship with the one- and two-liter bottles of tonic water that I buy for making vokda tonics. Now and then, I'll have occasion to cut the top off one of these bottles and use it as a funnel for putting salad dressing ingredients into a bottle. I'll also cut off the bottoms of tonic bottles and use them as containers for soaking rusted mechanical parts in solvent or freezing fish fillets. Perforated, they make good bait canisters for crab trapping. Sometimes I'll ice my catch of fish with tonic bottles that were filled with water and placed in the freezer overnight. It keeps the water inside clean, so after the ice melts, you can still drink the water. Once you drink the water, you can put the lid back on and tie monofilament around the neck of the bottle and use it as a buoy to mark the place where you caught the fish.

So, as you see, one could argue that I use every last part of my tonic bottles. The truth is, though, I only need so many funnels and bait cans. Nine times out of ten, I'll just drink the tonic and toss the bottle into the recycling bin. In the same way, Indians only needed so many implements and decorations. If a tribe drove three hundred buffalo over a cliff, they wouldn't feel obligated to make twenty-four hundred buffalo-hoof spoons and six hundred buffalo-horn charcoal carriers. Rather, they might just take the meat and hides from the best-looking female buffalo, those that weren't too smashed up or buried under other buffalo. That might be all they touched. After all, their time and energy had value, just as ours does.

The Indians' relationship to the buffalo was complex and beautiful, not because of the Indians' unwavering frugality with the buffalo but because of their unwavering inventiveness with the animal. Describing this inventiveness tests the limits of my tonic bottle analogy. While I might use tonic bottles for many purposes, I do not know how to cut tonic bottles with knives made from tonic bottles; I'm not wearing a tonic bottle right now, and I'm not living inside a tonic bottle house.

Indians would use untanned skins, or rawhide, to make buckets, mortars, war shields, drums, splints, cinches, lariats, packing straps, knife sheaves, saddles, blankets, stirrups, masks, ornaments, quirts, snowshoes, boats, and moccasin soles. They'd use tanned buffalo hides to make moccasin uppers, blankets, beds, winter coats, shirts, leggings, dresses, belts, bridles, quivers, backrests, bags, tapestries, sweat lodge covers, tipi covers, and tipi liners. The skin from the hind leg could be taken directly off the buffalo and used as emergency footwear. Indians would make baby cradles with tanned buffalo hides, and they'd make buffalo-skin sacks for carrying their babies on trips. If an infant was orphaned, it might be wrapped in a buffalo robe and left in the arms of its dead mother on a burial scaffold lashed together with strips of buffalo hide.

Indians would use buffalo hair, particularly the hair on the buffalo's forehead, to stuff pillows, dolls, sleeping pads, and medicine balls.* They'd insulate their moccasins with buffalo hair. They'd braid buffalo hair into ropes and use the ropes to make head-dresses, bracelets, hairpieces, bridles, and halters. The Comanche wove lariats from such coarse buffalo hair that the ropes appeared to be growing hair, like a caterpillar. Left together, the tailbone and its covering of hair were used as fly swatters, whips, decorations, and children's toys. The Indians would remove the buffalo's beard and use it as a decoration.

The shoulder blades of the buffalo were crafted into boat paddles and gardening implements, such as shovels and hoes. Other bones made good fleshing tools, smoking pipes, arrowheads, sled runners, saddle frames, war clubs, scrapers, awls, paintbrushes, sewing needles, gaming dice, knives and knife handles, and forks and spoons. The horns were used as ladles, head ornaments, bow laminates, powder horns, arrowheads, and decorative flourishes on headwear.

Buffalo teeth were used as ornaments for clothing. Brains and livers were used to treat leather. Indians would wash out a buf-

---

*The fuzzy, tangled hair on the buffalo's forehead was used as stuffing in commercially manufactured pillows as well. Because hide hunters didn't usually skin the buffalo's heads, people would sometimes follow in their wake to shave the hair away and collect it in sacks to sell by the pound.

falo's stomach and use it as a kettle, a washing basin, a water bucket, or as packaging material for meat. When dried out, buffalo tongues become prickly; Indians used these tongues as hair combs. They'd dry the scrotums out and use them as rattles. The rattle's handle might be a buffalo bone. Bladders were made into balloons, flotation devices, and waterproof pouches. They'd also use bladders to store buffalo marrow or buffalo fat. The fat would be used as a pomade-like hair treatment, as a base for medicine or cosmetics, and as a cooking oil, a food item, and a waterproofing agent. Indians would cook the hooves and noses down into glue. They'd use tendons and sinews from the buffalo to make bowstrings and cords. The best and most durable sinews came from alongside the spine. These could be split into fine, strong threads for sewing clothes. The thread was also used to lash points and feathers to arrows that could be used to kill more buffalo.

As I'm handling the dead buffalo, I have a desire to experiment with some of these ideas. I'd like to make a balloon with the bladder and let it float in the river. I'm also curious what it would look like if I painted my face with buffalo fat that's been dyed black with the ash from buffalo chips. In a way, though, doing those things seems like a form of cultural hijacking. I could learn what it feels like to have my face smeared with buffalo fat, but that wouldn't tell me what it's like to believe that I was harnessing the power of the buffalo. And without feeling both of those things, I imagine that it's difficult to properly feel either one of them.

With the tongue removed, I prop the buffalo's chin on a rock and cut through the hide all the way around the neck. My incision is just behind the ears. I cut through the meat of the neck and sever the spine with my bone saw. The head is heavy and hard to lift. I straddle it in a bowlegged stance and grab the horns, so that the buffalo's head and I are facing the same direction. Lifting with my legs, I waddle down the hill to the edge of my fire. I skipped breakfast, so I cut a couple of alder whips and spear a few strips of meat on the end of each. I poke the other ends into the ground and position the meat over the fire to cook. It curls in the heat.

Skinning the head takes an hour or so. The frozen hide and muscle are especially hard to work with. When my fingers get too cold, I stop to warm them over the fire while I chew a couple pieces of meat. It takes me longer than I think it should to pry the severed vertebrae away from the skull's foramen magnum. It's also very difficult to remove the lower jaw because the buffalo's powerful jaw muscles had clenched in death like a pair of locking pliers. I have to wiggle my knife blade up into the bone pockets that encase the jaw hinges and then blindly pry and poke until things start to loosen up. Eventually the jaw has a bit of wiggle to it. Sitting on the ground with the buffalo head standing on its neck between my knees, I hold the horns with my hands and use my boot heel to push away on the front teeth of the lower jaw. The jaw snaps free with a crunching and popping noise.

I run my fingers over the teeth. A buffalo has molars on its upper and lower jaws, but it has incisors only on its lower jaw. The incisors press against the dental pad of the upper jaw to snip off pieces of vegetation. To a trained eye, a buffalo's age can be determined by the condition of the incisors.* The emergence and wear patterns are somewhat standard on buffalo until the animals are about five or six years of age. After that, the particular environment where the buffalo lives will affect its teeth as much as its age does. Buffalo living in areas with short grass will crunch more dirt

---

*The same set of methods works for aging horses. That's where the old saying "Don't look a gift horse in the mouth" comes from. To do so is like asking how much a present cost.

and sand than buffalo living in areas with taller grass; as a consequence, their teeth will wear down sooner. Because a buffalo cannot outlive its teeth, its life expectancy is influenced by its grazing conditions. This is one of the reasons domesticated buffalo live longer than wild buffalo. If a buffalo eats cut hay and doesn't have to scrape every meal off the ground, it can easily live into its twenties or thirties. If a buffalo living in the wild is really careful and really lucky, it will survive long enough to enter old age—around twelve to fifteen years; they seldom last longer than that.

I slice away as much of the flesh as possible from the head and then empty out the eye sockets. The fat behind the eyes has an unusual texture. I read somewhere that Plains Indians liked to eat this fat along with the eyeballs when the animal was fresh dead. I once ate the olive-sized eyeballs out of a roasted hog, but I can't stomach the idea of eating an eye that's as big as a small plum. You'd have to bite into it and tear out a piece instead of sucking it back like an oyster. I toss the eyes toward the bird pile but save a tablespoon of the fat in my cooking pan.

The head begins to look like a skull, clean and white. Buffalo skulls were put to various uses by Indians, most of a spiritual or metaphysical nature. The buffalo skull was an especially potent symbol to many Plains Indians tribes, but not because it equaled death. Rather, a skull represented a form of rebirth to many tribes. To reduce a buffalo to its skeleton was like ushering the animal back to a sort of primordial starting line, or beginning. The clean skull allowed for continuity, like a blank canvas upon which future buffalo could be created. In 1875, travelers along the Platte River found a spot where Indians had arranged buffalo skulls in "circles, curves and other mathematical figures" across the prairie. Indians explained that the practice pleased buffalo and encouraged them to come near. The Arikara of the Missouri valley would stuff the eye sockets of buffalo skulls with sage leaves and then set the skulls in lines across the prairie. The lines might be fourteen skulls long. An Arikara man explained to a white man that this treatment appeased the skulls and dissuaded them from issuing warnings to their brother buffalo about the dangers of approaching an Arikara village. In conducting Sun Dances, men would tie leather cords to buffalo skulls and then fasten those cords to their skin with bone needles. They would dance, pulling the skulls behind them, until their skin ripped away and freed the skulls. The self-mutilation was considered by some to be a sacrifice to both the sun and the buffalo, which were not entirely separate entities. Each was a sort of co-sponsor of life on earth, and they were bound together by their generosity toward man.

I'm not a particularly religious person, though I do sense an inkling of the spiritual when I look at this buffalo skull. Many people have tried to explain to me what they feel when they look at a crucifix or Torah scroll; it's an emotion often described as a mixture of gratitude, devotion, continuity, and awe. Looking at a buffalo skull is probably the closest I'll ever come to experiencing those feelings, however faintly, and I'm glad to have a taste of that. I imagine this skull sitting next to my old skull from Montana, and I like the image very much. To thwart trophy hunters, it's illegal in Alaska to transport an animal's skull, horns, or hide ahead of its meat. So this skull will be the last thing out of here, and I probably won't be able to haul it until tomorrow. For now, I give it a nice home against a tree so that I can look up and admire it while I work.

It's getting toward noon and I still haven't finished butchering the upward-facing half of the buffalo. The ribs and neck are all that remain. With my large knife, I make a cut straight down into the center of the back of the neck. The cut runs lengthwise,

starting where I severed the head, and I begin slicing away the fil-
let of neck meat as one large piece. I'm removing an eight- or
nine-pound slab of meat shaped like a large dictionary. The neck
bone is left mostly clean. With that done, I cut the meat from over
and between the ribs, which leaves them looking like bars on a jail
cell window.

I figure that I should take one or two loads down to the
Chetaslina now, in order to spread out the misery of lugging
the weight. Plus, I want to make sure that nothing's disturbing the
meat. Getting the back leg into my pack is like trying to stuff a
really fat kid into a sleeping bag while he's lying on the floor and
playing stiff-as-a-board. The thickest part of the leg, near the fe-
mur's ball joint, is too big around for the pack's opening. I undo
the clasp on the pack's draw cord, and the aperture increases just
enough to accommodate the leg. After reassembling the draw
cord, I get the leg strapped into place so it doesn't wobble too
much. I sit with my back to the pack and pull the straps on, then
struggle to my feet and grab my rifle.

There's a tricky spot along my trail to the Chetaslina. From the
ridgetop, the kill site looks like it's close to the valley floor.
Actually, though, it's on a bench of land about twenty feet above
the valley floor. The drop-off is steep, and yesterday I went back
and forth looking for a good place to climb down. But there's only
one good route within a couple hundred yards in either direction,
a narrow game trail trampled into the hillside on a steep pitch.
The first two times I used the trail it was fine, but now it's starting
to get icy. I take a couple of steps downhill while using a few small
saplings as handholds. Suddenly my feet swing out from under
me as easily as they would in a weightless chamber. The sapling
slips from my hand and I come down fast. The weight on my back
makes it feel as if I've fallen off an extension ladder. I hit so hard

that my teeth knock together and gash my tongue, and then I'm sliding and rolling down the hill with the pack on my back and the rifle barrel somehow tangled in my legs. I hit the bottom of the hill with my wind knocked out. I catch my breath and roll clear of the pack. The gash on my tongue feels deep and tastes like metal. I spit up a mouthful of blood. There's a bunch of snow packed beneath the rifle's scope. I clear that out with a stick and use a corner of my shirt to wipe down the rifle's action. I'm sure that I probably knocked the hell out of my scope, but that hardly matters now. If I need to shoot at something, it's going to be close. There's a throbbing pain in my hip when I stand up. I don't want to let it get too stiff, so I hurriedly chase down some ibuprofen with a handful of snow and start walking.

I stay at the Chetaslina just long enough to fill my water bottle and unload the buffalo's back leg. There aren't any new grizzly tracks around. Maybe the bears have given up and will just wait until I leave; maybe they'll come back once it gets dark. When I start back into the woods, headed toward the carcass, I can feel the air warming up. The snow load is coming out of the spruce trees like rainwater. My pants get soaked from climbing over tree trunks and brushing against wet limbs. I take it easy while climbing the hillside that I just fell down. At the top I start scrounging around for dry wood. The fire is burned down to ash, but I wake it up with a few spruce twigs and then pile on the sticks I collected. Soon it's ripping enough that my pants and shirt are rolling with steam while I stand next to it. Once the fire burns down a bit, I'll put the pan of fat on the coals and fry some scraps of meat.

It takes a long time to get the carcass rolled over and the hide and remaining two legs removed. I get lost in the work and lose track of the hours. I stop just long enough to look for bears and chew a few scraps of the meat. The hide is almost too heavy to lift.

The buffalo hide on fleshing beam.

There's a lot of meat and gristle stuck to it, especially around the shoulder hump. The edges of the belly are coated in fat. My guess is that fleshing the hide down to bare leather will reduce the weight by almost half. That won't happen until tomorrow, though, so I roll the hide up, like an old-fashioned sleeping bag. Then I get to thinking that it might freeze into a cylinder and I won't be able to get it open. I cut a pole with my saw and lash the pole between two trees at the height of my throat. The pole is thick, about four inches in diameter, a good size for a fleshing beam. I drape the hide over the pole like I'm putting laundry out to dry. Hair side down, skin side out, the hide hangs nearly down to the forest floor.

I spend another half hour hauling the second back leg down to the Chetaslina. It's funny, carrying another creature's leg when my own leg is hurting so bad. It feels like something's clicking inside my hip every time I take a step. Once I'm ready to head back toward the kill site, I notice that I have a problem. It's already close to dusk, and it's obvious that I'm going to be out here messing around in the pitch black. I can't sleep up here, because I stupidly left my sleeping bag and tarp down at my main camp along the Copper. I'd have to spend the night lying next to the fire and would be awake all night, freezing my ass off while embers landed on my clothes and burned a bunch of holes in them. I'd almost rather get mauled by rabid coyotes than go through that. My other option would be to head to the Copper now, without going back to the carcass, but I left my gear lying around. If it snows tonight, it'll get covered up and lost, and the clothes that I left out will get wet. The only thing that makes sense, I suppose, is to go up there and get my stuff and then walk back to camp in the dark.

I keep moving as quick as I can up to the carcass, then gather my gear and load up the front shoulder and a few other cuts of meat. When I start back toward the Chetaslina, it's almost fully dark. The cloud cover has been thinning out, and now the moonlight is filling the woods. I can't see the moon, but the sky is bright enough to cast thin, faint shadows. Walking along, I think of how animals tend to be more active on moonlit nights. I wonder if that's actually true, or if it's just that you see more animals on moonlit nights because it's not so dark and you can see more of everything. I'm annoyed with myself because of the fear, though it does seem well-founded. My clothes are full of blood, and I'm carrying one hundred pounds of red meat in bear country. When I get to the steep slope with the slick trail, I sit on my ass and slide down. At the bottom I hear a cracking limb off to my side, and I wonder if it's a clump of falling snow or a footstep. I haven't chambered my rifle all day, but I work the bolt and load a round. After a few more steps I hear it again; this time there's no mistake. I stop to listen. It's walking off through the woods, headed away from me. Whatever it is, it's moving slowly, as though going about its usual business.

I click on my headlamp, and the illumination is stopped short by the misty haze and thick timber. I continue along, following my tracks from earlier. The going is rough, with lots of downed timber. A bear would have to make a lot of noise coming through here. I stop to listen, and again I hear footsteps. This time they're coming from the other side of the trail. Just a few at first, and then the noise explodes in a flurry of footsteps and crashing brush. I crouch down next to a tree trunk, fearing that something's coming my way. But the footfalls get farther and farther away and then make a sudden stop. The air is still and noiseless. I replay the noise in my mind. It didn't sound like hooves. It sounded like padded feet.

When I'm scared in the woods, I tend to think of other times when I've been freaked out. It's soothing for some reason. When I was a little kid, my family bow hunted for deer on a large tract of farmland owned by a man named Allen Zerlaut. We hunted out of trees, because deer are less likely to detect your presence when you're above them. You have to be twelve to legally hunt deer in Michigan, so for many years my brothers and I sat up in my dad's tree with him. He stole street signs and made platforms out of them that could be bound to tree limbs with chain binders, and we must have looked like a mother raccoon and her pups spread out in the limbs of those big beech and maple trees. When my brother Matt turned twelve, Danny sat in his tree with him to keep him from being afraid. When Danny turned twelve, Matt was all alone and I sat with Danny. Two years later and I became a legal hunter, too, so from then on we all had to be out in the woods by ourselves.

In discussions, we divided the Zerlaut farm into toplands and bottomlands. The toplands supported woodlots of maple and beech, fields of corn and alfalfa, and apple orchards. The bottomlands were deep, dark ravines shadowed beneath thick canopies of hemlock. I'd sometimes have to go down into those ravine bottoms in the mid-afternoon and then sit in my tree until total darkness. If I got down early, I might ruin my dad's hunt, which I didn't want to do, because at that point he was the meanest, most unpredictable man I'd ever known. So I'd wait until I could barely see the ground beneath me, and then I'd climb down out of my tree and start heading uphill. The woods sounded as if they were crawling with dangerous creatures. I'd carry an arrow in my hand to defend myself against who knows what, and I'd say the alphabet under my breath just to give myself something to think about. I'd worry about Matt and Danny coming out of the woods where they were hiding. It seemed like I had to go miles to get out of there. I wouldn't feel any safer until I entered the fields on the toplands and caught a glimpse of my dad's flashlight across the field. My dad used to whip me and my brothers now and then with his belt until we wet our pants, one time just because one of us left a pair of bull-nose pliers lying out in the yard. That I'd actually feel safe with that man coming out of the woods says a lot about my irrational fears of the wilderness.

I get down to the Chetaslina and unload the front shoulder on top of the other legs that I already hauled down. I don't want to wrestle that thing all the way back to my camp in the dark, but I do load a few smaller cuts so that I'm not going back empty-handed. Once I'm loaded up, I turn off my headlamp and wait for my eyes to adjust to the dark. I don't hear any more footsteps or cracking brush. The river is quieter now, too, as the slush melted during the warmth of the day. The moon is hidden behind the ridge on the other side of the river, but its light is bright as it comes through the open sky above the water. The crusted snow makes it even shinier. The gravel crunches under my feet as I move downriver. I measure my downstream progress against the ridge of land that rises up between the two branches of the Chetaslina. I pass the ridge, and I know that I've covered about a mile of ground. I'm downstream of any fresh bear tracks, and I start to relax a bit. I've got to cross the Chetaslina in the dark, which will be a pain in the ass, but at least I won't have to think about grizzlies until tomorrow. Then something bizarre happens. It hits me like a flash of light on the left side of my head, and I duck to the right as I let out a yell and throw up my arm. The burst of fright has barely left my mouth when I realize what has attacked me. There's a bright blob hanging in the sky, peeking out from the edge of the ridge. I just tried to dodge the moon.

— 14 —

AT FRONTIER SETTLEMENTS on the Canadian prairie, men used to dig gigantic square pits in the ground before the winter freeze. These pits were as big as basements. Then, when it got cold and the rivers froze, they'd cut blocks of ice with saws and pave the floor of the pits. They'd pour water into the cracks between the blocks and let it freeze up and cement everything together. After the floor was prepared, the walls were built up in the same way. With everything ready, hunters would go out and kill hundreds of buffalo and cut the carcasses into quarters with the skin still on. When the meat froze, they'd pack it into the pit as tight as possible, cap it off with straw and then cover it with a roof to keep out rain and sun. The meat would stay frozen all through the next spring and summer, and it would be more tender and flavorful than fresh game.

I'm reminded of this now because all of the meat is frozen stiff. I just took my second-to-last load of meat down from the kill site to the Chetaslina. I had the skull strapped to the outside of my pack, and I was extra careful coming down the slick hill with those sharp horns jutting out. Now I'm heading back up to fetch the hide, and my hip's still making that clicking noise from when I fell. Thankfully, my trail gets better and better with each pass. I drop my pack in the area where I heard something crashing around in the brush the night before. I check for tracks, but it's hard to find any because half of the snow is melted and the rest is all crusted over and dappled from yesterday's dripping slush. If I hadn't actually seen those two bears a few days earlier, I'd be tempted to think of them as ghosts by now. On the edge of a meadow I do find a patch of rose hips that are frozen and not dried out too badly. I haven't eaten anything sugary in a few days, so I stop long enough to have some. They've got waxy skins and lots of seeds, but they're not bad if you're in the right mood.

The hide's frozen as stiff as thick waxed cardboard, which actually makes it easier to handle. After putting a fresh sharpen on my large knife, I start filleting away the gristle and meat and orange-tinged fat. I throw the gristle into the bushes and the pieces of fat into a sack that I've been filling. The process leaves behind nice clean leather, white and soft. I kindle a small fire off to the side of where I'm working, so when my fingers get too cold I can flick them through the flames.

When archaeologists dig up ancient buffalo kill sites, they'll sometimes uncover buffalo skeletons that are still "articulated," meaning that whoever killed the buffalo hadn't cut them into pieces. All of the bones will be lying in their proper places, the way you'd imagine a human skeleton inside a casket. Often, articulated skeletons will be missing their tailbones. This used to puzzle archaeologists, but then someone realized that Indians removed the tails along with the hides when they skinned buffalo. The tailless, articulated skeletons were likely killed for skins.

Traveling through North Dakota, I once visited a kill site along the Missouri River where Indians corralled buffalo into a trap at the bottom of a coulee a few hundred years ago. There's a flat bench of land next to the coulee where archaeologists believe that the Indians fleshed the hides using small flint knives known as thumb scrapers. Now the site happens to be on land administered by the Nature Conservancy, and there's a small herd of buffalo living behind a fence there. The buffalo like to hang out on that bench of ground, and they've scratched out big wallows there. The wallows are the only places not covered in thick grass, and when I was digging around in the dirt in the bottoms, I found all kinds of flint shards and broken thumb scrapers left over from those people fleshing buffalo all those years ago. It was one of those bizarre collisions of present and past that seem to occur whenever you spend time around buffalo.

As I'm fleshing, I now and then have to put my hand against the fur side of the hide in order to provide some back pressure against my knife's blade. The fur feels good against my hand, especially in the area of the animal's rump and midsection. The hair is velvety and thick, luxuriant. Buffalo can exhibit a variety of hair types, in the same way that humans have wavy hair or straight hair, or thick or thin hair. The rarer varieties were often quite valuable. Hunters were always on the lookout for what they called mouse robes, which were more bluish in color and had long, fine fur. In Montana, maybe one out of a hundred buffalo had a mouse robe. Another popular type of buffalo hide was known as a beaver hide. These were chestnut brown and had exceptionally fine, wavy fur. Indians liked so-called beaver robes because of their beauty and comfort; hide hunters liked beaver robes because they could sell them for up to twenty-five times the price of a normal buffalo hide.

By far, the most valuable buffalo hides were taken from white, or albino, buffalo. These were extraordinarily rare.* Albino calves have a difficult time surviving into adulthood because the lack of protective melanin in their eyes is a vicious detriment on the sun-drenched, shadeless prairie; most white buffalo probably died from complications of blindness long before an arrow or bullet found them. Most Plains tribes, including the Blackfoot, Mandan, Lakota, and Cheyenne, considered the white buffalo a figure of great religious significance.† They believed in variations of the same story line; the Lakota version holds that the tribe's sacred ritual of the pipe was given to them by a beautiful woman known as White Buffalo Cow Woman (sometimes White Buffalo Calf Woman). After instructing the tribal ancestors in the sacred rituals, White Buffalo Cow Woman walked toward the setting sun. She stopped and rolled over in the dirt and turned into a black buffalo. She rolled again and turned into a brown buffalo, and then into a red buffalo. After her fourth and final roll, she emerged as a white buffalo and disappeared.

While many Plains Indians revered the white buffalo and anticipated the return of White Buffalo Cow Woman, they maintained the seemingly paradoxical habit of killing every white buffalo they ran into. If one of the animals was killed, its hide was handled with great caution. According to a Euro-American explorer, the Gros Ventre Indians believed that if a white buffalo died in a buffalo jump, they could not touch any of the animals that it perished with.

---

*Today, there's a much higher percentage of white buffalo than there was in historic times. Many of the "sacred white buffalo," a fixture of Western tourist traps, are the result of crossbreeding between buffalo and white breeds of cattle.

†It's been reported that the Crows feared and respected white buffalo hides, but would not use or touch them. Hunters from tribes that did not consider the white buffalo sacred, such as the Cree and Assiniboin, would attempt to kill white buffalo in order to sell the hide to a tribe that did.

If a Cheyenne hunter killed a white buffalo, it was forbidden for him or anyone in his tribe to eat the meat.* The hunter himself was not permitted to skin the animal. Instead, he had to hire another man to do it. Women were not allowed to handle the white hides, ever. There was a Mandan chief named White Buffalo Robe Unfolded whose people were particularly avid connoisseurs of white buffalo hides. In the early 1830s, the German explorer and ethnologist Prince Maximilian passed through the Mandan villages along the Missouri River. He explained that the mere ownership of a white buffalo hide trumped all other accomplishments that a person could strive for in life. "Suppose two men to be disputing about their exploits," wrote the prince, "the one an old veteran warrior, who has slain many enemies, the other, a young lad

---

*Legend has it that the Cheyenne chief Roman Nose rode into battle dressed in a white buffalo robe. This is probably not true, as it stems from a completely fanciful narrative written by a relatively unknown U.S. Army general by the last name of Fry. Of Roman Nose, Fry writes, "The shock of battles and scenes of carnage and cruelty were as of the breath of his nostrils . . . with a single eagle feather in his scalp-lock, and with the rarest of robes, a white buffalo, beautifully tanned, and soft as cashmere, thrown over his naked shoulders, he stood forth the war chief of the Cheyennes." The rumor of Roman Nose's white buffalo robe has been perpetuated by the circumstances of his death. He was gunned down while leading a daylight charge against a heavily armed contingent of U.S. soldiers who were dug in on Beecher Island, along the Arikaree River in eastern Colorado. The charge was brazen, almost suicidal in a kamikaze sense of the word. Apparently, Roman Nose made the fatal mistake of believing that he had magical protection from bullets. Some say that this belief stemmed from his own good looks; his enemies were so stunned by Roman Nose's appearance that they couldn't concentrate on shooting him. Others have suggested that Roman Nose's protection came from the white buffalo robe as described by General Fry. The most provocative version of events is that Roman Nose was assured of his protection from bullets by a medicine man named White Bull, who gave Roman Nose an elaborate headpiece. As a condition of ownership for the headpiece and its protection, Roman Nose was forbidden to use the white man's cooking implements. The day before his death, he made the mistake of eating a piece of meat that a woman had poked with an iron fork.

without experience; the latter reproaches the other with never having possessed a white buffalo cow hide, on which the old man droops his head, and covers his face for shame."

According to the famed hide hunter J. Wright Mooar, only six or seven white buffalo were ever killed by white men. He himself shot two of those. He downed his first white buffalo in Kansas; his second came out of Scurry County, Texas, in October 1876, the only white buffalo ever killed by a white man in that state. The animal's

Author with the world's largest buffalo, July 2007.

hide was featured at the 1904 World's Fair in St. Louis, and Teddy Roosevelt offered Mooar $5,000 for it. After selling twenty thousand hides for a couple dollars apiece, Mooar for some reason turned down Roosevelt's offer.

I've never seen a white buffalo, though not because I haven't tried. One summer, I took a long weekend and drove almost a thousand miles round trip just to attend a white buffalo's eleventh birthday party at the National Buffalo Museum in Jamestown, North Dakota. I flew into Minneapolis and drove west along I-94 to exit 258, mostly following signs for the world's largest buffalo. I was picturing an actual creature, pumped full of bovine growth hormones. Instead, it's a beast built of steel beams, wire mesh, and stucco: twenty-six feet high, forty-six feet long, and weighing in at sixty tons. The animal is anatomically proportioned, right down to the scrotum. A kid pointed at the painted stucco sac and asked his dad, "What the heck is that?" The dad said, "That's a *male* buffalo."

Down the hill from the giant buffalo was the albino White Cloud's home, a large fenced pasture containing grassland and a heavily wooded creek bottom. The albino buffalo was born on July 10, and in honor of her birthday the museum had established the Tatanka Festival. I was there early in the morning, which I'd heard was a good time to catch a glimpse of White Cloud—she's known to abhor direct sunlight and prefers to graze early in the morning or late in the evening, when the sun's angle isn't so fierce. A dozen or so people were lined up along the fence, staring toward the creek bottom and, beyond, I-94. However, White Cloud seemed to be taking her birthday off. I saw a pair of coyotes, and my gaze on the animals was intent enough that a couple of other tourists stopped to ask me if I saw White Cloud. We stood around and watched the coyotes as they skulked around in the grass, but eventually everyone left.

I'd come a long way, and I had no intention of leaving without a glimpse. The festival included free pony rides, an old car show, a horseshoe tournament, a piano recital, a breakfast sponsored by the American Legion, and a grilled-buffalo luncheon. I was perfectly prepared to miss all of that. I walked back and forth along the fence, seeking an angle of view into the thickest thickets along the stream. I saw another coyote and realized that they had a den back in there. The temperature touched into the eighties. I left long enough to get a bottle of water and a buffalo steak and then hurried back. At one point, when no one was looking, I jumped a fence into an off-limits area to have a look around, but I didn't have the nerve to jump the main fence into White Cloud's pasture. I imagined flushing her out of the brush and giving everyone a good look. I also imagined getting hauled off in a squad car.

The sun traveled across its path toward the western half of the sky. I could hear the talent show taking place off in the distance. A while later I heard the talent show end. A worker started going around and locking up the buildings in Frontier Village. The coyotes came out and sat on a mound of dirt behind their den. Someone told me that it was lockup time and the museum was closing. I nodded but didn't budge. Thirty minutes later another guy came in a pickup to tell me to leave. I said sure, but he idled there like he wanted to see it happen. I still haven't seen a white buffalo.

YOU'LL SOMETIMES HEAR modern-day hunters use the word "collect" as a euphemism for "kill"; for instance, a guy might come back from an African safari and brag that he "collected thirteen head." Trophy hunters are particularly inclined to say that word, and I used to hate trophy hunters. I felt that they were reducing the notion of a species down to nothing more than large horns and overgrown hides, and that their ethic was vulgar and wasteful and a general discredit to hunters. I've begun to see that the issue is actually much more complicated now and that collecting is not necessarily antithetical to wise usage. After all, I'm going to eat hundreds of pounds of this buffalo's meat, right down to the marrow inside its bones. But someday, probably in a year or so, the meat will be gone. If it weren't for this buffalo hide, which I'll likely sleep under and take naps on top of for the rest of my life, I wouldn't have anything tangible to remind me of the wonderful days that I've spent out here. In that sense, it's a trophy and I'm a trophy hunter. However, it's not one of those special emblems that would only come from a lifetime of handling thousands or millions of buffalo hides; it's not a beaver robe or a mouse robe or a magical white buffalo robe. I don't believe that I've earned one of those. I don't believe that I'm so experienced with these animals that I require abstractions as a way of understanding their deepest meaning. All the meaning and symbolism that I'll probably ever need is right here: a perfectly typical hide taken from a perfectly typical buffalo, the first and last buffalo that I will ever kill.

I spend a few hours fleshing the hide. I slice away all the heavy stuff, the large blocks of fat and the thin layers of meat that pulled away from the carcass. It's still not perfect, but I reduced the weight by at least a quarter. I pull the hide down off the fleshing beam and spread it across the ground. I place it hair side down, because the flesh side's sticky and it will pick up spruce needles. It's a little bigger than a comforter for a queen-sized bed. I roll it from head to tail into a five-foot-tall cylinder as big around as a basketball. I snake one end of the cylinder into my pack, which accommodates about half of the length. The hide weighs seventy pounds. With the pack on my back, the upper end rides way up above my head. I reach back and try to fold it down over my shoulder so that it doesn't snag on limbs. It doesn't want to stay down, so I loop a rope over the top and pull it down to my shoulder strap. I turn to look at the bones on the ground, and I wonder about their fate. The bears will eat some, for sure, but the heavier bones will likely lie here scattered about for a very long time.

IT'S LATE INTO AFTERNOON when I get across from my camp along the Copper. I pull on my dry suit and start wading across the Chetaslina. As I'm climbing out on the opposite bank, the actor Willem Dafoe steps from the willows in a pair of camouflage waders. I don't know if I should run the other way or dig into my pockets for a scrap of paper for an autograph. I'm still thinking about what a strange turn of events this is when Jeff Jessen emerges out of the willows behind Dafoe and gives me the thumbs-up. We meet each other on the gravel bar, and I'm just getting ready to tell Dafoe how much I liked him in *The Last Temptation of Christ* when Jessen tells me that the Dafoe look-alike standing in front of me is actually none other than the infamous Hardcore Jeffy.

I've never met Hardcore Jeffy before, but I've certainly heard stories about him. His name often pops up in Anchorage outdoors social circles. At forty-seven, he's fifteen years older than most of his friends but also in better shape. No one ever talks about getting drunk with Hardcore Jeffy or of providing Hardcore Jeffy with a shoulder to cry on. Instead, stories involving Hardcore Jeffy are invariably set in uncomfortable wilderness circumstances, and they usually involve an anecdote or two about Hardcore Jeffy's obsessive gear-organizing tendencies. Jessen and Hardcore Jeffy were once stuck inside a snow cave on a climbing trip that was interrupted by a blizzard. Hardcore Jeffy managed the cave's organization right down to the frozen Baggies of human waste. Jessen once called Hardcore Jeffy on the phone and caught him in the midst of dipnetting sockeye salmon. During the conversation, Hardcore Jeffy had to excuse himself for a moment to scold his dog. Jessen heard him holler, "Georgia, you're fucking up the system!"

Jessen and Hardcore Jeffy had anticipated the situation I'm in, or at least they hoped I was in. They'd brought along two Alpacka pack rafts, which are small Alaska-made inflatable boats that are five and a half feet long and weigh less than a house cat. Inflated, pack rafts resemble a pool toy for little kids, if kids' pool toys cost $800 and came with advice on hauling moose meat and a warning about puncturing the hull on mine tailings. I've never been in a pack raft, but I've been warned about them. My two brothers once flew thirty miles into the Alaska Range with their rifles and backpacks and a pair of pack rafts. They carried their pack rafts with them while they hunted in the mountains for a week. After killing a Dall sheep, they hiked back down to the river and started floating out. Within five miles they'd capsized a raft and nearly lost their sheep. Matt's life jacket turned up missing. So they deflated the rafts and started walking with the dead sheep and the boats strapped to their backs. After twenty-five miles of hiking, they emerged on the Parks Highway and picked up a cell phone signal to call a taxicab in the town of Healy. Matt came away with the impression that pack rafts are best treated as what they appear to be: pool toys. I express this reservation, but Jessen and Hardcore Jeffy assure me that the pack rafts are tickets to ease. We could either spend two full days arduously hauling meat down the banks of the Chetaslina to the Copper, they say, or else spend a couple hours floating the meat down the canyon. They describe all of the dozens of rivers they've floated without suffering a single drowning incident.

In truth, there isn't really a decision for me to make. Hardcore Jeffy has to get back to work; he's already spent one full day on the Copper River getting this far, and we have to spend another day on the Copper to get out of here. There's no time for screwing around. After organizing our gear and getting the big raft secured on the bank with ropes, we strap the deflated, rolled-up pack rafts to our backs and begin heading upriver. The sun's setting by the time we get back up to the meat cache. It's already been a pretty long day for me, and I'm feeling suspiciously cold. My clothes got wet from sweat and exertion. The sun's dropping, and the temperature is going along with it. I pull on some extra clothes and zip up my dry suit, but I'm still shivering.

The buffalo's front shoulder makes the inflated pack rafts look like something a buffalo might use as water wings. Hardcore Jeffy is undeterred by this, and we begin fitting the pieces and parts of the buffalo into the rafts. Getting everything to fit is like trying to put kernels of corn back on a cob. The legs are frozen stiff and can't be arranged very well, and we try a dozen configurations before settling on a haphazard arrangement by which meat is mounded twice as high as each raft and lashed down with a woven network of rope. We lash the hide to one of the pack rafts, and I lash the skull to the front of the other. Now each boat has about 350 pounds aboard. When I try to yank the loaded pack raft into the river, I can't even get it to budge. We all three grab the lines on the raft and do a 1-2-3 count before yanking it toward the water. A dozen or so of these yanks and we get the first raft out into the current. It floats, with just a few inches of freeboard. We get the other raft into the water, and I secure the collar on my dry suit and step into the river.

The current is gushing at the highest rate it will hit all day. The slush from the morning is gone, but with the temperature dropping back down, it's freezing over again. The quiet water along the edges of the river is forming into ice that looks like honeycomb, and the boulders in the river are getting capped in opaque layers of frozen froth that remind me of shower caps from cheap motels. Starting out, we've got this idea that we'll take it slow and easy. Because Hardcore Jeffy doesn't have his dry suit, he'll stay on the bank with the rifle and a headlamp for shining into the river in case we hit a problem in the dark. Jessen and I will guide the loaded pack rafts along the river's edge with ropes.

It takes me approximately thirty seconds to see that this plan is utter nonsense. I step out into the river with my wrist tethered to the pack raft by a length of rope. As soon as the current grabs the raft, it feels like I'm trying to walk a pack of mastiffs. Rather than me guiding the raft along, the raft is yanking me. And its path is not the path that I want to take. I'm plunged into water up to my chest. The rope is wrapped around my wrist, and the pack raft feels like it's going to take my hand and my glove with it. If I let go, who knows how we'll catch the thing. I yell to Jessen, but he's having the same problem. As I bounce along behind the boat, I manage to scramble toward the bank and get my feet locked behind a big boulder. I lean into the rope and steer the raft toward another rock. It beaches, and then a wave of water rushes over the rubber gunwale. The raft manages to stay afloat, but only in the way that a piece of wet bread manages to stay afloat when you toss it into a duck pond.

I climb onto the bank and struggle to open my suit. I must have gone into deeper water than I've been in yet, because my clothes beneath the suit are wet, especially around the waist, and now water is trickling down into my socks. I try to find the leak. It looks like the seam near the belt line is shot and letting water in. Stupidly, I zip back up and stumble into the water again. As I'm yanking on the raft to get it off the rock, I see that ice is forming on the outside of the meat bags. If I punch the blocks of meat, ice breaks away like paper-thin shards of glass. I make several more attempts to guide the raft downriver with the ropes, but each attempt leads to me being dragged over rocks and filling my dry suit with even more water. It's darker now, and I can't see how deep the water is. The bottom of the river drops out from my feet, and I wrap my fingers under one of the ropes securing the load. I kick in the water as I try to pull myself up. I get my armpits up over the raft, and I'm clinging to it like someone holding on to a life ring in the ocean. If I climbed in, the high center of gravity would flip the raft for sure. Everything below my armpits is underwater, and my dry suit continues to fill up, but at least I'm not busting my knees open while getting dragged across rocks. I shoot down the river at a good clip and pass up Jessen as he's struggling to get his raft off an exposed rock. We're in a rapid, and the current's roaring loudly. Hardcore Jeffy must have had to go around some obstacle or another, because I haven't seen him or the LED beam from his light.

After a half hour of floating along, kicking off rocks, and trying to keep the pack raft from capsizing, I can hardly feel my legs. I send messages to them, but the messages don't instantly compute. I'll tell the legs to move down and catch the bottom of the river, but they don't do the motion with any vigor. This ain't good, I tell myself. The next time I hit a slow, shallow spot, I dig my knees into the bottom and stop the raft in a calm pocket of water behind a rock. The rope trailing in the water is as stiff as heavy-gauge wire and my hands will barely work, but I manage to get the rope looped around the rock well enough to hold it in place. I'm in the shallow water, on my hands and knees. I've got a pair of rubber pipe fitter's gloves on, and they're all full of water and cold. I can't even see across the river. Holy shit is this stupid, I think.

I get my legs in place beneath me and walk awkwardly up to the gravel bar. I attempt a few half-assed jumping jacks, but it feels like someone forced steel reinforcement rods into the hollows of my bones. I walk up and down the gravel bar, stiff as a robot, keeping an eye on the river to see if Jessen comes floating past. There are flakes of ice forming on my clothes. I stumble around for five minutes and never see him. I can't tell if I'm getting colder or warmer. I wonder if Jessen somehow passed me up, and now he and Hardcore Jeffy are below me and I'm up here freezing my ass waiting for them. But how could they be below me? I passed Jessen. Or didn't I? I realize that I'm not thinking too clearly. The cold's getting to my head. How long have I been in the water? An hour? I haven't even passed where the two forks of the Chetaslina come together. Why is this taking so long? I start thinking how thirsty I am. I know that's not a good sign, but I honestly am thirsty. Or maybe I'm not. I think about a beer. A beer and a cold glass of water. It occurs to me that I could drink the water right here, out of this river, but that water looks too goddamned cold. I stumble back out to my raft. My backpack is lashed to the load. The knots holding it down are frozen and bound up. I try to snake my hand inside the pack to feel around for my water bottle. As I'm groping for it, I realize that there isn't any difference. Just drink any water. Then my thirst fades and I'm consumed again by how cold I am. I feel for the Ziploc bag with my waterproof matches and a lighter, but everything's soaking wet. Finding it seems impossible. Nothing feels like plastic in there. Besides, my fingers are way too numb to work a lighter. I could start walking down the riverbank, but then I'd have to leave everything here and risk the grizzly situation all over again.

I undo the rope, grab the raft, and kick off into the current. I hear Jessen let out a whoop ahead of me. Through the darkness I see him bucking over the waves. He's going right down the middle, where the current stands up in a frothy strip like the hair on the back of a pissed-off dog. Jessen vanishes ahead of me. I realize that we're in the narrowest part of the canyon, where the river passes beneath a steep cliff. It's deep from here on out. My boat's pulled into the same route that Jessen took and it pulls me along with it. I try to put my feet down to grab the bottom, but they just bounce off the rocks like I'm dragging two big hunks of firewood from my torso. My hands are frozen into two hooks. The hooks are latched onto strings. The thirst comes back really hard until I feel like I'm dying of thirst. The pain in my feet is gone; there's nothing there now, just numb, tingling blocks. Several times I hit

boulders that I think are going to capsize the raft and sink me under, but somehow the rubber bounces off and stays upright.
Another rock smacks into my knees, but it feels like a dull thud,
no different from if it smacked one of the buffalo's legs up in the
boat.

Now I'm just hanging on, going where the water tells me to go.
My boat gets hung up in a back eddy beneath the cliff, and I swirl
there for a few minutes; in all, I've been in the water two hours
now, and I imagine spinning here until daybreak. The river grabs
me out of the back eddy like someone pulling a piece of laundry
from a still-spinning clothes dryer. I continue downstream, trying
to imagine what I'll do when I float past camp. How will I stop the
boat before I float into the Copper and on toward the Pacific
Ocean? But I can't really grasp the concept of it. It's almost like
I'm in a dream and can't wake up. I shoot through a fast stretch of
water, and I see a large cliff looming ahead of me. I don't remember that cliff, and I can't tell where I am, but I hear Jessen yelling,
"Whoa! Stop! Stop!" He's got his boat beached on the bank of the
river. I realize that I'm looking across to the other side of the
Copper. We've made it down to camp! The Chetaslina is loud and
rushing here, and I shoot past Jessen. I tell my legs to go down to
the bottom of the river, to hook the rocks or drag along, but they
won't do it.

I go over a gushing rim of water, and the Chetaslina spits me
out into the darkened gray swirl of the Copper. It's bottomless and
perfectly quiet. There is no more gushing water, no more rocks
bumping my legs. I think it's still, too, but a patch of snow against
the cliff goes shooting past, and I see that I'm moving quite
quickly. My dry suit is full of water, a bucket made of fabric, and I
wonder if there's a life jacket in camp. I wish I had one. I can't see
anything up that way. No tent, no trees. I wonder where yester-

day's moon went. How did it get so dark? Again I tell my legs to do something, and again they don't. I'm unbelievably thirsty, and while I realize that I must be very cold, I don't actually feel cold anymore. I feel more like I'm ready for a long nap. The thought that I've got two arms and two hands comes to me as a sort of vague recollection. I leave one of those hands hooked to a rope and yank the other free. I use it to paddle, languidly at first but then with more gusto. It doesn't seem to be helping. I feel exhausted, and I imagine falling asleep out here in the water. Where will I wake up? At the bottom of the river? And what will happen to the buffalo?

— 15 —

THE MOSQUITOES ARE THICK in the warm June air, buzzing around my ears and crawling across the mesh of my head net. Danny's stretched out on the ground just ahead of me, belly down, his feet next to my head. His left pant leg has risen up to his calf, and the skin above the top of his boot is red and puffy from so many bites. I smash a cluster of the mosquitoes with my gloved hand and leave a tangle of broken legs and wings sticking to his sweaty skin. I tuck his pant leg back into his boot. Danny looks over his shoulder and motions me forward. I crawl along, following the crest of a beaver dam. The mosquitoes lift away from our clothes like dust rising from a shook rug. Once I move forward a few body lengths, I can see the direction that the buffalo are coming from. Off a ways, toward the river, a wallowing bull kicks up a poof of dry glacial flour. We hold steady, and soon I can see their backs coming in over the tops of the willows, heading into the wind and toward us. About fifty of them. Fist-sized clumps of chocolate brown wool are shedding away from their humps. Their tails swat back and forth, chasing bugs. As the herd draws near, I begin to see the reddish glimpses of what I've been hoping to find: buffalo calves. The closest should pass within a few yards.

It's been eight months since I killed the buffalo. My feet still aren't right. When my weight is off of them, like now, I can feel the tingling numbness of frostbite creeping back into my toes and the backs of my heels. The sensation always reminds me of that cold night when I floated into the Copper River. Hardcore Jeffy climbed into the water and snagged the buffalo's severed knee joint as I floated past. My ice-crusted pack raft swung around in the current downstream from his body, and he pulled me to the bank. I writhed on the floor of the tent while wrapped in sleeping bags, the heat moving back into me like a hot wire brush going through the veins of my legs.

In the morning I was back on my feet. We rafted the meat and gear down the Copper River and then loaded it into a pickup near the village of Chitina. I spent the next three days at Danny's house in Anchorage butchering the buffalo meat, converting the hunks of red flesh into wrapped and frozen steaks, roasts, sausages, and burgers. I minced the scraps of gristle and boiled them into dog food for my friends' pets. I sawed the marrowbones into inch-and-a-half disks, then baked the disks on a cookie sheet until the fatty white insides spilled out like banana slugs; they tasted like buffalo-meat concentrate. I pickled the tongue and braised it in homemade sauerkraut from cabbages grown in my brother Matt's garden. I sawed up the shank bones and made osso buco with my own homegrown tomatoes, then took the leftover bits of picked-clean bone and boiled them down into an assortment of stocks and glazes. I bleached the skull for a decoration and sent the hide to a commercial tannery.

Finally, months later, I thawed out some bags of the carotene-rich fat and rendered them down into a few quart-sized jars of lard the color of diluted carrot juice. One night I took a handful of the liquefied fat and styled my hair into a wild shape, some kind of crazed buffalo warrior. By then I knew that I had to come back up here. Remembering the cold air and the death of the buffalo made me want to witness the opposites, warmth and birth. Bushpilot Dave made two separate trips to fly Danny and me up the Chetaslina valley in his Super Cub, going low and slow at eight hundred feet. We traveled some twenty miles beyond the old kill site, all the way up to the herd's summering grounds at the foot of the glacier. Dave dropped us off on a gravel bar with our backpacks and a couple days' worth of food. We took a GPS waypoint on the improvised landing strip and then set off in search of the animals.

Of the twenty-four hunters who were issued permits for DI454, only four of us killed a buffalo by the end of the seven-month season. The replacements for those animals are coming toward me now. There are a dozen calves in all, maybe more, though the adults are leading the herd. A young bull locks its eyes on me, some strange mound sticking out of a beaver dam. I don't

A bull and cow along the upper Chetaslina, June 2006.

move, and I control my breath so that my back doesn't rise and fall. When the bull goes back to eating, I can hear its teeth ripping the willow leaves. Its breath is like a soft snore, rising and falling. A calf passes so close that I could jump out and touch it, though that would likely get me a major ass kicking from its mother. It abandons a willow that it's been nibbling in order to nurse. The cow is getting tired of this routine. She brings her back knee forward to smack his head and chase him off; the calf protests by charging back in. He bangs the top of his skull against her udder until she relents and lets her milk drop. The calf feeds frantically for a few seconds and then trots off away from the herd, bucking and kicking. It occurs to me that this buffalo calf has probably never seen a human. Most likely, a human has never seen it.

There's beauty in the young calf's unknowingness, in the mystery of its wild and remote existence. My quest to understand the buffalo has carried me across several years and thousands of miles, yet only rarely have I been able to see the animal in the way that I see this calf—as an untethered beast living outside human context and beyond the reach of human history. But my enjoyment of this animal as a simple biological being is short-lived; within seconds, my concentration is broken by a question that I've been struggling with for the past few months—how can I claim to love the very thing that I worked so hard to kill? I've thought of this often lately, yet I haven't been able to answer it with force and conviction. For now, I rely on a response that is admittedly glib: I just do, and I always will.

In a historical sense, I suppose that my confused and convoluted relationship to the buffalo is nothing new. For the entirety of man's existence in North America, we've struggled with the meaning of this animal, with the ways in which its life is intertwined with our own. I think of the first hunters who walked through some long-ago gap between glaciers and stumbled onto a landscape populated with strange and massive creatures. The buffalo was just one of many then, a giant among a host of other giants, but over time these many animals were whittled away by the forces of man and nature. Eventually the buffalo stood alone, the continent's greatest beast, like the winning contestant in a game show.

Herd crossing the upper Chetaslina, June 2006.

Its prize was humanity's never-ending attention, which was ultimately a bittersweet award. For thousands of years, the first people of North America fed on the buffalo's meat and wore the buffalo's skin, and then made a deity of the animal as a way of reconciling their need to slaughter the thing that granted them life. My own European ancestors came to the New World and scoffed at the heathen nature of the Indians' ideas, then stood by as the buffalo nearly vanished from the earth beneath their notion that the animal was an expendable gift of their own God, a commodity meant to get them started before stepping aside and letting "civilization" bloom in the wilderness.

I sometimes imagine that we saved the buffalo from the brink of extinction for the simple reason that the animal provided a handy mirror in which we could see our innermost desires and failures, and our most confounding contradictions. Our efforts to use the buffalo as a looking glass have rendered the animal almost inscrutable. At once it is a symbol of the tenacity of wilderness and the destruction of wilderness; it's a symbol of Native American culture and the death of Native American culture; it's a symbol of the strength and vitality of America and the pettiness and greed of America; it represents a frontier both forgotten and remembered; it stands for freedom and captivity, extinction and salvation. Perhaps the buffalo's enduring strength and legacy come from this chameleonic wizardry, this ability to provide whatever we need at the given moment. Maybe that's what the sculptor James Earle Fraser had in mind when he put the buffalo on the American nickel. In pursuit of a timeless design, he gave us an image that will never lose its meaning, whatever that meaning might ultimately be.

I think of a day last February when I went to Yellowstone National Park, at a point about forty miles away from where I unearthed the buffalo skull years before on that warm September af-

Buffalo calf along the upper Chetaslina, June 2006.

ternoon. I'd come to the park to watch Nez Percé Indians kill buffalo near the northern border as a way to exercise treaty rights that their forefathers had negotiated with the U.S. government many generations ago. The Nez Percé had not hunted the park since 1877, and their plans to kill buffalo generated a firestorm of local interest. Along with dozens of spectators, including hunters, game wardens, protesters, tribal police, Department of Homeland Security officers, county sheriffs, and the merely curious, I watched as a group of young hunters, many of them teenagers, gunned down five buffalo amid a long volley of firing. The animals staggered around in the snow, leaving vivid trails of blood that flowed from poorly placed head shots. When the fifth buffalo finally fell, everyone, no matter their reason for being there, breathed a long sigh of relief.

I returned to the place in the morning, hoping to watch wolves clean up the tidbits of the buffalo's remains. Instead, another small party of Indian hunters was there. They'd just killed another buffalo down the mountain from the first five carcasses. Several vehicles carrying protesters pulled in next to a truck that was loaded with meat; they'd come to pay their respects to the fallen animals. The hunters and I joined the protesters and walked up to what was left of the freshly butchered carcass on the snow. Without talking, we joined hands around the animal's severed insides and a small offering of meat and burned sweetgrass laid out by the hunters. A woman next to me was crying uncontrollably, her hand shaking in mine. Down from me, an Indian man was singing a song of thankfulness that made me think of triumph. One of the hunters had bloodied hands, and his face bore a look of inner peace and contentment. He would eat well this winter, the meal of his fathers. High above, a cluster of ravens circled in the air. They were waiting. I looked at the buffalo's remains on the snow, and I could sense that this animal would live on in a new form, forever and ever.

THE BUFFALO PASS BY THE BEAVER DAM where Danny and I are hiding, and soon there's nothing for me to see but their twitching tails. We quietly back up and enter a line of trees. We stop to sit in a small hillside clearing where we can look out across the valley. The herd arrives at the end of the willow flat. They move across the dry gravel bars of the riverbed, their hooves kicking up dust that gets swept upstream by the stiff wind. They come to the river's channel and pause. The adults walk back and forth to find a good spot and then start climbing in. At first it's just one at a time, but then there are groups of five or six plunging in together. As the buffalo emerge from the river, they shake the water away like wet dogs. By the time that half of the herd has crossed, they've created a house-sized patch of wet gravel. It looks like the shadow of a small cloud. Soon there's just one buffalo left on our side of the river, a young calf. She paces back and forth and several times enters up to her knees before backing out. She watches the herd move away and then dives in. Her jump is so frantic that she disappears beneath the surface. When her head pops up, the current rushes her downriver. She swims hard and climbs out on spindly legs. When she shakes dry, she leaves her own little patch of wet gravel just downstream of the others. As she runs to catch up, a feeling of joy rises from deep inside me. The joy turns to words. I don't want to destroy the silence, so I just think them to myself.

Let the buffalo roam.

ACKNOWLEDGMENTS

First and foremost, I'd like to thank my agent and friend, Marc Gerald, for placing me with the perfect editor and collaborator, Cindy Spiegel. Thanks to Cindy and everyone else at Spiegel & Grau, especially Gretchen Koss, Hana Landes, and Meghan Walker, for taking such good care of my project and me.

I am indebted to many professionals, agencies, and self-taught experts who offered me physical assistance and personal time while I was researching this book. Thanks to Tony Baker for showing me "the really old shit"; Reverend Grant of Garrett County, Maryland, for giving me a firsthand introduction to President George Washington; Mike Kunz of the U.S. Bureau of Land Management's Arctic Field Office for the banjo songs, helicopters, and twenty-four-hour sunlight; Paul Picha of the State Historical Society of North Dakota for showing me the earthen mounds and weird holes in the ground along the Missouri River; David Eck and Commissioner Patrick H. Lyons of the New Mexico State Lands Office for the use of a truck, a knowledgeable guide, and keys to the gates; geneticist Beth Shapiro for putting me up and removing two grams of my skull at the Henry Wellcome Ancient Biomolecules Centre at Oxford University; Stephen Sautner, Steve Johnson, and everyone else at the Wildlife Conservation Society for letting me come to Denver and introducing me to that precious stash in the library at the Bronx Zoo; Bob Stephenson of the Alaska Department of Fish and Game in Fairbanks, Alaska, for showing me some old skulls, taking me to see a cool painting, and giving me a glimpse into the buffalo's bright future in Alaska; Jason Labelle of Colorado State University for showing me a bunch of Ice Age kill sites; Dan Flores, an environmental historian and my one-time professor at the University of Montana, for taking a day off to visit Clovis, New Mexico; Ray the Rock Man Baker of Miles City, Montana, for his unique cultural insights and cool hunks of rock; Dan Brister and Mike Mease of the Buffalo Field Campaign in West Yellowstone, Montana, for sharing a couch and meals.

Many historians, scientists, and knowledgeable laypeople gave me valuable insights and answers when called upon via phone, e-mail, or office visits, including Ryan Byerly and Judith Cooper of Southern Methodist University in Dallas, Texas; Wes Olson of Elk Island National Park in Alberta, Canada; Stuart MacMillan and Rhona Kindopp of Wood Buffalo National Park in Canada's Northwest Territories; Kenneth P. Cannon of the Midwest Archeological Center in Lincoln, Nebraska; Michael C. Wilson of Douglas College in British Columbia; Tom Groneberg, of northwest Montana; Faber the taxidermist, of Miles City, Montana; Jim Matheson of the National Buffalo Association; Shelly Toenniges of Ebonex Corporation in Melvindale, Michigan; Darden Hood of Beta Analytic, in Miama Florida; Nola Davis of the Texas Parks and Wildlife Department; and George Hamell of the New York State Museum in Albany, New York.

Finally, and most important, a huge thanks to my personal friends and family who offered me their particular blends of muscle power and brain power, especially Katie Finch (Catherine Rinella, that is), Danny Rinella, Dr. Matt Rinella, Matt Rafferty, Jeff Jessen, Hardcover Jeffy, Dr. Matt Carlson, Dr. Eric Kern, and my mother, Rosemary. You guys have made this world a very interesting place to hang out.

NOTES AND BIBLIOGRAPHY

Chapter Two

8 *"an exercise in assumption, conjecture, and surmise."*: McMurtry, Larry. *Crazy Horse.* New York: Viking Penguin, 1999.

9 *"And, in my search for symbols . . ."*: Text accompanying Buffalo Nickel Exhibit at National Cowboy Hall of Fame, circa 1972, quoting James Frazer. Biographical/historical file on Black Diamond, Bronx Zoo Library.

13 *"Its head droops as if it had lost all hope in the world"*: Personal correspondence between William T. Hornaday and Martin S. Garretson, secretary of the American Bison Society, in 1918. Collected in biographical/historical file on Black Diamond, Bronx Zoo Library.

NUMBERS OF BUFFALO AND HISTORIC DISTRIBUTION

Allen, J.A. "The American Bisons, Living and Extinct." *Memoirs of the Museum of Comparative Zoology,* vol. 4, no. 10. Cambridge: Cambridge University Press, 1876.

Belue, Ted Franklin. *The Long Hunt: Death of the Buffalo East of the Mississippi.* Mechanicsburg: Stackpole Books, 1996.

Dodge, Col. Richard Irving. *The Plains of the Great West and Their Inhabitants.* New York: G. P. Putnam's Sons, 1877.

Flores, Dan. "Bison Ecology and Bison Diplomacy: The Southern Plains from 1800 to 1850." *Journal of American History,* vol. 78, no. 2, September 1991, pp. 465–485.

Hamell, George. Personal correspondence with the author. Hamell is a former senior historian with the New York State Museum in Albany, New York.

Hornaday, William T. *The Extermination of the American Bison.* Washington and London: Smithsonian Institution Press, 2000.

Lott, Dale F. *American Bison: A Natural History*. Berkeley: University of California Press, 2002.

Roe, Frank G. *The North American Buffalo: A Critical Study of the Species in Its Wild State*. Toronto: University of Toronto Press, 1951.

Weber, Bill. "Buffalo Visions: Bringing Back the American Bison—Symbol of the Great Plains." *Wildlife Conservation Magazine*. September/October 2006.

CORTÉS AND CABEZA DE VACA

Cabeza de Vaca, Alvar Nunez. "The Account and Commentaries of Governor Alvar Nunuz Cabeza de Vaca, of what occurred on the two journeys that he made to the Indies." Online book made available through the Southwestern Writers Collection of the Texas State University—San Marcos, http://alkek.library.tx state.edu/swwc/cdv/index.html.

De Solis, Don Antonio, translated by Thomas Townsend. *The History of the Conquest of Mexico by the Spaniards*. London: T. Woodward, J. Hooke, and J. Peele, 1724.

Prescott, William H. *History of the Conquest of Mexico, with a Preliminary View of Ancient Mexican Civilization, and the Life of the Conqueror, Hernando Cortes*. New York: Harper and Borthers, 1843.

CRAZY HORSE

Ambrose, Stephen E. *Crazy Horse and Custer: The Parallel Lives of Two American Warriors*. New York: Doubleday, 1975.

Frazier, Ian. *Great Plains*. New York: Farrar, Straus & Giroux, 1989. Chapter 6 encompasses a factual, though moving, account of the life and death of Crazy Horse.

Sandoz, Mari. *Crazy Horse: The Strange Man of the Oglalas*. Lincoln: University of Nebraska Press, 1961.

THE BRONX ZOO AND BLACK DIAMOND

Bridges, William. *Gathering of Animals: An Unconventional History of the New York Zoological Society*. New York: Harper and Row, 1974, pp. 145–49.

Sanborn, Elwin R. "The National Bison Herd: An Account of the Transportation of the Bison from the Zoological Park to the Wichita Range." *Zoological Society Bulletin,* no. 28, January 1908, pp. 400–412.

SIGNIFICANCE OF THE BUFFALO IN PLAINS INDIAN MYTHOLOGY

Barsness, Larry. *Heads, Hides & Horns: The Compleat Buffalo Book*. Fort Worth: Texas Christian University Press, 1985.

Grinnell, George Bird. *Blackfoot Lodge Tales: The Story of a Prairie People.* Lincoln: University of Nebraska Press, 1967.

———. *By Cheyenne Campfires.* Lincoln: University of Nebraska Press, 1971.

———. *Pawnee Hero Stories and Folk-Tales with Notes on the Origin, Customs and Character of the Pawnee People.* New York: Forest and Stream Publishing Co., 1889.

Marriot, Alice, and Carol K. Rachlin, *Plains Indian Mythology.* New York: Thomas Y. Crowell Co., 1975.

Chapter Three

24 *"The passion for buffalo is a regular fever among them and could not be stopped.":* As quoted in Farr, William E. "Going to Buffalo: Indian Hunting Migrations Across the Rocky Mountains, Part 1." *Montana: The Magazine of Western History,* Winter 2003.

25 *"as good an investment as real estate.":* As quoted in Barsness, Larry. *Heads, Hides & Horns: The Compleat Buffalo Book.* Fort Worth: Texas Christian University Press, 1985. Original text from Allard, Charles. "Breeding Buffaloes." *Self-Culture,* May 1895, pp. 81–82.

30 *"short on services but big on wilderness.":* National Park Services website for the Nabesna Road, http://www.nps.gov/wrst/planyourvisit/the-nabesna-road.httm.

30 *"East of the Copper River, south of the Nadina River . . .":* "DI 454 Bison Hunt: Copper River Land Status and Public Access." Pamphlet produced by Alaska Department of Fish and Game, August 2000.

32 *"Dear Hunter: Congratulations on winning a Copper River Herd Bison Permit . . .":* Letter from Alaska Department of Fish and Game, July 19, 2005.

INTROGRESSION OF CATTLE GENES INTO BUFFALO HERDS

Derr, Jim. "Genetic Considerations: American Bison—the Ultimate Genetic Survivor." *Ecological Future of the Bison in North America: A Report from a Multi-Stakeholder, Transboundary Meeting,* ed. Kent H. Redford and Eva Fearn. Wildlife Conservation Society, May 2007.

Robbins, Jim. "Out West, with the Buffalo, Roam Some Strands of Undesirable DNA." *New York Times,* January 9, 2007.

INTRODUCTION AND MANAGEMENT OF COPPER RIVER BUFFALO HERD

Burris, Bud (Oliver). Personal correspondence with author. Bud Burris is a long-time Delta Junction resident and retired employee of the Alaska Department of Fish and Game.

Burris, Oliver E., and Donald E. McKnight. "Game Transplants in Alaska." Alaska Department of Fish and Game pamphlet published in December 1973.

"Delta Junction State Bison Range: History of Bison in Alaska." Alaska Department of Fish and Game Web site, http://wildlife.alaska.gov/index.cfm?adfg=refuge.delta-bison.

Elrod, Morton J. "The Flathead Buffalo Range: A Report to the American Bison Society." *Report of the American Bison Society.* New York: American Bison Society, 1908.

Robert, Bigart, ed. "I Will Be Meat for my Salish: The Montana Writers Project and the Buffalo of the Flathead Indian Reservation." Salish Kootenai College Press and the Montana Historical Society, May 2002.

"Southcentral Bison Population Management." Performance report completed in 2000 by the Alaska Department of Fish and Game.

Chapter Four

39 *"I felt the most dreary forebodings":* Parkman, Francis. *Oregon Trail.* Boston: Little, Brown and Company, 1880.

40 *"well aged but still a little tough.":* Guthrie, Dale. *Frozen Fauna of the Mammoth Steppe: The Story of Blue Babe.* Chicago: University of Chicago Press, 1989.

47 *"altered body proportions":* Geist, Valerius. "The relation of social evolution and dispersal in ungulates during the Pleistocene, with emphasis on the Old World deer and the genus *Bison."* *Quaternary Research,* 1971: 1, pp. 283–315.

48 *"cranial characteristics and horn-core morphology":* From e-mail and telephone correspondence with Ryan Byerly, a graduate student with the Department of Anthropology at Southern Methodist University.

49 *"rostral width at maxillary-premaxillary suture":* Shackleton, D.M., L.V. Hills, and D.A. Hutton. "Aspects of Variation in Cranial Characters of Plains Bison (*Bison bison bison* Linnaeus) from Elk Island National Park, Alberta." *Journal of Mammology,* vol. 56, no. 4, 1975, pp. 871–887.

54 *"dudes riding three-wheeled ATVs on a hill":* "Quarter Designs Come Rolling In." *Billings Gazette,* August 4, 2005.

55 *"That quarter is UG-LY":* Taken from online comments posted to the *Billings Gazette* website (www.billingsgazette.net) in response to "Bison Skull Selected for State Quarter." *Billings Gazette,* June 30, 2006.

57 *"Statistically, this bison likely died in the early to mid-18th century":* Cannon, Kenneth. " 'They Went as High as They Chose': What an Isolated Skull Can Tell Us about the Biogeography of High-altitude Bison." *Arctic, Antartic and Alpine Research,* vol. 39, no. 1, 2007, pp. 44–56.

TORONTO BUFFALO SKULL

"May Have Roamed Ontario: Skull 10,000 Years Old Found." *Edmonton Journal,* June 11, 1932.

ARTIFACT-BEARING BUFFALO SKULL FROM BOW RIVER

Roe, Frank G. *The North American Buffalo: A Critical Study of the Species in Its Wild State*. Toronto: University of Toronto Press, 1951.

GLACIATIONS, PLEISTOCENE MAMMALS, MIGRATIONS, AND BISON EVOLUTION

Allen, J. A. "The American Bisons, Living and Extinct." *Memoirs of the Museum of Comparative Zoology*, vol. 4, no. 10. Cambridge: Cambridge University Press, 1876.

Guthrie, Dale. *Frozen Fauna of the Mammoth Steppe: The Story of Blue Babe*. Chicago: University of Chicago Press, 1989.

Lange, Ian. *Ice Age Mammals of North America: A Guide to the Big, the Hairy, and the Bizarre*. Missoula: Mountain Press Publishing Co., 2002.

Shapiro, Beth et al. "The Rise and Fall of the Beringia Steppe Bison." *Science*, vol. 306, November 2004.

Van Zyll De Jong, C. G. "Origin and Geographic Variation of Recent North American Bison." *Alberta*, vol. 3, no. 2, 1993, pp. 21–35.

Weiner, Jonathan. *The Beak of the Finch*. New York: Knopf, 1994.

Wilson, Michael C. "Late Quaternary Vertebrates and the Opening of the Ice-Free Corridor, with Special Reference to the Genus *Bison*." *Quaternary International*, vol. 32, 1996, pp. 97–105.

———. Personal correspondence with author.

———. and James A. Burns. "Searching for the Earliest Canadians: Wide Corridors, Narrow Doorways, Small Windows," in *Ice Age People of North America: Environments, Origins and Adaptations*, ed. Bonnichsen and Turnmire. Tucson: University of Arizona Press, 1999. Oregon State University Press and Center for the Study of the First Americans, 1999.

Chapter Five

67 *"that had fallen victims to the embrace of the flames"*: Kelly, Fanny. *Narrative of My Captivity Among the Sioux Indians, with a Brief Account of Sully's Indian Expedition in 1864, Bearing Upon Events Occurring in My Captivity*. Hartford: Mutual Publishing Co., 1871.

68 *"staggering about, sometimes running afoul"*: as quoted in McHugh, Tom. *The Time of the Buffalo*. New York: Alfred A. Knopf, 1972.

69 *"we began to notice more particularly the great number of drowned buffaloes"*: Bradbury, John. "Bradbury's Travels in the Interior of America, 1809–1811." As collected in volume 5 of *Early Western Travels, 1784–1846*. New York: A. H. Clark Co., 1904–1907.

70 *"as many as 10,000 of their putrid carcasses lying mired in a single ford"*: Sir George Simpson, as quoted in Frank G. Roe's *The North American Buffalo: A Critical Study of the Species in Its Wild State*. Toronto: University of Toronto Press, 1951.

70 *"whole herds were often drowned in the Missouri"*: Maximilian, Prince of Wied. "Maximilian, Prince of Wied's Travels in the Interior of North America, 1832–1834." As collected in volumes 22–25 of *Early Western Travels, 1784–1846*. New York: A. H. Clark Co., 1904–1907.

70 *"drowned buffalo continue to drift by in whole herds throughout the month"*: This is a line from the journals of an explorer known as Alexander Henry the Younger, as quoted in Frank G. Roe's *The North American Buffalo: A Critical Study of the Species in Its Wild State*. Roe's original source for the quote is an obscure, difficult-to-find volume of collected journals, *New Light on the Early History of the Great Northwest: Henry-Thompson Journals,* Francis P. Harper, 1897.

71 *"attracted an immense number of turkey buzzards"*: Maximilian, Prince of Wied. "Maximilian, Prince of Wied's Travels in the Interior of North America, 1832–1834." As collected in volumes 22–25 of *Early Western Travels, 1784–1846*. New York: A. H. Clark Co., 1904–1907.

FLOW RATES AND SEDIMENT DISCHARGE OF
THE COPPER RIVER AND ITS TRIBUTARIES

Brabets, T. P. "Geomorphology of the Lower Copper River, Alaska." U.S. Geological Survey Professional Paper #1581.

Embick, Andrew. *Fast & Cold: A Guide to Alaska Whitewater*. Helena: Falcon Press, 1994.

THERMOREGULATORY ATTRIBUTES OF BUFFALO

Christopherson, R. J., and R. J. Hudson. "Effects of Temperature and Wind on Cattle and Bison." 57th Annual Feeder's Day Report, 1978.

Christopherson, R. J., R. J. Hudson, and R. J. Richmond. "Comparative Winter Bioenergetics of American Bison, Yak, Scottish Highland and Hereford Calves." *Acta Theriologica,* issue 23, 1978, pp. 49–54.

———. "Feed Intake, Metabolism and Thermal Insulation of Bison, Yak, Scottish Highland and Hereford Calves During Winter." 55th Annual Feeder's Day Report. 1976, pp. 51–52.

Lott, Dale. *American Bison: A Natural History*. Berkeley: University of California Press, 2002.

Meagher, Mary. "Bison bison." The American Society of Mammalogists, *Mammalian Species,* no. 266, 1986.

Olson, Wes. Personal correspondence with author. Wes Olson is a private buffalo rancher whose day job is working with the buffalo herd at Canada's Elk Island National Park.

FREAKISH CAUSES OF MASS BUFFALO DEATH

Barsness, Larry. *Heads, Hides & Horns: the Compleat Buffalo Book.* Fort Worth: Texas Christian University Press, 1985.

Bradley, Mark, and John Wilmshurst. *The Fall and Rise of Bison Populations in Wood Buffalo National Park.* Published on the NRC Research Press Web site, http://cjz.nrc.ca on September 23, 2005.

Larter, N. C., Nishi, J. S., et al. "Observations of Wood Bison Swimming across the Liard River, Northwest Territories, Canada." *Arctic,* vol. 56, no. 4, 2003, pp. 408–12.

Maximilian, Prince of Wied. "Maximilian, Prince of Wied's Travels in the Interior of North America, 1832–1834." *Early Western Travels, 1784–1846,* vols. 22–25. New York: A. H. Clark Co., 1904–1907.

Parkman, Francis. *Oregon Trail.* Boston: Little, Brown and Co., 1880.

Roe, Frank G. *The North American Buffalo: A Critical Study of the Species in Its Wild State.* Toronto: University of Toronto Press, 1951.

Sandoz, Mari. *The Buffalo Hunters: The Story of the Hide Men.* Lincoln: University of Nebraska Press, 1978.

Townsend, John K. "Townsend's Narrative of a Journey Across the Rocky Mountains, to the Columbia River." *Early Western Travels, 1784–1846,* vol. 21, ed. Reuben Gold Thwaites. New York: A. H. Clark Co., 1904–1907.

Chapter Six

81 *"so long as the buffalo may range thereon in such numbers as to justify the chase"*: From the Medicine Lodge Treaties, as quoted in Isenberg, Andrew, *The Destruction of the Bison: An Environmental History, 1750–1920.* Cambridge: Cambridge University Press, 2000.

84 *"were utterly erratic and unpredicatable and might occur regardless of time, place, or season"*: Roe, F. G. *The North American Buffalo: A Critical Study of the Species in Its Wild State.* Toronto: University of Toronto Press, 1951.

86 *"We hunt the Buffalo and kill them with the Bows and Arrows"*: Hendry, Antony. *The Journal of Antony Hendry,* ed. L. J. Burpee. Royal Society of Canada Transactions, 3rd Series, no. 1, 1907.

86 *"the gradual decadence of the slight civilization which the people had acquired"*: Shaler, Nathaniel. *Nature and Man in America.* New York: Scribner's Sons, 1891.

87 *"it is the same thing in a Savage to wish to become sedentary and to believe in God"*: From Father Le Jeune's *Relacion,* as quoted in Roe, Frank G. *The North American Buffalo: A Critical Study of the Species in Its Wild State.*

87 *"buffaloes were so plenty in the country that little or no bread was used"*: Cumings, Fortescue. *Cumings' Tour to the Western Country, 1807–1809.* New York: A. H. Clark Co., 1904.

90 *"cherished the fond delusion that the great herd had only 'gone north' "*: Hornaday, William T. *The Extermination of the American Bison.* Washington and London: Smithsonian Institution Press, 2000.

91 *"huge herd reduction sale"*: http://www.highadventureranch.com. Accessed winter 2007.

91 *"We drive you out into a 2500 acre pasture and you shoot the buffalo you want"*: www.rockin7ranch.com/buffalo_hunting. Accessed spring 2008.

91 *"fair-chase" hunt*: http://www.thbison.com. Accessed spring 2008.

92 *"the passion . . . the drive . . . the determination"*: http://www.northstargameland.com. Accessed spring 2008.

92 *"the mighty American Buffalo still roams the virgin prairie"*: http://www.two-heartbuffalohunt.com. Accessed winter 2007.

92 *"slip back in time to when pioneers were filtering into Kansas"*: http://www.huntinfo.com/pipecreek2. Accessed spring 2008.

THE IMPACT OF THE HORSE ON NATIVE AMERICAN BUFFALO HUNTING AND WARFARE

Farrs, William E. "Going to Buffalo: Indian Hunting Migrations Across the Rocky Mountains, Part 1." *Montana: The Magazine of Western History,* Winter 2003.

Flores, Dan. "Bison Ecology and Bison Diplomacy: The Southern Plains from 1800 to 1850." *Journal of American History,* vol. 78, no. 2, September 1991, pp. 465–485.

Hornaday, William T. *The Extermination of the American Bison.* Washington and London: Smithsonian Institution Press, 2000.

Isenberg, Andrew. *The Destruction of the Bison: An Environmental History, 1750–1920.* Cambridge: Cambridge University Press, 2000.

Chapter Seven

99 *"in which were tied three fine horses, was picked up like chaff, torn to pieces"*: Untitled article. *La Epoca,* August 31, 1908.

GEORGE MCJUNKIN AND THE FOLSOM FLASH FLOOD

Folsom, Franklin. *Black Cowboy: The Life and Legend of George McJunkin.* Topeka: Tandem Library, 2000.

Hillerman, Tony. *The Great Taos Bank Robbery and Other Indian Country Affairs.* Albuquerque: University of New Mexico Press, 1973.

McNaghten, Allcutt. "The Flood as Experienced by Allcutt McNaghten." *Folsom*

1888–1988: Then and Now. Centennial Book Committee, 1988. (Note: as of spring 2008, portions of the accounts are available on the Folsom Museum's Web site, http://folsommuseum.netfirms.com/index.htm.)

Preston, Douglas. "Fossils and the Folsom Cowboy." *Natural History,* vol. 106, 1997, 16–22.

THE ARRIVAL AND IMPACT OF PALEOINDIANS IN NORTH AMERICA

Baker, Tony. Personal correspondence with the author. Tony Baker is a Folsom expert and projectile point enthusiast in Denver, Colorado.

Boldurian, Anthony T., and John L. Cotter. *Clovis Revisited: New Perspectives on Paleoindian Adaptations from Blackwater Draw, New Mexico.* Philadelphia: University of Pennsylvania Museum, 1999.

Diamond, Jared. *Guns, Germs, and Steel: The Fates of Human Societies.* New York: W. W. Norton, 1999.

Eiseley, Loren. *All the Strange Hours: The Excavation of a Life.* New York: Charles Scribner's Sons, 1975.

Flannery, Tim. *The Eternal Frontier: An Ecological History of North America and Its Peoples.* New York: Atlantic Monthly Press, 2001.

Freedman, Russell. *Who Was First?: Discovering the Americas.* New York: Clarion Books, 2007.

Frison, George. *Survival by Hunting: Prehistoric Human Predators and Animal Prey.* Berkely: University of California Press, 2004.

———. *Prehistoric Hunters of the High Plains.* New York: Academic Press, 1991.

Haynes, Gary. *The Early Settlement of North America: The Clovis Era.* Cambridge: Cambridge University Press, 2002.

Kunz, Michael, Michael Bever, and Constance Adkins. *The Mesa Site: Paleoindians Above the Arctic Circle.* BLM-Alaska Open File Report 86, April 2003.

Martin, Paul S., and Richard G. Klein, eds. *Quaternary Extinctions: A Prehistoric Revolution.* Tucson: University of Arizona Press, 1984.

Meltzer, David J. *Folsom: New Archaeological Investigations of a Classic Paleoindian Bison Kill.* Berkeley: University of California Press, 2006.

Stanford, D. J., and Jane S. Day, eds. *Ice Age Hunters of the Rockies.* Denver Museum of Nature and Science and University Press of Colorado, 1992.

Tankersley, Kenneth. *In Search of Ice Age Americans.* Layton: Gibbs Smith, 2002.

Wilmsen, Edwin N., and Frank H. H. Roberts. *Lindenmeier, 1934–1974: Concluding Report on Investigations.* Washington, D.C.: Smithsonian Institution Press, 1984.

Chapter Eight

125 *"public roads in a populous country":* From the journal of Nicholas Cresswell, 1775, as quoted in Belue, Ted Franklin. *The Long Hunt: Death of the Buffalo East of the Mississippi.* Mechanicsburg: Stackpole Books, 1996.

130 *"between a dark umber and liver-shining brown"*: Hornaday, William T. *The Extermination of the American Bison*. Washington and London: Smithsonian Institution Press, 2000.

Chapter Nine

140 *"crushed deep into the mud of the earthen floor by the cruel hoofs"*: Shoemaker, Henry W. *A Pennsylvania Buffalo Hunt*. Middleburg: Middleburg Post Press, 1915.

145 *"We saw a great many wolves in the neighborhood of these mangled carcasses"*: Clark, William, and Meriwether Lewis. *The Journals of Lewis and Clark*. Whitefish: Kessinger Publishing, 2004.

150 *"Not being good travelers sideways"*: *Buffalo Jones' Forty Years of Adventure*. Compiled by Colonel Henry Inman. Dalton: Crane and Co., 1899.

151 *"I have risked the sending of a party of hunters"*: Officer Daniel Brodhead to General George Washington. Quoted in Busch, Clarence M. *Report to the Commission to Locate the Site of the Frontier Forts of Pennsylvania*. State Printer of Pennsylvania, 1896.

151 *"owes its origen to Buffaloes, being no other than their tracks from one lick to another"*: *The Writings of George Washington from the Original Manuscript Journals 1745–1799*, ed. John C. Fitzpatrick. Electronic edition. Washington Resources at the University of Virginia Library, http://etext.virginia.edu/washington/fitzpatrick/.

156 *"not clothed from the waist up and was missing a shoe"*: *Morbidity and Mortality Weekly Report*. Centers of Disease Control and Prevention, March 5, 2004.

156 *"his jacket and neck chain were recovered a short distance away."*: *Morbidity and Mortality Weekly Report*. Centers of Disease Control and Prevention, February 25, 2005.

156 *"partially dressed in a pullover, T-shirt, pants, and one sock."*: *Morbidity and Mortality Weekly Report*. Centers of Disease Control and Prevention, March 17, 2006.

INTERACTIONS BETWEEN WOLVES AND BUFFALO

Carbyn, L. N., and T. Trottier. "Responses of Bison on Their Calving Grounds to Predation by Wolves in Wood Buffalo National Park." *Canadian Journal of Zoology*, vol. 65, 1987, pp. 2072–2078.

Fuller, W. A. "Behavior and Social Organization of the Wild Bison of Wood Buffalo National Park, Canada," www.pubs.aina.ucalgary.ca.

Franke, Mary Ann. *To Save the Wild Bison: Life on the Edge in Yellowstone*. Norman: University of Oklahoma Press, 2005.

Hornaday, William T. *The Extermination of the American Bison*. Washington and London: Smithsonian Institution Press, 2000.

Isenberg, Andrew. *The Destruction of the Bison: An Environmental History, 1750–1920.* Cambridge: Cambridge University Press, 2000.

Laundre, John W., Lucina Hernandez, and Kelly B Altendorf. "Wolves, Elk, and Bison: Reestablishing the 'Landscape of Fear' in Yellowstone National Park, U.S.A." *Canadian Journal of Zoology,* vol. 79, no. 9, 2001, pp. 1401-1409.

Lott, Dale F. *American Bison: A Natural History.* Berkeley: University of California Press, 2002.

Roe, Frank G. *The North American Buffalo: A Critical Study of the Species in Its Wild State.* Toronto: University of Toronto Press, 1951.

Seton, Ernest T. *Lives of Game Animals.* New York: Doubleday, Doran and Co., 1929.

THE INFLUENCE OF BUFFALO ON THE ROUTING OF AMERICAN RAILROADS AND HIGHWAYS

Belue, Ted Franklin. *The Long Hunt: Death of the Buffalo East of the Mississippi.* Mechanicsburg: Stackpole Books, 1996.

Roe, Frank G. *The North American Buffalo: A Critical Study of the Species in Its Wild State.* Toronto: University of Toronto Press, 1951.

MCCULLOUGH'S PACK HORSE PATH

Unsigned article. "McCullough's Pack Horse Path." *Glades Star.* September 30, 1948.

Chapter Ten

164 *"to the banks of the Missouri and, by gradual approaches, confine them into a narrow space where the ice was weakened . . .":* From the journals of Charles Mackenzie. Translated from French and quoted in Roe, Frank G. *The North American Buffalo: A Critical Study of the Species in Its Wild State.* Toronto: University of Toronto Press, 1951.

164 *"except some passage which they leave on purpose, and where they take post with their bows and arrows.":* Hennepin, Louis. *A New Discovery of a Vast Country in America.* Chicago: A. C. McClurg and Co., 1903 (original edition 1683).

168 *"as many as we can get.":* Hunt, James W. *Buffalo Days: Stories from J. Wright Mooar.* Abilene: State House Press, 2005.

178 *"there was not a hoof left.":* Smith, Vic. Quoted in Wayne Gard's *The Great Buffalo Hunt: Its History and Drama, and Its Role in the Opening of the West.* New York: Alfred A. Knopf, 1959.

180 *"Buffalo bones was laying around on the ground as thick as cones under a big fir tree":* McKeown, Martha F. *Them Was the Days.* Lincoln: University of Nebraska Press, 1950.

BUFFALO JUMPS

Bamforth, Douglas B. *Ecology and Human Organization on the Great Plains*. New York: Plenum Press, 1988.

Barsness, Larry. *Heads, Hides & Horns: The Compleat Buffalo Book*. Fort Worth: Texas Christian University Press, 1985.

Bement, Leland C. *Bison Hunting at the Cooper Site: Where Lightning Bolts Drew Thundering Herds*. Norman: University of Oklahoma Press, 1999.

———. "Excavation of the Late Pleistocene Deposits of Bonfire Shelter, 41VV218, Val Verde County, Texas." Archaeology Series 1, Texas Archaeology Survey, University of Texas, 1986.

Byerly, Ryan M., Judith R. Cooper, et al. "On Bonfire Shelter (Texas) as a Paleoindian Bison Jump: An Assessment using GIS and Zooarchaeology." *American Antiquity*, vol. 70, 2005, pp. 595–629.

Clark, William, and Meriwether Lewis. *The Journals of Lewis and Clark*. Whitefish: Kessinger Publishing, 2004.

Frison, George. *Prehistoric Hunters of the High Plains*. New York: Academic Press, 1991.

———. *Survival by Hunting: Prehistoric Human Predators and Animal Prey*. Berkeley: University of California Press, 2004.

Gard, Wayne. *The Great Buffalo Hunt: Its History and Drama, and Its Role in the Opening of the West*. New York: Alfred A. Knopf, 1959.

Isenberg, Andrew C. *The Destruction of the Bison: An Environmental History, 1750–1920*. Cambridge: Cambridge University Press, 2000.

Malouf, Carling, and Stuart Conner. "Symposium on Buffalo Jumps. Memoir 1." Montana Archaeological Society, 1962.

Roe, Frank G. *The North American Buffalo: A Critical Study of the Species in Its Wild State*. Toronto: University of Toronto Press, 1951.

EUROAMERICAN HIDE HUNTERS

Branch, E. Douglass. *The Hunting of the Buffalo*. New York: D. Appleton and Co., 1940.

Dixon, Billy. *Life and Adventures of Billy Dixon of Adobe Walls*. Co-operative Publishing Company, 1914.

Dixon, Olive K. *Life of Billy Dixon*. Dallas: Southwest Press, 1927.

Dodge, Col. Richard Irving. *The Plains of the Great West and Their Inhabitants*. New York: G. P. Putnam's Sons, 1877.

Gard, Wayne. *The Great Buffalo Hunt. Its History and Drama, and Its Role in the Opening of the West*. New York: Alfred A. Knopf, 1959.

Hornaday, William T. *The Extermination of the American Bison*. Washington and London: Smithsonian Institution Press, 2000.

Hunt, James W. *Buffalo Days: Stories from J. Wright Mooar.* Abilene: State House Press, 2005.

O'Connor, Richard. *Bat Masterson.* New York: Doubleday and Co., 1957.

Roe, Frank G. *The North American Buffalo: A Critical Study of the Species in Its Wild State.* Toronto: University of Toronto Press, 1951.

Roosevelt, Theodore. *Hunting Trips of a Ranchman: An Account of the Big Game of the United States and Its Chase with Horse, Hand, and Rifle.* New York: G. P. Putnam's Sons, 1885.

Sandoz, Mari. *The Buffalo Hunters: the Story of the Hide Men.* Lincoln: University of Nebraska Press, 1978 (original publication, 1954).

Vestal, Stanley. *Queen of the Cowtowns: Dodge City.* New York: Harper and Brothers, 1952.

BONEPICKERS

Barsness, Larry. *Heads, Hides and Horns: The Compleat Buffalo Book.* Fort Worth: Texas Christian University Press, 1985.

Hunt, James W. *Buffalo Days: Stories from J. Wright Mooar.* Abilene: State House Press, 2005.

McCreight, Major Israel. *Buffalo Bone Days.* Sykesville: Nupp Printing, 1939.

McKeown, Martha F. *Them Was the Days.* Lincoln: University of Nebreska Press, 1950.

Toenniges, Shelly. Personal correspondence with the author. Shelly Toenniges works as a manager at Ebonex Corp.

Chapter Eleven

188 *"vast clouds of dust rising and circling in the air ...":* Townsend, John K. "Townsend's Narrative of a Journey Across the Rocky Mountains, to the Columbia River." *Early Western Travels, 1784–1846,* vol. 21, ed. Reuben Gold Thwaites. New York: A. H. Clark Co., 1904–1907.

191 *"These animals are by no means plentiful ...":* Dodge, Col. Richard Irving. *The Plains of the Great West and Their Inhabitants.* New York: G. P. Putnam's Sons, 1877.

BOB STEPHENSON AND THE PROPOSED INTRODUCTION (OR, PERHAPS, REINTRODUCTION) OF WOOD BUFFALO IN ALASKA

Gates, C. Cormac, Robert Stephenson, et al. "National Recovery Plan for the Wood Bison (*Bison bison* athabascae)." National Recovery Plan No. 21, a publication of Recovery of Nationally Endangered Wildlife (RENEW), October 2001.

Stephenson, Robert O., S. Craig Gerlach, et al. "Wood Bison in Late Holocene Alaska and Adjacent Canada: Paleontological, Archaeological and Historical Records."

People and Wildlife in Northern North America, ed. S. Craig Gerlach and Maribeth S. Murray. BAR International Series 994, 2001.

"Wood Bison Restoration in Alaska: A Review of Environmental and Regulatory Issues and Recommendations for Project Implementations." A Public Review Draft from the Alaska Department of Fish and Game, July 2006.

BUFFALO WALLOWS

Gerlanc, Nicole M., and Glennis A. Kaufman. "Use of Bison Wallows by Anurans on Konza Prairie." *American Midland Naturalist,* vol. 150, no. 1, July 2003, pp. 158–168.

Fritz, Ken M., and Walter K. Dodds. "The Effects of Bison Crossings on the Macroinvertebrate Community in a Tallgrass Prairie Stream." *American Midland Naturalist,* vol. 141, no. 2, April 1999, pp. 253–265.

McKeown, Martha F. *Them Was the Days.* Lincoln: University of Nebraska Press, 1950.

Vinton, Mary Ann, David C. Hartnett, et al. "Interactive Effects of Fire, Bison (*Bison bison*) Grazing and Plant Community Composition in Tallgrass Prairie." *American Midland Naturalist,* vol. 129, no. 1, January 1993, pp. 10–18.

Chapter Twelve

INTERACTIONS OF BUFFALO AND GRIZZLY BEARS

Clark, William, and Meriwether Lewis. *The Journals of Lewis and Clark.* Whitefish: Kessinger Publishing, 2004.

Dodge, Col. Richard Irving. *The Plains of the Great West and Their Inhabitants.* New York: G. P. Putnam's Sons, 1877.

Franke, Mary Ann. *To Save the Wild Bison: Life on the Edge in Yellowstone.* Norman: University of Oklahoma Press, 2005.

Isenberg, Andrew C. *The Destruction of the Bison: An Environmental History, 1750–1920.* Cambridge: Cambridge University Press, 2000.

Lott, Dale F. *American Bison: A Natural History.* Berkeley: University of California Press, 2002.

Mattson, David J. "Use of Ungulates by Yellowstone Grizzly Bear." *Biological Conservation,* vol. 81, July–August 1997, pp. 103–111.

Roe, Frank G. *The North American Buffalo: A Critical Study of the Species in Its Wild State.* Toronto: University of Toronto Press, 1951.

Wyman, Travis. "Grizzly Bear Predation on a Bull Bison in Yellowstone National Park," *Ursus,* vol. 13, 2002, pp. 375–377.

Chapter Thirteen

225 *"circles, curves and other mathematical figures . . .":* Irving, Washington. *The Adventures of Captain Bonneville.* New York: John B. Alden Publishers, 1886.

INDIAN USES OF BUFFALO

Belue, Ted Franklin. *The Long Hunt: Death of the Buffalo East of the Mississippi.* Mechanicsburg: Stackpole Books, 1996.

Cabeza de Vaca, Alvar Nunez. "The Account and Commentaries of Governor Alvar Nunez Cabeza de Vaca, of what occurred on the two journeys that he made to the Indies." Online book made available through the Southwestern Writers Collection of the Texas State University—San Marcos, http://alkek.library.tx state.edu/swwc/cdv/index.html.

Dary, David A. *The Buffalo Book.* New York: Avon Books, 1974.

Dodge, Col. Richard Irving. *The Plains of the Great West and Their Inhabitants.* New York: G. P. Putnam's Sons, 1877.

Frazier, Ian. *Great Plains.* New York: Farrar, Straus and Giroux, 1989.

Grinnell, George Bird. *Blackfoot Lodge Tales: The Story of a Prairie People.* Lincoln: University of Nebraska Press, 1967.

———. *By Cheyenne Campfires.* Lincoln: University of Nebraska Press, 1971.

———. *Pawnee Hero Stories and Folk-Tales: With Notes on the Origin, Customs and Character of the Pawnee People.* New York: Forest and Stream Publishing Co., 1889.

Maximilian, Prince of Wied. "Maximilian, Prince of Wied's Travels in the Interior of North America, 1833–1834." *Early Western Travels, 1784–1846.* vols. 22–25. New York: A. H. Clark Co., 1904–1907.

McCreight, Major Israel. *Buffalo Bone Days.* Sykesville: Nupp Printing, 1939.

Sandoz, Mari. *The Buffalo Hunters: The Story of the Hide Men.* Lincoln: University of Nebraska Press, 1978 (original publication, 1954).

Chapter Fourteen

238 *"Suppose two men to be disputing about their exploits . . .":* Maximilian, Prince of Wied. "Maximilian, Prince of Wied's Travels in the Interior of North America, 1833–1834." *Early Western Travels, 1784–1846.* vols. 22–25. New York: A. H. Clark Co., 1904–1907.

238n *"The shock of battles and scenes of carnage and cruelty were as of the breath of his nostrils . . .":* Fry, General James B. *Army Sacrifices: Briefs from Official Pigeon-Holes.* Mechanicsburg: Stackpole Books, 2003.

WHITE BUFFALO

Fleron, Julian, and Donald Hoagland. "Miracles and Mathematical Biology: The Case of the White Buffalo," in *Environmental Mathematics in the Classroom*, ed. B. A. Fusaro and P. C. Kenschaft. Mathematical Association of America, 2003.

Grinnell, George Bird. *Blackfoot Lodge Tales: The Story of a Prairie People*. Lincoln: University of Nebraska Press, 1962.

———. *By Cheyenne Campfires*. Lincoln: University of Nebraska Press, 1971.

———. *Pawnee Hero Stories and Folk-Tales: With Notes on the Origin, Customs and Character of the Pawnee People*. New York: Forest and Stream Publishing Co., 1889.

Hunt, James W. *Buffalo Days: Stories from J. Wright Mooar*. Abilene: State House Press, 2005.

Maximilian, Prince of Wied. "Maximilian, Prince of Wied's Travels in the Interior of North America, 1833–1834." *Early Western Travels, 1784–1846*. vols. 22–25. New York: A. H. Clark Co., 1904–1907.

Meagher, Mary. "Bison bison." The American Society of Mammalogists, *Mammalian Species*, no. 266, 1986, pp. 1–8.

Roe, Frank G. *The North American Buffalo: A Critical Study of the Species in Its Wild State*. Toronto: University of Toronto Press, 1951.

ABOUT THE AUTHOR

Steven Rinella is the author of *The Scavenger's Guide to Haute Cuisine* and a correspondent for *Outside* magazine. His writing has also appeared in *The New Yorker, American Heritage,* the *New York Times, Field & Stream, Men's Journal,* and Salon.com. He grew up in Twin Lake, Michigan, and now splits his time between Anchorage, Alaska, and New York City.